Australian Studies

Australian Studies

Acquisition and Collection Development for Libraries

Edited by
G. E. Gorman

MANSELL

First published 1992 by
Mansell Publishing Limited. *A Cassell Imprint*
Villiers House, 41/47 Strand, London WC2N 5JE, England
387 Park Avenue South, New York, NY 10016-8810, USA

British Library Cataloguing in Publication Data
A catalogue record for this book is available from the British Library.
ISBN 0-7201-2134-5

Library of Congress Cataloging-in-Publication Data
Australian studies : acquisition and collection development for libraries / edited by G. E. Gorman.
p. cm.
Includes bibliographical references and index.
ISBN 0-7201-2134-5
1. Libraries—Special collections—Australia. 2. Australia—Bibliography—Methodology. I. Gorman, G. E.
Z688.A95A9 1992
025.2′994—dc20 92-10382
CIP

Printed and bound in Great Britain by
Biddles Ltd, Guildford and King's Lynn

Contents

Introduction

For many centuries, certainly earlier than Captain Cook's voyages across the Pacific, some of the world's more ancient libraries have been collecting documentation descriptive of the Antipodes. Slightly more recently many newer libraries have been collecting publications *from* – and not only *about* – the Australian colonies. Between the wars, but particularly after the Second World War, this rather desultory collecting became more purposeful with the advent of Australian studies in American and European universities. In Australia, especially since the gradual withering of the 'cultural cringe' in the enthusiasm generated by the Whitlam era, there has been growing recognition that Australian publications, by Australians and about Australia, deserve to be read and therefore ought to be in libraries. In other words, in various parts of the world there is growing interest in Australia's publishing output, whether this be for study or research, for leisure or simply to satisfy an acquisitive urge.

However, for the most part libraries responsible for collecting materials of and about Australia have been functioning independently, without benefit of shared information on why, where and how best to acquire Australiana. Accordingly, this publication for the first time seeks to address the needs of librarians charged with collecting and managing collections with an Australian content. It does this through eighteen papers arranged in five parts, covering the growth of Australian studies, Australian publishing, selecting and purchasing Australiana, experiences in developing Australiana collections and such special aspects as multiculturalism and cooperative copying projects. Each paper has been prepared by a specialist in his field, with emphasis on information that will facilitate more efficient acquisition and use of Australiana in libraries wherever they may be located.

The essays open in Part 1 ('The Demand for Australian Collections') with two papers which indicate the growing need for attention to collections of Australian publications. The first, 'Australian Studies, Australian Publications and Library Provision', offers a brief overview of the nature of Australian studies and its documentation together with a less than optimistic view of the future that awaits collectors in this field.

In 'No Bushfires Yet: Australian Studies in the United States' Robert Ross offers a concise history of the development of Australian studies programmes in the USA, concentrating on recent developments in teaching and research at American universities. His conclusion, that the future of Australian studies in the United States is bright, could apply equally to the situation in Britain, Europe and Australia, all of which have thriving academic 'industries' devoted to Australian studies – hence the warrant for this collection.

Part 2 ('Australian Publishing') looks at the various sources of Australian publishing and at a number of types of Australian documentation. Wallace Kirsop's opening paper, 'Modern Australian Publishing: An Historical Perspective', provides a solid study of the development of printing and publishing in Australia. In the last forty years Australian publishing has increased from 20 to 50 per cent of indigenous requirements, but mere figures mask an often complex history of trade relations with Britain and the USA. Dependence on overseas publishers remains a major characteristic of Australian publishing, and the uncertain future of the Australian economy can do little for the confidence of those who argue for greater national independence in terms of information creation and dissemination. Nevertheless, the fact that Australia currently produces 50 per cent of its own literature means that collectors of Australiana must take this output seriously.

At the pinnacle of Australian publishing in terms of output is government; accordingly, Michael Harrington in 'Government Publishing in Australia' discusses publishing activities and trends in the different levels and forms of government in Australia: the Commonwealth, the states, local government, self-governing and non-self-governing territories. He also treats the mode of publishing, including sales and distribution, and concludes with descriptions of the major tools for identifying, selecting and acquiring government publications. Much smaller in terms of volume is Australian serial literature, although in a comparatively short history Australia has produced a significant quantity of such documentation. This subject is treated in 'Serial Publishing in Australia', in which Toby Burrows discusses newspapers, literary magazines, government and legal serials, women's magazines, radical and satirical periodicals, scholarly and scientific journals. Each of these types is considered from both historical and current perspectives. Burrows concludes with comments on bibliographic access to Australian serials, a topic taken up thoroughly by John Mills in 'An Introduction to Australian Reference Publishing'. Here Mills outlines the role of non-governmental reference publishing in Australia but devotes most of his discussion to bibliographic control titles, ready reference titles, indexing and abstracting services and databases. Nearly all reference publishing stems from institutional or larger commercial imprints, but there is still a significant amount of other publishing in the hands of individuals. Indeed, some of the most creative publishing in Australia, both in terms of subject matter and format, has been done by small private presses or self-publishing. In her inimitable and highly entertaining fashion, Wendy Lowenstein investigates the world of self-publishing through case studies of seven key players, concluding that they are 'happy but not rich'. These papers in Part 2 offer a solid perspective on the range of literature published in Australia, by whom and how identified.

With these papers on Australian publishing as background, Part 3 then turns to 'Selecting and Purchasing Australian Publications'. This opens with Jerelynn Brown's 'Selecting In-print Australian Material', which explores the question, 'What is an Australian book?' The answer, it appears, may be something of a moveable feast, depending on the source of figures for Australian publishing output. Brown also describes the processes used to select material for the Bennett Australian Blanket Order Service and provides information on average Australian book prices. In this regard her paper offers interesting contrasts to the views expressed by Carol Mills in the final paper of this section. Brown concludes her essay with a select list of Australian selection aids, which is the topic of John Arnold's more detailed treatment in 'Resources for Collecting Australiana'. His contribution surveys the bibliographic record of the Australia's publishing output from the viewpoint of book purchasers, whether bookshop proprietors, librarians or general readers. Emphasis is also given to retrospective and out-of-print material. The paper concentrates on resources for collecting monographs, with some attention to newspapers, serials and reformatted texts.

Finally, in Part 3 Carol Mills addresses important issues surrounding the supply and pricing of foreign books in Australia. As she points out, a range of market forces makes English language foreign titles unavailable from Australian bookshops when they are readily available in other countries. These same market forces give rise to book prices which are higher in Australia than their original price abroad warrants. Mills offers an overview of the present situation, its origins, and factors for change which have failed to redirect the situation. Taken together, these three papers offer important insights into the problems faced by librarians when selecting and acquiring Australian publications, whether within Australia or elsewhere.

Part 4 then investigates how a number of libraries – in Australia, Britain and the United States – have actually built their collections of Australian publications, with some emphasis on Australian literature as the earliest component in Australian studies. This section begins with two papers on Australian experiences, beginning with the country's premier Australian collection. In 'The Acquisition of Australiana in the National Library of Australia' Richard Stone describes the various means by which 'The National' has developed its collections, including legal deposit, formed collections and other deposit arrangements for government publications. At present, however, introduction of the Distributed National Collection means that the National Library can redefine its comprehensive Australiana collection development policies. (This concept is also addressed in Part 5 by John Horacek.) In 'Australiana in the British Library' James Egles and Graham Cornish do not discuss acquisitions procedures, which differ little from those at the National Library of Australia, but rather describe the many impressive collections with an Australian content. Given the august history of the British Library and Britain's colonial links with Australia, these collections are historically the most significant Australiana repositories in the anglophone world.

In contrast to the broad Australiana collections at the national libraries are the subject-specific collections in academic and research libraries. Typical of these is the Australian creative writing collection at Flinders University, described by G.A. Stafford in 'Collecting Australian Literature: An Australian Perspective'. This began, along with the University, in 1966 to support teaching and research in the field of Australian literature and received further impetus with the foundation of the Centre for Research in the New Literatures in English. In less than thirty years Flinders University has been able to create a literature collection noted for its breadth and depth; this example, and the means to achieve it, should be instructive for any institution seeking to create an Australiana collection today. While serendipity and reliance on personal visits may suit a library close to the source of Australian publishing, more formal means are the norm for libraries far removed from Australia. Thus Patricia Larby offers excellent guidance on selection and acquisition resources from a British perspective in 'Collecting Australian Literature: A British Perspective'. Additionally, and following the descriptive emphasis of her fellow countrymen in the British Library paper, Mrs Larby offers a thorough description of Australiana collections in Britain. (These two papers, incidentally, provide an excellent service for Australianists working in Britain.) Part 4 concludes with 'Developing an Australian Literature Collection: An American Perspective'. In it Ross Atkinson takes an eminently sensible and thoroughly professional approach in discussing how to begin developing and to maintain an Australian literature collection. Although he purports to be focusing on the North American scene, his advice applies to professionals in any environment and covers collection scope and level, bibliographic and synoptic sources, subject vocabulary, collection maintenance and other collection management issues.

In a first collection on any subject there are bound to be a number of 'loose ends' that warrant at least passing attention, partly to provide the full flavour of the field and partly to indicate directions to be pursued in later collections. These are the dual purposes of Part 5 ('Special Needs and Their Solution'), which opens with a discussion of the Australian Joint Copying Project (AJCP). In 'Historical Sources and the Tyranny of Distance: The Achievements of the Australian Joint Copying Project' Graeme Powell and Adrian Cunningham explore the history of Australian copying projects in Britain, outline the operation and administration of the AJCP, discuss the types of records filmed and the repositories searched, summarize the finding aids available to researchers, and elaborate on the future of the Project. The AJCP could well serve as a model for cooperation in the provision of scarce resources in fields other than history. A second topic of growing importance in Australia is multiculturalism; accordingly, Derek Whitehead in 'Documenting Multicultural Australia' outlines the issues, problems and current directions in collecting documentary materials of Australia's ethnic minorities. He also examines the different levels and types of collecting, surveys what is published and its bibliographical control and summarizes problems of acquiring multicultural materials. As multicultural documentation published within Australia becomes increasingly important to any library that collects Australiana, this paper may offer important guidelines for collecting such literature.

Among the enduring problems that vex libraries in their attempts to share resources, collections and experiences is the matter of incompatible descriptions of their collections. Conspectus, because of its increasingly wide acceptance in the anglophone world, offers a future in which collection managers speak the same language. With this in mind, John Horacek in 'Conspectus and Australiana Collections, with Some Comments on the Distributed National Collection' concludes this collection of essays with a discussion of Conspectus in relation to Australiana collections. Although several major Australian libraries have adopted Conspectus, their Australiana collections tend to be treated as a special case – that is, outside Conspectus. Nevertheless, it is likely that Conspectus will continue to attract converts and that all collections will be described in this common language, thereby facilitating communication not only within Australia but overseas as well. At the same time, the spectre of what in Australia is termed the Distributed

National Collection (DNC) may well affect the future of Australian collections. Unlike the old Farmington Plan in the USA or the SCOLMA area specialization scheme in the UK (both for African studies), there is little genuine cooperation built into the DNC, nor is there any proposed funding for it. This may mean that gaps in collections will widen, with no safety net at national level.

In these eighteen papers the overriding aim has been to encourage dialogue among those libraries around the world which seek to collect publications from and about Australia. To achieve this we have presented information on the current state of Australian studies, specific aspects of Australian publishing, features that characterize the selection and purchase of Australian materials and experiences of libraries in several countries with the development of Australiana collections. To the extent that useful information has been disseminated and dialogue begun, this collection will have achieved its purpose.

G.E. Gorman
Charles Sturt University - Riverina

Part 1. The Demand for Australian Collections

1 Australian Studies, Australian Publications and Library Provision

G. E. Gorman and Lyn Gorman

This paper examines the emergence of Australian studies as a recognized academic discipline, the accompanying cultural climate and the institutional infrastructure. The 'raw materials' for Australian studies are then considered. It is shown that libraries catering to Australian studies have an active publishing industry to draw on, in a climate where there is much encouragement of Australian publishing; and they have the benefit of generally sound bibliographical control and many well established selection tools. However, there are problems relating to library provision, and the paper concludes by discussing several: the possible long-term effects of the generous number of literary awards available; the dearth of quality non-fiction Australian publications; and various areas in which libraries and the librarianship profession have been remiss in collecting and preserving the material for Australian studies.

Australian Studies

Following the Second World War, area studies emerged as a discipline in recognition of Western countries' inadequate knowledge of the developing world; this was particularly true in North America and in the former colonial centres of Britain and France, where emphasis was placed on political, economic and anthropological matters. Gradually area studies developed into a truly multidisciplinary field, covering literally every aspect of the history, culture and society of a region; today area studies generally encompasses the literature and linguistics, history and politics, economics and policy studies, cultural and social studies of a specific geo-political entity.

As area studies has become more refined and more successful in terms of the generation of new knowledge, the smaller the areas under investigation have become. 'The more that is known about an area, the smaller the area under institutionalized study is likely to be.'[1] In the instance of Asian and Pacific studies this is certainly the case. In the 1940s the Australian National University in Canberra established its geographically broad Research School of Pacific Studies; in the 1980s Monash University founded the much more narrowly focused National Centre for Australian Studies.

As an academic discipline Australian studies has been recognized in Australia from the mid-1970s. It is convenient to date formal recognition from 1977, the founding year of the *Journal of Australian Studies*. Succeeding years saw the establishment of such primary and secondary serials as *Antipodes, Australian Cultural History, Australian Journal of Cultural Studies, Australian Studies, Index to Journal Articles in Australian History, Reference Australia, Australasian Religion Index* and a number of other Australiana reference guides.

Today the commonly accepted definition of Australian studies seems to be that proposed by David Stockley in the third issue of the *Journal of Australian Studies*: 'a study of those activities of people, and the localities that interact with them, in a culturally identifiable Australian whole'.[2] More recently James Walter has defined the field more succinctly, but still within the same broad framework: the '...systematic study of Australian culture and society.'[3] These definitions, encompassing the arts, humanities and social sciences, exclude the pure and applied sciences; this may be unacceptable to many and may even be incorrect, but it is the reality nevertheless. The reason for it is quite straightforward. In Elizabeth Morrison's words, it arises '...from the fact that Australian studies...is a field of study which happens to have grown up within the arts/humanities/social sciences confines of academic structures....'[4]

In the decades prior to the mushrooming of interest in Australian studies Australians had been struggling to overcome the inferiority complex known by the unfortunate catchphrase, 'cultural cringe'. That they have largely succeeded in this, due in no small part to the 1988 Bicentennial, can be seen in the growing confidence of Australian cultural activities and in the general acceptance of Australian culture internationally. As Linda Christmas so aptly stated in her paper delivered to the 1988 British Australian Studies Association Conference, 'No one today could accuse Australia of cringing. In fact it is more likely in the year of the Bicentennial to be suffering from cultural strut.'[5] If one makes allowances for the hyperbole and exaggeration that naturally accompany new-found confidence of any kind, it is safe to say that Australian cultural life (and, by extension, Australian intellectual endeavours) has reached a watershed in its development. We can now look forward to the refinement of a uniquely Australian contribution to the arts and letters, to social and cultural understanding, to the humanities and the social sciences.

In the words of Jim Davidson, 'Although there are many creative artists who could not be identified with it, there are signs of an emerging Australian aesthetic: wry, spiky and minimalist, often reached by a paring back, a discarding of imported or superfluous assumptions, and marked by an eagerness to come to grips with the spirit of place.'[6] Never mind that this aesthetic might be rejected by those who predominate in the cultural mafia and who, despite their protestations otherwise, cannot accept cultural innovation at the expense of possibly vested interests, the fact is that it is emerging.

This emergence has been accompanied by development of the study of Australia at both school and university levels; this is most evident in courses devoted to Australian society, history and culture, but there are many more references to Australia buried in subjects which cannot be identified as specifically or solely Australian - for example, the treatment of Australian fiction in courses on contemporary creative writing. More readily identifiable has been the emergence of Australian studies as an academic discipline. In Australia alone there are literally dozens of courses, programmes, academic majors and research degrees in Australian studies; many of these are described in Walter's *Australian Studies: A Survey.*[7] At school level perhaps the best example of the growing interest in Australian studies is the introduction in Victoria of Australian studies units in the final two years of secondary education.

In the same period a number of academic and professional associations devoted to Australian studies have been established, both in Australia and overseas – the Australian Studies Association of North America, Association for the Study of Australian Literature, American Association of Australian Literary Studies, British Australian Studies Association, European Association for Studies on Australia. All of these point to the vigour of a new addition to the range of cross-cultural geo-political disciplines that began in the immediate postwar era with African studies and Asian studies. As these associations suggest, Australian studies is certainly not a uniquely Australian phenomenon. Indeed, the National Centre for Australian Studies at Monash University is at least matched in the quality of its work by similar centres overseas, at the University of Texas and the University of London, for example. And on a more modest scale, if many Australian universities now include Australian subjects in the curriculum, so too do many universities overseas. Who, for example, would have expected to find Australian studies being taught at Hungary's Eotvos Lorand University and Lajos Kossuth University? Many of these overseas focal points are described in Amanda Lohrey's *Australian Studies Overseas.*[8]

Australian Publications and Library Provision

If Australian studies as a field of study in universities and schools has grown exponentially in recent years, and if an Australian studies infrastructure now exists in terms of scholarly bodies, degree programmes and research centres, the same is true of the raw information on which these activities are based – that is, information in the form of books and the apparatus to control this information bibliographically. Indeed, it is here that the earlier parallel between area studies and Australian studies breaks down, for in terms of publishing and distribution infrastructures there are few similarities between Australia and the developing nations that are the subject of area studies.

Like North America and Western Europe, Australia has the benefit of an expanding and generally well documented publishing industry. Cecily Johns characterizes area studies librarianship thus: 'typically the area studies librarian is faced with building a collection without a systematic bibliographic apparatus, and in spite of government restrictions that make it difficult and sometimes impossible to purchase publications. In addition to these obstacles there is often no effective distribution system.'[9] In none of these respects does Australian publishing or book distribution resemble the developing world. On the contrary Australia resembles Britain and North America more than any other country – and some would say that Antipodean publishing is but a branch of Anglo-North American publishing in any event.

To begin with, Australia has a very healthy publishing industry for such a small population base. According to Jerelynn Brown (in her paper in Part 3 of this volume), Unesco reports 12,235 original Australian titles published in 1990. Although other sources provide vastly different figures, ranging from 2000 or 3000 to more than 20,000, the reality is that Australia produces a very respectable number of publications each year – and this says nothing of Australiana publications from other countries, Britain and the USA in particular. There is, in other words, a significant amount of documentation on which Australian studies can draw for its inspiration.

At the same time within Australia there is a well established infrastructure for encouraging Australian publications, most notably in creative writing through the Literature Board of the Australia Council. Also, awards abound, from those of state governments (the Victorian Premier's Literary Awards, for instance) to those sponsored by major newspapers (*The Australian*/Vogel National Literary Award and *The Age* Australian Book of the Year Award, among others).[10] There is also a growing number of specialist awards, the most highly publicized being for children's literature: the Children's Book Council alone offers awards in three categories: best picture story books, books for younger readers, books for older readers. In addition there are various '...state student choice trophies – such as Victoria's...Young Australians' Best Book Award (YABBA)....'[11]

To record and select these materials which receive an increasing range of awards, Australia has a highly developed information infrastructure, including a long-established national bibliography (the *Australian National Bibliography)*, a listing of federal government publications *(Australian Government Publications)*, a listing of in-print materials *(Australian Books in Print)* and a wide range of general *(Australian Book Review, Guide to New Australian Books*, etc.) and specialist (*Magpies* and *Reading Time* in the field of children's literature, for example) reviewing and indexing sources. As these and many other resources are described elsewhere in this collection of papers, they need not be discussed here. The important point is that, for selection purposes, Australia's publishing output is well documented and reported upon, making it quite feasible for selectors to choose items individually rather than abrogating responsibility through blanket orders and other devices. Except for libraries aiming to collect comprehensively in all areas of Australiana, this country's publishing output is small enough to permit item-by-item selection.

These selection sources focus on new titles, which has been the major interest of most libraries. However, there is growing interest in older publications, particularly as libraries outside the country seek to create retrospective collections of some breadth and depth. Consequently, a significant amount of Australiana is available through the antiquarian and secondhand book trade. In Australia there are nearly 200 dealers in this field – a large number of traders for a country with a relatively brief publishing history and small output. This aspect of Australiana book supply, too, is replete with information resources, ranging from a list of dealers, *Antiquarian and Secondhand Book Dealers in Australia*, to price guides such as *Australian Book Auction Records* and *Guide to Fine and Rare Australasian Books.* [12]

Yet all is not well in Camelot, and there are increasing signs that publishing and information professionals recognize this. To begin with, there is growing uneasiness about the long-term effects of the plethora of Australian literary awards. In particular there is concern that the tendency to treat 'the best' as the only literature for library shelves is doing a great disservice to the reading public. As Haigh asks, '...are academics, teachers and critics foisting "worthy", and often quite weighty, literature on a readership mostly craving entertainment?'[13] If the answer is yes, and there is much evidence that it is, then many literary awards and their recipients are unmerited – and perhaps unreadable by a large proportion of the public. '...English critic Rob Leeson warned in his 1985 "Reading and Righting": "Survival of literature depends upon expansion, upon winning new readers. 'Filling the shelves with the best' may simply be placing books in a time capsule for future archaeologists."'[14]

Equally disturbing is the fact that non-fiction, particularly of the scholarly or academic variety, is simply inadequate in terms of number of titles. 'The dearth of Australian textbooks in all areas of study is as well recognised as the alibi that the small market makes many otherwise worthwhile projects commercially uninteresting.'[15] This comment by Turner appears in his review of the CRASTE (Committee to Review Australian Studies in Tertiary Education) report, which itself came to the general conclusion that Australian publishing aimed at the educational market was well below expectations.[16] That being the case, there is little defence against Lambert's view that 'area studies programs cannot survive without adequate library resources. A great library collection does not of itself guarantee the excellence of an area studies program, but there can be no strong instructional or research program without one.'[17] This may be one of the great difficulties with Australian studies programmes in Australia and overseas, although the quality of non-Australian publications does compensate significantly for the poor showing of indigenous materials.

If the materials are non-existent in some areas, this is certainly not true of others – Australian fiction, for example, which has enjoyed a well-deserved reputation in recent years. Here, however, it appears that Australian libraries at least have been remiss in their collecting activity. In *Libraries and Australian Literature*, an admirable study of fiction in Australian libraries, the researchers found that 'the largest purchaser of Australian works of creative writing was the South Australian [public library] system, with a total of 13000 volumes for the two years – a proportion of 2.7% of its total acquisitions. On average, roughly one in thirty-eight books bought is a work of Australian creative writing.'[18] Even by limiting the survey to commercially available titles listed in *Australian Books in Print* the public library average for coverage of Australian fiction was only 50 per cent at the time of the survey.[19]

Somewhat defensively, Isaacs and her colleagues ask the question, '...are Australian titles so consistently impressive that a library, even if it was [sic] able, would want to buy all of them?'[20] Of course a library would not want to buy all of them any more than it would want to have all novels by Barbara Cartland or Frederick Forsyth, but it would certainly want to have all 'good' novels and a large percentage of many less notable titles. That neither can be true should be obvious from the figures just cited.

If librarians are not selecting and purchasing Australian titles where they do exist, these same people are also failing to exercise proper custodianship in a number of respects. The CRASTE report included the following condemnatory observations: 'In general the Committee was disturbed to note the profound threat posed by the physical decay of collections, the limited physical and intellectual control over and access to records, and the uncoordinated nature of collection policies.'[21] In other words individual librarians in individual libraries are not selecting Australian titles, nor are they purchasing them; furthermore, where Australian collections of note do exist, they are not being properly managed. This is as much the fault of the profession as a whole as it is of individual professionals. As Elizabeth Morrison suggests, 'committed individuals alone cannot ensure that the collective responsibility of the librarianship profession for providing the bibliographic infrastructure for education and research is met. Articulated policy, organizational structures and financial support are required.'[22]

It is this collective responsibility that no one seems willing to assume in Australia. There are exceptions, of course – notably the tireless work by the Acquisitions Section of the Australian Library and Information Association – but frankly this is the result of sustained commitment by a small number of individuals rather than by the profession as a whole, or by cooperation across relevant industries and professions. For example, as long ago as 1987 CRASTE recommended investigating the prospects for Australian Book Centres as commercial ventures in Asia, Europe and North America, and also the establishment of a Book and Periodicals Development Council to promote the production of scholarly Australian books and their distribution.[23] That neither has occurred more than four years later is a sad indictment of all concerned, from government to lobby groups.

A brief example of one book and its unavailability in bookshops or libraries indicates a great deal about the present state of Australian publishing, book supply and library provision. In Adelaide at the end of 1991 Gillian Mears' *The Mint Lawn* (North Sydney: Allen and Unwin, 1991) was available in only one of four of the city's major bookshops, and it was not to be found on the shelves of a single suburban library in the city; yet this same novel was winner of the 1990 *Australian*/Vogel National Literary Award and had enjoyed a reasonably high profile in the media. If this is typical case of Australia's casual approach to its literary heritage, there is a long road ahead before we can state that Australiana and Australian studies are in a secure position in this country. Overseas, of course, there are great Australiana collections, particularly in Britain and in several American states. But how long will these continue to grow successfully? Without effective support and improvement within Australia, one suspects that collecting Australiana overseas will become as frustrating as collecting Africana from obscure central African states has been for the past three decades – not a comforting thought.

Notes

1 *International Encyclopedia of the Social Sciences,* ed. David L. Sills. New York: Macmillan Company and Free Press, 1969-1979, Vol. 1, p. 402.

2 David Stockley, '"Australian Studies": Seamless Whole or Formless Confusion?' *Journal of Australian Studies,* 3 (1977): 1-13.

3 James Walter, 'Nation and Narrative: The Problem of General History.' In *Australia towards 2000,* ed. Brian Hocking (London: Macmillan Press, 1990).

4 Elizabeth Morrison, 'Australian Studies and the National Centre in the Bicentennial Era,' *Australian Academic and Research Libraries,* 21 (1990): 188.

5 Linda Christmas, 'Images from the Outside,' in *Australia towards 2000,* ed. Brian Hocking. London: Macmillan Press, 1990, p. 61.

6 Jim Davidson, 'The Manufacture of Australian Culture,' in *Australia towards 2000,* ed. Brian Hocking. London: Macmillan Press, 1990, p. 40.

7 James Walter, ed., *Australian Studies: A Survey.* Melbourne: Melbourne University Press, 1989, quoted in Elizabeth Morrison, 'Australian Studies and the National Centre in the Bicentennial Era,' *Australian Academic and Research Libraries,* 21 (1990): 188.

8 Amanda Lohrey, comp., *Australian Studies Overseas: A Guide.* Compiled for the Committee to Review Australian Studies in Tertiary Education. Canberra: Australian Government Publishing Service, 1988.

9 Cecily Johns, ed., 'Introduction,' in her *Selection of Library Materials for Area Studies. Part I. Asia, Iberia, the Caribbean and Latin America, Eastern Europe and the Soviet Union, and the South Pacific.* Chicago, Ill.: American Library Association, 1990, p. x.

10 These and many other literary awards are now recorded in the excellent *Australian Literary Awards and Fellowships; with Winners of Australian and Overseas Awards*. 1st ed. Port Melbourne: D.W. Thorpe, 1991.

11 Gideon Haigh, 'Kid Literati: Deciding What Children Should Read,' *The Age Tempo Magazine*, 20 November 1991, p. 1.

12 Brian R. Howes, *Antiquarian and Secondhand Book Dealers in Australia: A Directory*. 3rd ed. Angaston, SA: Magpie Books, 1990; *Australian Book Auction Records* (N.S. 1983/1985-); Brian R. Howes, *Guide to Fine and Rare Australasian Books*. Wagga Wagga, NSW: The author, 1986.

13 *Op. cit.*, p. 1.

14 *Ibid.*, p. 4.

15 Graeme Turner, 'Pleasing Some of the People, Some of the Time: A Study of Australian Studies.' [Review of *Windows onto Worlds: Studying Australia at Tertiary Level. The Report of the Committee to Review Australian Studies in Tertiary Education*]. *Australian Book Review* (October 1987): 11.

16 Committee to Review Australian Studies in Tertiary Education. *Windows onto Worlds: Studying Australia at Tertiary Level. The Report of the Committee to Review Australian Studies in Tertiary Education*. Canberra: Australian Government Publishing Service, 1987.

17 Richard D. Lambert *et al.*, *Beyond Growth: The Next Stage in Language and Area Studies*. Washington, DC: Association of American Universities, 1984, p. 236.

18 Margaret Isaacs, Linda Emmett and Jean P. Whyte, *Libraries and Australian Literature: A Report on the Representation of Australian Creative Writing in Australian Libraries*. Melbourne: Ancora Press, 1988, p. 26.

19 *Ibid.*, p. 37.

20 *Ibid.*

21 Committee to Review Australian Studies in Tertiary Education, *op. cit.*, p. 208.

22 Elizabeth Morrison, 'Australianizing the Librarianship Agenda,' *Australian Academic and Research Libraries* 21 (1990): 167.

23 Committee to Review Australian Studies in Tertiary Education, *op. cit.*, pp. 267-268.

2 No Bushfires Yet: Australian Studies in the United States

Robert L. Ross

Although Americans have during recent years shown enthusiasm for Australian popular culture, this interest has been slow to translate into formal Australian Studies programmes in American universities. Yet progress is being made, stemming in part from the pioneer work of US scholars from the 1930s onward. Literature has so far received the greatest share of attention through the establishment of an association and journal, but a similar interdisciplinary association is now being formed. Two Australian Studies Centres have been established at major US universities and others are in the planning stage. Library materials are widely available and the Australian Discussion Group of the American Library Association stresses continued acquisition. Considering the progress made recently, the future of Australian studies in the United States is bright.

During the past decade ordinary Americans have embraced things Australian: film, wine, television, fashions, books, sports, music and other elements of popular culture. Many hold a romanticized view of Australia as a rugged frontier not unlike what they believe the United States once was. This somewhat inaccurate but ever colourful vision and version of Australia was created in part by the astounding success a few years ago of *The Thorn Birds*, first as a novel then as a television series; by films such as the *Crocodile Dundee* instalments and *Gallipoli*, both depicting in their own ways manliness and downhome courage; by the revived mystery novels of Arthur Upfield and their celebration of the outback; by the film *Picnic at Hanging Rock* that captured so brilliantly an Australian mystique; by Robert Hughes' *The Fatal Shore* and its tale of suffering and fortitude, the kind of story Americans relish. Recently Aboriginal culture has come into vogue; 'culture' is the key word, not 'Aboriginal'. For the fascination lies with metaphysics and art, rather than with the social plight of a downtrodden, colonized people. After all, Americans are besieged by their own social problems and would rather not be bothered with those of other nations.

So the US has woven Australiana into the fabric of its popular culture, and the Antipodean strand will surely endure. For one thing, many Americans dream of visiting Australia, and many do, especially with the new direct flights that make the long trek less arduous. These tourists are for the most part ordinary folk attracted to a faraway country, foreign yet familiar, where they speak English (often a major criterion for Americans travelling abroad) – even if the English does sound a little funny.

Consul-General Chris Hurford said in a newspaper article (*The Australian*, 24 October 1990) that 'Australia's relationship with New York [City?] and the US was much easier in the past' and 'admits a decline in the relationship between the two countries.' Mr Hurford knows more about politics than I do, but I have observed the cultural scene for the past twenty years from an American's vantage point and I find things much 'easier', both in New York and the rest of the US, of which the City is a part. It has been my observation also that while Australians are sensitive to US politics and the way decisions made in Washington might affect them, Americans show little interest in US-Australian relations on matters of trade, defence, alliances and such. Neither hostility nor condescension are causes, but a lack of awareness and concern – both singular American qualities when it comes to politics. Memories of the Second World War are fading as well, and consequently so does that connection with Australia as fewer veterans are around to recollect the good times in Brisbane and Kings Cross. Mr Hurford also understands more about business and trade than I do, but two things I know for certain: US business will go where there is money to be made regardless of the relationship between the sometimes reluctant host and home; Americans will buy anything that strikes their fancy and worry little about the goods' national origin.

I see the ties, then, as cultural, mainly popular and at times illusory as they stem from what I called earlier a romanticized view of a country that supposedly still holds what America has lost. Most people who ask about Australia want to hear nothing of cities, sophisticated and intellectual circles, art, fine hotels and restaurants, business and trade, theatre, politics and the like. They want to know about the outback, about kangaroos and real-life 'Crocodile Dundees', about the landscape and weather, about Aboriginal mysticism, about male chauvinism, about the men and women who struggle valiantly on a barren land shearing sheep and cutting cane and getting drunk on Saturday night in a pub with a tin roof and a verandah to which they have driven a hundred or so miles.

The academy in the US always remains a step or two behind the larger world it serves, but is slowly awakening to the popular interest in Australia. Through what is generically called 'Australian studies' these days, the academy can correct misapprehensions and increase American understanding and appreciation of Australia as it really is, warts and all. That is happening now, granted on a small scale, but serious study is increasing. When I entered the field in the 1970s by way of a PhD dissertation on Patrick White's fiction, consideration of Australian matters in universities was scant indeed. To receive graduate committee approval for my proposed dissertation, I was required to compare White with what one professor called 'real writers' – those from England and Europe. That could still happen, but it is less likely as Australian literature has slowly gained respect among English professors. More dissertations have appeared in recent years: several on White, as well as ones on David Williamson, A.D. Hope, Christina Stead, Shirley Hazzard, and comparative studies with American writers. Masters theses have also been written on Australian literature, but information on them is difficult to obtain.

There are two other early White dissertations that helped to break the ice: those of Marian Arkin and Thomas Warren. I suppose the three of us could be called pioneers. (Ironically, Arkin's study at New York University was also directed to be comparative in nature.) We were following, though, in the footsteps of true pioneers: C. Hartley Grattan who published in 1928 the first American critical study of Australian literature; Joseph Jones at the University of Texas at Austin; Bruce Sutherland at Pennsylvania State University; Herbert Jaffa at New York University. These scholars and teachers left a legacy. Texas and Pennsylvania State have emerged in recent years as two of the prime movers in Australian studies, and through the establishment of Australian centres have extended the focus beyond literature into political, historical and social areas. The English Department at New York University now engages an Australian writer to teach from time to time, past guests being Thomas Keneally and Peter Carey.

On another front, a small private liberal arts college in Florida, Rollins College, has quietly gone its own way for many years, sending students to Australia for courses arranged by Rollins, hosting Australian artists, composers, writers and scholars, and teaching Australian-related courses in various departments. These student sojourns, as well as similar ones to other countries, are offered through Rollins' International Programs. On the eastern seaboard the Australian government funds a chair at Harvard, and distinguished Australian painters, writers, historians and critics occupy it on a yearly basis. The impact of this well intended effort on the Harvard community remains in question; as America's oldest and most prestigious university, Harvard entertains multiple demands for attention, and the Australian guests – no matter how distinguished at home – may well be swallowed in the traffic.

In the past and currently, isolated courses in Australian literature crop up at such diverse places as Indiana and Tulsa universities in the American heartland, at the University of Utah out in the desert, at Stanford and the University of Oregon on the Pacific coast, at Vassar College in the east, and at Auburn and Memphis State down south; the literary tradition still holds at Pennsylvania State but has vanished at Texas with Professor Jones' retirement. These courses, though, are occasional, most often undergraduate, sometimes given through continuing education departments, and not an established part of a curriculum still largely devoted to American and British literature – areas jealously guarded by the traditionalists who dominate English departments. Syllabi for the courses show that current fiction dominates – that of White, Randolph Stow, Elizabeth Jolley, Thea Astley, Mudrooroo Narogin, David Malouf, Thomas Keneally, Peter Carey; when poetry sneaks in, it is usually by Judith Wright, A.D. Hope and Les Murray, while drama is limited to David Williamson's plays. Henry Lawson finds a place now and then. Recently, through a faculty exchange programme with the University of Sydney, the University of Texas has scheduled history and literature courses and plans others in additional fields on a one-time basis.

Some enterprising Australians must have concluded that studies of their country were not penetrating American academia fast enough, so they decided to transport Americans to Australia to learn things firsthand. Sending US graduate students and 'honours year students' (the latter concept is not a part of US degree plans) to Australia is one of the major thrusts of Mr Hurford's ambitious plans for the American Australian Studies Foundation he has established. Already in action, Curtin University has opened an office in Minneapolis to entice students to Western Australia. The University of Oregon, Pennsylvania State and the University of Texas do send undergraduate students to Australia for a year of work, but they are few in number.

However, unless the highly structured and complex degree requirements in US universities change radically, the likelihood of a mass exodus of increasingly pragmatic American students seems farfetched. Even when transferring from one American university to another, undergraduates often face problems, sometimes losing credits and repeating courses that differ only in catalogue name and number. US graduate study is much more structured than that in Australian universities, with a specific number of coursework hours required before beginning a thesis or dissertation, which is then supervised by a resident adviser. Another factor to consider is that since America gained independence from Great Britain, study abroad – except for short, well regulated periods – has not been a tradition.

After many telephone calls, numerous faxes and letters, and attendance at two gatherings of American 'Australianists', the above is about all I have to report. Although the picture may appear gloomy at first – suggesting that Australia is more often apprehended mythically through popular culture than seriously through academic study, I consider it a hopeful and encouraging state of affairs, one with promise and potential. Yet it would be erroneous and unfair to suggest that Australian studies are spreading like a bushfire across US campuses. Whether they ever will remains doubtful, for the US is a vast and heterogeneous country where attention is diffused. This diffusion is reflected in the academy, which has all manner of special interests demanding resources: Asian, African-American, South American, Chicano, Eastern European, African, Jewish, Native American – all of which have larger constituencies and possibly more immediate relevance than do Australian interests.

So, from a realistic standpoint, I see Australian studies continuing to grow in the US, but gradually. Further, I see it as a grass-roots movement, not one unfolding only at the 'big-name' universities like Harvard or Columbia, Stanford or Texas, Princeton or Penn. State. Important, too, are the schools with names less familiar overseas, but not inferior because of that, institutions like Rollins College, Indiana and Tulsa universities, like Humboldt State in far northern California, Auburn in Alabama and Memphis State, like the Universities of Oregon and Utah. Often in these places a lone faculty member has developed an interest in Australia and through dogged perseverance manages to teach a related course occasionally.

Now that I have generalized outrageously, I will deal more specifically with the concrete work that has been done and that is being carried on, and at the same time examine the important matter of research sources.

Literary Studies

Because my connection with Australian studies has been in literature, it may sound self-serving to say that literary studies have made the greatest progress in the US. This conclusion is backed up, however, by a summary of 'Australian Studies in Academic Institutions in the United States', prepared by Chris Lamb of the Australian Embassy in

Washington. I have cited earlier several universities that have offered courses in Australian literature, even if not on a regular basis.

Why, then, has literature been in the forefront? First, much of it is simply very good, and some of the writing has been published in the US for many years; for example, Patrick White and Christina Stead both had American publishers long before their work appeared in Australian editions, and Henry Handel Richardson's trilogy was a Book-of-the-Month Club selection during the 1940s. Literature also moves easily from one country to another; this has something to do with it being universal, even if that term has fallen into disrepute among fashionable critics. As I have already mentioned, it was the first field to receive serious academic attention. I recall Professor Jaffa telling me how in the 1960s he gave lectures at New York University evening extension courses on Australian poetry; after all, in those days such a renegade subject had no place in the English department. There has long been scattered interest in what was once called 'Commonwealth literature', that is, the writing from the old Empire, of which Australian is a part; that interest is solidifying, so Australian books are often included in courses now called 'World Literature Written in English' or 'Post-Colonial Literature', names less suggestive of imperialism. Further, the work of White and Stead has found its way into courses on the modern novel alongside that of 'real writers'. Because feminist critics consider Stead's fiction meaningful, they sometimes include her novels – most often *The Man Who Loved Children* – in women's studies courses.

In addition, the Literature Board of the Australia Council has recognized US readers as a potential audience for the writers it serves and has carried on an extensive programme to help get books published, to promote them, and to assist writers in making personal appearances in the US. The Board has even hired a New York publicist, Selma Shapiro, but exactly what she does is not altogether clear. While the work of the Literature Board has been most admirable, the emphasis placed on New York City is a mistaken one. Although it is the centre for publishing and Australian writers' interests there must be promoted and guarded, New York does not speak for the whole country. Most Americans live west of the Hudson River and there lies the larger audience. The idea that all the bookstore windows along Fifth Avenue will someday be brimming with Australian books is an unrealistic and impractical one. Take, for instance, Thea Astley's American tour in the spring of 1990 to promote her new novel, *Reaching Tin River*. Her small New York City audience consisted mainly of the already converted, while her appearance in Richmond, Virginia, turned into a special event for that city. The well attended reading and the writer's mingling with the community there undoubtedly did much to make Americans aware of Australian literature. A retired businessman and patron of the arts, Saul Viener, who arranged Astley's appearance in Richmond, told me that those attending Astley's reading are still talking about it – and more importantly are reading her books and others by Australians. That story could be repeated across the US where various Australian writers have been seen and heard. Again, much depends on the grass-roots movement.

Australian novels are regularly reviewed in major US publications, both academic and popular, including *The New York Times Book Review, The Book World (Washington Post)* and *The Los Angeles Times Book Review*. Writers receiving such attention include Elizabeth Jolley, Jessica Anderson, Thomas Keneally, Peter Carey, Rodney Hall, Thea Astley and Janette Turner Hospital, all of whom have American publishers. Penguin Books, through its international distribution system, releases work by writers well known in Australia but not so in the US, but they do not tend to be reviewed. Poetry and drama, on the other hand, have not fared so well: David Williamson's plays have been produced on Broadway and in major regional theatres, and work by other Australian dramatists has received off-Broadway productions; the poetry of Les Murray, Chris Wallace-Crabbe, Mudrooroo Narogin and others has been published either in book form or in magazines, and some anthologies have appeared. Such major academic journals as *Prairie Schooner* and *Journal of Popular Culture* have devoted issues to Australian literature, and other prestigious publications like *Modern Fiction Studies* and *World Literature Today* regularly publish articles and reviews on Australian writing. The printed programme for the annual meeting of the Modern Language Association provides an accurate gauge for what is happening in academic circles. Not long ago an isolated paper on Patrick White might show up, but at recent meetings entire sessions have been devoted to Australian literature. A regional meeting of the Modern Language Association, the South Central MLA Conference, organized an Australian session in 1984 and has offered a programme of papers and guest appearances by Australian writers each year since. In 1988 an organization at Yale, the Common Wealth of Letters, sponsored a conference on Australian literature as part of a series of such meetings devoted each year to the literature and art of a former Commonwealth country. In 1990, for instance, the focus was on Indian film.

Once it was difficult to buy an Australian book in most US bookstores – even one by Nobel Laureate Patrick White after the first edition had disappeared. I recall scouring used bookshops, depending on inter-library loans and coercing Australian friends into sending books to me at extraordinary air mail rates. But that is not necessary today – and part of the fun has disappeared. If the local shop does not have the book, then an excellent mail order service, The Australian Book Source, operated by Susan Curray in Davis, California, can provide almost any Australian publication in print.

In 1985, with the encouragement and support of the Literature Board, the American Association of Australian Literary Studies (AAALS) was organized when twenty academics from all parts of the US met at Columbia University. The enthusiasm displayed at that casual meeting led to a formal organization, which currently has over 150 members world-wide, holds an annual conference, and publishes a newsletter and a journal, *Antipodes*, which just completed its fifth year of publication. The lively conferences, drawing delegates from the US, Canada, Europe and Australia, have been held at Penn. State, New York University, University of Texas at Austin, Rollins College and Indiana University. The University of Oregon will host the 1992 gathering. The AAALS not only serves as a network for American academics and others interested in Australian literature but also operates on the international scene so that ties have been formed with Australian, Asian, African, British and European scholars.

Although I have been closely associated with the founding of AAALS and *Antipodes*, I am not embarrassed to say the the organization and its publications have had a wide influence on behalf of Australian literature and its writers, not embarrassed because the success of the organization has depended on so many people how have given their time and talents to its development. *Antipodes* published in 1989 a retrospective bibliography of Australian literature and criticism in North America, compiled by Julia Duffy, and its winter 1990 issue offers a similar bibliography for 1989, its several hundred entries compiled by Nan Bowman Albinski. The journal will continue publishing the yearly bibliography, a most revealing document that shows Australian literature has indeed carved out a deserved place in American readership, both academic and general.

Studies Centres

Although talk of Australian studies centres in American universities does occasionally spread like a bushfire, in truth only two are fully operational, at Penn. State and at the the University of Texas; another, at the University of Oregon, remains in the planning state; the fourth, at the University of Hawaii, is being organized.

Established in 1982, the Australia-New Zealand Studies Center at Pennsylvania State University was founded by Henry Albinski, Professor of Political Science, who directs the diverse programme along with Associate Director Robert A. Brand, a retired Minister-Counsellor of the US Foreign Service. The Center's objective rings with clarity: 'To promote the systematic study of and the dissemination of information about Australia and New Zealand, and to clarify and enhance the Australian-American and New Zealand-American relationships.'

The 1989-1990 report tells how the Center realizes this objective. For one thing, it promotes the teaching of Australian and New Zealand subject matter throughout the university, for it is not a teaching centre; the report cites courses in political science and literature as ones focusing on Australian-New Zealand materials, as well as an interdisciplinary course on the two countries' culture and civilization offered through the Humanities Program but developed by the Center; also visiting Australian academics sometimes teach courses in their fields, examples being sociology, film and labour/industrial relations.

Research projects of various kinds, involving Penn. State and Australian-New Zealand academics, have been undertaken and are planned, through funding by grants from the USIA, the Myer Foundation in Melbourne and other sources. The arrangement of conferences comprises another of the Center's activities, which has resulted in meetings that have addressed topics ranging from 'Australian Energy Resource Development' to 'Australian and New Zealand Health Policies and Their Administration'. The Center also plays host each year to Australian and New Zealand academics, professionals and 'public persons', who during brief visits present lectures and seminars. On the cultural side the Center has sponsored and co-sponsored Australian film festivals, literary readings, the production of Australian plays, musical performances and art exhibitions.

Publications also play a part. Two significant recent works are *Australian/New Zealand Literature in the Pennsylvania State University Libraries: A Bibliography* and *A Calendar of Australian Letters, Documents and Manuscripts in the Pennsylvania State University Libraries*. The Penn. State libraries hold one of the most extensive American collections of Australian/New Zealand materials, as these two bibliographical guides prove, thus making the University a prime place for research in almost any field. The archives of the AAALS and *Antipodes* have been acquired by the Penn. State library and will be developed there on a continuing basis.

The second centre to emerge is the Edward A. Clark Center for Australian Studies at the University of Texas at Austin, which was established in 1988 under the co-directorship of John Higley and Desley Deacon, and opened formally by Prime Minister Bob Hawke when he visited Austin in 1988. Its objective resembles that of the Penn. State Center, except that it does not include New Zealand studies. How it works to fulfil the objective also differs little from the other centre. Funded by a special endowment and various grants, the Center is sponsoring faculty and student exchanges between Texas and the University of Sydney and is carrying on a comparative study of American and Australian immigration policies in cooperation with the Australian Bureau of Immigration Research. In the spring of 1991 the Center held a conference on immigration policies, which was attended by Australians, Canadians and Americans. Also, in cooperation with the AAALS, the Center publishes *Antipodes*. Another project includes the fostering of North American links with the future American Studies Centre at the University of Sydney. The Clark Center inaugurated the R.J.L. Hawke Annual Lecture in October 1990 when Senator Gareth Evans, Australian Minister for Foreign Affairs and Trade, spoke on 'Alliances and Change'. The Center has published that speech in the first of a series of occasional publications. In 1992 the Center will sponsor a production of David Williamson's *The Removalists*.

Like those at Penn. State, the Texas libraries offer impressive Australian materials, including the C. Hartley Grattan Collection, which contains over 25,000 books, as well as archival materials on all aspects of Australia. In addition to the literary manuscripts that comprise part of the Grattan collection, the Harry Ransom Humanities Research Center holds the Howarth Papers and Christina Stead's correspondence with Stanley Burnshaw. With the Center's encouragement and direction, the libraries are adding to their Australian holdings and working to fill gaps. In 1988 the Center assisted with the publication of *Perspectives on Australia: Essays on Australiana in the Collections of the Harry Ransom Humanities Research Center*, which provides a good sampling of some of the materials available. Another resource of the University is the Harold E. Mertz Collection of 150 Australian paintings, which is considered the major assemblage of contemporary Australian art in America.

Australian visitors – academics, government officials, writers – also add to the Center's visibility, with many of the guests offering lectures, readings and seminars to the University community. The Center offers no courses on its own, but encourages such work throughout the University curriculum.

Although the third centre, at the University of Oregon, remains in the planning stage, it emerges as a scene of activity in Australian studies. In addition to his regular position in the office of student affairs, Jack Bennett supervises various projects, which includes encouraging classes with Australian content, teaching literature courses intermittently and arranging forums for Australian guests. The University of Oregon sponsors a student exchange programme and has been the host for two Australian Fulbright scholars, Brian Matthews and John McLaren. Although endorsed by the University, the Center's development has been hampered by lack of financial support. While not on a par with the Penn. State and Texas libraries, research sources at the University of Oregon, in literature especially, are excellent.

The University of Hawaii has launched a plan to create a centre that would be much like the ones on the mainland. Now surveying faculty to determine interests, a committee, headed by Brian Murton, Professor of Geography, looks forward to future development in this handy and strategic location.

In 1986 Bernard Hickey published an article in *Quadrant* (30, pp. 49-51) entitled 'Things Fall Apart: The Centers Cannot Hold', in which he lamented the deteriorating state of Australian studies in the US and called for increased support. Now, however, that support appears to be forthcoming, and the centres are holding.

Other Developments

Library Organization

An Australian Discussion Group was added in 1987 to the American Library Association (ALA), and holds meetings at the ALA Conventions. Organized by William Schenck, Library of Congress, the Group stresses the acquisition of Australian materials. Murray Martin, a library consultant from Massachusetts, was recently elected as the chair, replacing Schenck. The Group publishes a newsletter, edited by Cheryl Malone, reference librarian and Australian bibliographer at the Perry-Castaneda Library, University of Texas.

According to information from the Group, US libraries, other than those at Penn. State, University of Oregon and Texas, that hold creditable amounts of Australian materials include the Universities of Iowa, Minnesota, North Carolina (Chapel Hill) and Cornell, Duke and Indiana Universities. In addition, the Library of Congress and the New York Public Library have sizeable collections.

Interdisciplinary Organization

Encouraged by the success of the AAALS in promoting literary studies, those interested in other Australian fields have set out to form the Australian Studies Association of North America (ASANA). Spearheaded by Henry Albinski, whose initial survey indicated interest among academics and others in the United States and Canada, ASANA published a newsletter in early 1991 and solicited membership. The new association looks toward conferences and an interdisciplinary journal. The formation of ASANA was first discussed at a general meeting of American Australianists sponsored by the Clark Center in 1989. A similar gathering took place at Penn. State in 1990, where those attending endorsed the plan and by their presence formed a steering committee. Another planning meeting was held at the University of Oregon in the fall of 1991.

As I conclude this chapter, I think of Walt Whitman's poem, 'When I Heard the Learn'd Astronomer'. After listening for a while to the expert 'add, divide, and measure' the heavens, the poet goes outdoors to experience the 'mystical moist night-air' and the stars in his own untutored way. Similarly, the Australianists, with their journals and conferences, resource materials and studies and analyses – adding, dividing and measuring – might well undermine the magic Australia holds for so many Americans. Let us hope that is not the case, for the experts – like their less informed fellow Americans – must once have approached this faraway land in mythical terms. May they not lose the indefinable spirit that imbues a first fascination.

Publications of Interest

(All prices are in US dollars unless noted otherwise. In some cases there may be an additional charge for overseas air mail if that is not specified. Prepayment in US funds is required unless noted otherwise.)

Bibliographies

Albinski, Nan Bowman. *Australian/New Zealand Literature in the Pennsylvania State University Libraries: A Bibliography*. Bibliographical Series No. 11. University Park: The PSU Libraries, 1989. 345 pp. pap. $15 (Available from the Office of the Dean, Pattee Library, Pennsylvania State University, University Park, PA 16802. Prepayment not required.)

Albinski, Nan Bowman. *A Calendar of Australian Letters, Documents and Manuscripts in the Pennsylvania State University Libraries*. University Park: Australia-New Zealand Studies Center, 1990. 25

pp. pap. $6 (Available from the Australia-New Zealand Studies Center, Pennsylvania State University, 314 Kern Building, University Park, PA 16802.)

Albinski, Nan Bowman. 'Bibliography of Australian Literature and Criticism Published in North America – 1989.' *Antipodes*, 4, 2 (Winter 1990): 150-162.

Duffy, Julia. 'Bibliography of Australian Literature and Criticism Published in North America: 1985-1988.' *Antipodes*, 3, 1 (Spring 1989): 71-79.

Ross, Robert L. *Australian Literary Criticism – 1945-1988, An Annotated Bibliography*. New York: Garland Publishing, 1989. $52 (Available from Garland Publishing, 136 Madison Avenue, New York, NY 10016.)

Journals

Antipodes – A North American Journal of Australian Literature. Two issues per year published by the American Association of Australian Literary Studies in cooperation with the Edward A. Clark Center for Australian Studies. (Subscription rates: $A32 individuals; $A40 institutions; back issues $A15; all rates include air mail postage; available from Brian Kiernan, English Department University of Sydney, NSW 2006; cheques payable to Antipodes.)

Daedalus, 114, 1 (Winter 1985). Special Australian issue entitled 'Australia: Terra Incognita'; articles on history, art, literature, society, communication, politics, ecology. ($10; available from *Daedalus* Business Office, PO Box 515, Canton, MA 02021.)

Journal of Popular Culture, 23, 2 (Fall 1989). Special Australian issue; articles on current research in earlier Australian literature, Catherine Helen Spence, Aboriginal literature, A.D. Hope, Xavier Herbert, Patrick White and Vincent Buckley, with an introduction on Australian literary development. ($7.50 plus $2.50 postage; available from Journals Department, Bowling Green University Popular Press, Bowling Green, Ohio 43403.)

Library Chronicle, N.S., 42/43 (1988). Special issue on Australian materials in the Harry Ransom Humanities Research Center at the University of Texas; articles on C. Hartley Grattan, Miles Franklin, Joseph Furphy, Alice Henry, Iris Milutinovic and Christina Stead, as well as a discussion of the paintings in the Mertz Collection. Illustrations. Reprinted as *Perspectives on Australia* (1989). ($18.95, plus $8.28 for Australian air mail or $2.50 surface; available from Harry Ransom Humanities Research Center, University of Texas, Austin TX 78713-7219.)

Prairie Schooner, 62, 4 (Winter 1988/89). Special issue entitled 'Writing from Australia'; seven short stories, fifty poems, two interviews, involving thirty-four Australian writers, including Elizabeth Jolley, Gwen Harwood, John Tranter, Munganye, Les Murray, Rosemary Dobson, Tim Winton, Bruce Dawe. ($7; available from Prairie Schooner, 201 Andrews Hall, University of Nebraska, Lincoln, NE 68588-0334.)

Newsletters/Reports/Other Items

Newsletter, American Association of Australian Literary Studies (twice yearly). (A$8 per year, includes air mail postage; available from Brian Kiernan, English Department, University of Sydney, NSW 2006.)

Yacker, newsletter of the Edward A. Clark Center for Australian Studies (twice yearly). (No charge; available from the Center, HRHRC 3.362, University of Texas, Austin TX 78713-7219.)

Newsletter, Australian Studies Association of North America (twice yearly). (No charge; available from Australia-New Zealand Studies Center, Pennsylvania State University, 314 Kern Building, University Park, PA 16802.)

Newsletter, Australian Studies Discussion Group of the American Library Association (twice yearly). (No charge; available from Cheryl Malone, Reference Department, Perry-Castaneda Library, University of Texas, Austin TX 78712.)

Annual Report of Activities of the Australia-New Zealand Studies Center, Pennsylvania State University. (No charge; available from Australia-New Zealand Studies Center, Pennsylvania State University, 314 Kern Building, University Park, PA 16802.)

Grattan, C. Hartley. 'Australian Literature.' *The Bookman*, 67 (1928): 625-631. Reprint. Seattle: University of Washington Chapbooks, 1989. Reprint. *Antipodes*, 2, 1 (Spring 1988): 20-24.

Jones, Joseph. 'Some Australian Scholars at Home and Abroad.' *Antipodes*, 2, 1 (Spring 1988): 27-29.

Jaffa, Herbert C. 'On Poetry and Poets – Beginnings.' *Antipodes*, 2, 2 (Winter 1988): 117-118.

Cromwell, Alexandra (ed.). *From Outback to City: Changing Preoccupations in Australian Literature of the Twentieth Century.* (Papers on Patrick White, Les Murray and Australian drama from the 1987 MLA session on Australian literature.) New York: AAALS, 1988. ($6 postpaid; available from AAALS, 190 Sixth Avenue, Brooklyn NY 11217.)

Evans, Gareth. *Alliances and Change*. Inaugural R.J.L. Hawke Lecture, 1990. Austin, Tex.: Edward A. Clark Center for

Australian Studies, 1990. (No charge; available from the Center, HRHRC 3.362, University of Texas, Austin TX 78713-7219.)

Sessions on Australian Literature

Modern Language Association Conventions
1984 Patrick White (1), 1986 General Topics (1), 1987 General Topics (1), 1988 General Topics (2), 1989 General Topics (1), 1990 Aboriginal Literature (1)

South Central Modern Language Association Conference (a regional division of the international Modern Language Association)
The first session was held in 1984 and has become a regular part of the yearly programme; a variety of papers on general topics has been presented; Australian writers participating include Rodney Hall, Chris Wallace-Crabbe, Thea Astley, Dorothy Hewett, Carmel Bird.

Addresses of Relevant Centres

Edward A. Clark Center for Australian Studies
University of Texas at Austin, HRHRC 3.362
Austin, Texas 78713-7219
Tel.: 512/471 9607; fax: 512/471 8869

Australia/ New Zealand Studies Center
Pennsylvania State University
314 Kern Building
University Park, Pennsylvania 16802

International Programs
Box 2759
Rollins College
Winter Park, Florida 32789-4496
Tel.: 407/646 2466; fax: 407/646 2600

Australian Studies Program
C/o International Studies
University of Oregon
Eugene, Oregon 97403

For information on Visiting Professor of Australian Studies at Harvard University, contact:
Professor L.R. Hiatt
Department of Anthropology
Peabody Museum
Harvard University
Cambridge, Massachusetts 02138

Part 2. Australian Publishing

3 Modern Australian Publishing: An Historical Perspective

Wallace Kirsop

Printing and publishing have been practised in Australia since the beginning of the nineteenth century. Until the 1950s the country imported four-fifths of its reading matter. Now it produces half of its needs. Behind the change indicated by these simple figures lies the complex history of trade relationships with Britain and the United States of America and of see-sawing levels of dependence or independence. The combination of global concentration in the publishing industry and of Australia's loss of markets for wool, wheat and minerals makes the future uncertain.

Anyone setting out to describe the publishing industry in Australia in the 1990s recognizes quickly that it is indispensable to understand some of the tensions and conflicts of interest that have marked the country's book world since European settlement in 1788. This is no polite gesture to antiquarianism or to the leisurely rhetorical conventions of another age. The present is embedded in the past in ways that can astonish people who see the nations of the so-called 'New World' as a sort of tabula rasa fit for experiments in the construction of hitherto unheard of societies. The supposed freedom to invent is constrained and limited by traditions imported from Europe. Language, the legal system, institutions, the cultural heritage, all these things are given in advance in the very act of colonization. The penal basis of the early Australian settlements was particularly determining in this respect. However, we need to remember that even where, as in South Australia, there were no convicts, ideas, songs, paintings, books and words were also transported to provide the comforting illusion of a reconstituted 'home'. The various media, with print foremost among them, are at the very centre of the complex interrelationships between the several former British colonies and the major English-speaking countries of the northern hemisphere. Proper attention to the historical context cannot therefore be avoided.

After a brief survey of developments in book distribution and production from the early period of settlement to the end of the 1980s, it will be necessary to concentrate on those conflicts, constraints and tensions that have been visible at every stage of the industry in Australia. These perennial themes provide the background to a present situation affected by all the centripetal pressures that are characteristic not only of the English-speaking world in the late twentieth century but also of international publishing in general. In giving an account of what Australian publishers are doing now and of how they are serving their market, one must also assess their position on the global stage.

From 1788 to 1988: The Gradual Australianization of Book Consumption and Production

From the start it had been assumed that some at least of the printing needs of the new British colony would be satisfied from local resources. Governor Arthur Phillip's First Fleet arrived in 1788 with a printing press on board. It was 1796 before this was put to use and then essentially for notices, playbills and such ephemeral items. After George Howe took over as government printer at the beginning of the nineteenth century, more elaborate work was undertaken and a pattern was established that was to remain valid for both New South Wales and Van Diemen's Land into the 1820s. Official tasks, notably the production of a weekly government gazette, predominated along with the level of control and censorship that one would expect, but Howe and his opposite number in Hobart, Andrew Bent, were able to develop a certain amount of normal commercial activity on the side. This included some rudimentary bookselling as well as a few ventures into general publishing, for example of locally composed verse and of almanacs. More ambitious works, frequently the testimonies of eye-witnesses of the great enterprise of European settlement in Australia, were destined for London booksellers and for readers on the other side of the Equator.

One has to remember the fragility of the Australian colonies until after the Napoleonic Wars. Before pastoral possibilities replaced the subsistence crises of the first period, the long-term future of the penal settlements was in some doubt and the population remained small. The dominance of the newspaper press – a parallel to the situation in many places in North America – was therefore to be anticipated. At bottom people made private arrangements for the importation of books, bringing them in their luggage or having them sent out later by friends, relatives and London booksellers. Loans from neighbours and infrequent auctions of the property of departing or bankrupt colonists gave opportunities for encountering unfamiliar books. Beyond the strictly utilitarian material being printed locally, trade distribution was virtually absent.

In the 1820s this first pioneering phase gave way to greater sophistication. However, it should be noted that the later major settlements in modern Western Australia, Queensland, Victoria and South Australia also went more briefly through similar deprivation before a regular trade was set up there, towards the middle of the century. The new time of expansion was marked by the creation of the institutions of civilized life in legislative councils, learned societies, secondary schools and – after 1850 – universities, museums, public and commercial libraries, clubs; and all of these stimulated publishing on the spot. An expanding audience of emancipists, free settlers, professional men and their families created a demand for polite literature that could not be satisfied locally but at least brought into being the first Australian essays in various genres.

After the confrontations of the 1820s between colonial governors and newspaper proprietors, the press was emancipated and flourished in consequence. Government activities proliferated and found appropriate expression in print. The innovation, at this time of much greater production than before 1820, was that now separate government and newspaper printeries were being joined by recognizable booksellers like Dowling of Launceston, who issued a piratical *Pickwick Papers* in 1838-1839. The ever-successful almanacs and directories – a staple of colonial publishers – were to come from more than one of these sources.

In the wider field of book distribution the characteristics of these decades were on the one hand the speculative consignment system, on the other the emergence of professional traders – importers, booksellers, circulating library proprietors – in the major colonial centres. London and other booksellers, especially those specializing in remainders, sensed that the colonial market was open for speculative consignments to be put up for auction to private persons and to retail booksellers in Sydney, Adelaide, Melbourne, Hobart, Launceston and even Port Fairy. Although the choice of items to be put in cases and catalogued either locally or in Britain was supposedly tailored to the needs of colonists, one would be rash to discount the convenience of exporters dumping excess stock. Taste was being imposed and dictated from outside. In contradistinction to this rather cynical traffic we have booksellers working in the colonial towns and bringing in material – often from sources to which they had privileged access by virtue of a shared denominational affiliation. The conscious building of a general trade network was to be left to James and Samuel Augustus Tegg, sons of the famous Cheapside bookseller. In Sydney, Hobart and Launceston between 1835 and 1847 they operated rather like James Rivington in North America in the late eighteenth century, pursuing all branches of the profession, including publishing. The sale of their businesses and the breaking of the London connection they represented made it easier for Australians to take a radically different direction in the 1850s.

The enormous increase in population that came with the gold rush to New South Wales and to a now separate Victoria showed up the grave deficiencies of the quite haphazard consignment system. The Walches, who had bought out Tegg in Hobart in 1846, and George Robertson, a Dublin-trained bookseller who arrived in Melbourne at the end of 1852, hit on the obvious solution to the problem: establish buying agencies in London to select books and export them to their wholesaler principals in the colonies. The rapid ascension of Melbourne to the status of premier city in Australasia in the second half of the century meant that Robertson became the dominant importer and wholesaler, with branch houses in Sydney and Adelaide and commercial travellers covering the whole region. His business was not a monopoly. Other firms continued to have their own sources of supply, and consignments still reached Australian ports. Nonetheless, most retailers in the cities and in country towns bought from Robertson's trade catalogs and sales. It was the great merchant's boast from relatively early that he could give discounts that would enable most small shops to sell books at London published prices. It was no accident, of course, that arrangements so favourable for booksellers' customers were made possible in the period of free trade from Lord Campbell's decision in 1852 till the Net Book Agreement of 1899.

Although importation was facilitated in this way, publishing in the colonies themselves continued to grow, with Melbourne the most important centre. Once again the crucial name is that of Robertson. However, if one reviews the quite long list of titles issued by the firm, it is hard to discern any sort of coherent policy or a guiding principle of choice. There were important books, for example the works of the political economist W.E. Hearn and Marcus Clarke's novel, *His Natural Life*, but Robertson's attempts to place them in the northern hemisphere market met with limited success. Much else was of more obviously local interest, and one suspects – in the absence of surviving business records – that authors frequently paid for or subsidized the publication of their texts. Those who sought a wider audience normally turned as before to London, Edinburgh or Glasgow houses. The lists of other Australian publishers, for instance H.T. Dwight, who was active in Melbourne from 1859 until his death in 1871, display the same disparate character in this period.

On the other hand the newspaper press thrived in the cities and far and wide in the countryside. As literary historians are beginning to discover, it played – notably through the serialization of fiction, some original and some placed by organizations like Tillotson's Fiction Bureau – a wider role in the colonies' cultural life. Unlike monthly and other journals, which often had predictably short careers, the weeklies associated with metropolitan dailies, foremost among them the Melbourne *Argus*'s *Australasian*, maintained over many decades high standards of serious writing. Government patronage through paid advertisements was valuable to the marginal provincial press, but the official contribution to publishing remained direct and massive as administrative functions became more and more diverse.

Despite the rich complexity of the Australian book world from the late 1850s to 1890, most reading matter continued to be imported. Without cringing, the people of Robertson's generation were conscious of their place in a wider English-speaking community. To be a colonial or a provincial was neither a matter of exaggerated pride nor the occasion of shame. It was a fact to be accepted and certainly no excuse for the diminution of striving. Paradoxically, as the colonies approached their Federation in 1901 and found in the *Bulletin* from 1880 an aggressively nationalist voice, they increased the Australian fervour of their publications and gradually lost control of their own book trade.

The fourth phase of Australian book history may have begun almost imperceptibly in the 1880s and been hastened by the great financial crash of the early 1890s, but it took decades to be fully installed. In its essentials it was still in place a century later at the end of the 1980s. In terms of book distribution it has gradually substituted a closed market for an open one. The legal and organizational steps towards this included the appearance in the Australian colonies during the 1880s and 1890s of a number of branches and representatives of British publishing houses – a parallel to the general supplanting of local merchant importers by manufacturers' agents – the adoption of the Net Book Agreement in Britain, the enshrinement in the Copyright Act of 1912 of the principle of 'territorial divisibility' and the gradual removal in most cases of the right to indent directly from Britain and the United States of America. Neither the outlawing of resale price maintenance by the Restrictive Trade Practices Act of 1971 – from which the trade unsuccessfully sought exemption in 1972 – nor the later breakdown of the old carve-up of North American and British and Commonwealth rights did much to change the industry's price structures. One hundred years after George Robertson Australian retail customers were and are normally paying well above northern hemisphere prices for imported books.

There is no doubt that the price differential has in recent decades had the same effect as a tariff in encouraging the expansion of local publishing. However, the ground was prepared in the late nineteenth century by new firms that had broken away from George Robertson and Company, especially in Sydney, which, less affected by the 1890s depression, was re-emerging as the nation's largest city. From 1888 Angus and Robertson, in which another and unrelated George Robertson was the moving spirit, began a programme of systematic publication of Australian writing. The fact that a new generation of native-born and often intensely patriotic authors had come to maturity in the 1880s and 1890s was no doubt more than a happy coincidence. The *Bulletin* school and the stable of popular novelists working for A.C. Rowlandson's New South Wales Bookstall Company between 1897 and 1922 gave some substance to the notion that a wide audience could be reached from an Australian base. Outstanding and enduring commercial successes like *Cole's Funny Picture Book*, first issued by the Melbourne bookseller E.W. Cole in 1879, indicated the market's potential. In spite of a dominance by Angus and Robertson that lasted at least into the 1960s, publishing in Australia came to attract more and more businesses.

It would be too simplistic to date the greater strength of local production from Federation in 1901. As Australia developed its own versions of British institutions, publishing needs grew in complexity, but progress remained relatively slow until after the Second World War. Melbourne University Press, created in 1922, was in the field a good quarter of a century before its fellows. Research was not strong in institutions overwhelmed by their undergraduate teaching responsibilities. The Commonwealth Council for Scientific and Industrial Research (CSIR), later to become the Commonwealth Scientific and Industrial Research Organisation (CSIRO), did not start until 1926. Scientific publishing before the 1920s was therefore the exclusive preserve of learned societies and of state-supported museums. Nonetheless, the role of Angus and Robertson, 'Publishers to the University' on the model of MacLehose in Glasgow, where Robertson did his training, should be noted. At least one trade publisher was prepared in this way to assume the duties and privileges of his profession, to cater not only for the consumers of novels, poems and children's stories, but also for the users of textbooks and for scholars or intelligent and educated general readers.

In a world in which many developed countries have stabilized their population size over the last half-century it is prudent to remember that demographic growth in Australia has kept pace with the overall trend of 150 per cent increase since the early 1930s. This, apart from all the other factors evident in modern societies, helps to explain the spectacular expansion of publishing in Sydney, Melbourne and elsewhere in the continent. The market, which before 1939 was the same size as that of Sweden, now encompasses 17 million people in Australia itself, as well as the still modest – but previously non-existent – academic clientele in Europe and North America. At the same time – and despite an explosion of interest at all levels in a national past highlighted in the 1980s by a series of sesquicentenaries and bicentenaries – local books accounted for at most one-half of the demand. The curiosity of the Australian reader extends well beyond family histories, guidebooks and chronicles of towns and districts up and down the country.

Given the Australianization of school and university curricula after 1945 especially, it is not surprising that local booksellers should have lost their virtual monopoly of publishing in New South Wales, Victoria and the other states. The example was set by Thomas Lothian, son of John Inglis Lothian, who had come to Melbourne in 1888 as the representative of Walter Scott of Newcastle-upon-Tyne. In 1905 the younger Lothian began a publishing business that is still controlled by the family and that has brought out a wide range of textbooks and general works. Oxford University Press, which established its Melbourne office in 1908 after regular selling trips from 1890, started its educational list in the 1930s and launched seriously into publishing after 1945. The last few decades have seen many other British and American firms take the same path. Importing and wholesaling have been complemented by direct competition for manuscripts to be printed in Australia or – more often – in Hong Kong, Singapore or Taiwan. Going even further, some northern hemisphere companies have simply bought out or taken over Australian ones.

Alongside the foreign presence in the Australian Book Publishers' Association, formed in 1949 by the merger of two smaller groups in New South Wales and Victoria, we have to recall the continuing function of official presses of various kinds. The state governments and their instrumentalities, the Australian Government Publishing Service and other Commonwealth bodies, public corporations, municipal administrations, all of these contribute to a very considerable flow of printed material that is now normally sold at full commercial rates and not at nominal figures. Add to this the part played by associations, political parties, religious groups and others and one sees something of the complexity of the Australian book world at the beginning of the 1990s. Assuredly, none of the more or less overt tensions noticed over two centuries is absent from this picture.

The Perennial Tension between the Local and the Imported in the Australian Book Trade

The inhabitants of the so-called 'New World', or more specifically those of them that claim descent from and identity with the European settlers who arrived at the earliest during the Renaissance, are prone to doubt and much introspection about their cultural status and their relationship with the societies from which their ancestors came. Australians are so far from being free from this ambivalence that it runs as a leitmotiv through their history since 1788. Discussion of issues in the book trade is coloured as much by this as is debate about the role of the monarchy, participation in foreign wars or appropriate international alliances. Suspicions of exploitation, resentment of patronizing attitudes, anger at failure to break into northern hemisphere markets, these are some of the facets of an ongoing conflict. No colonial or ex-colonial who remembers the imperturbable sense of European superiority that one used to find a generation ago in the pages of *The Times Literary Supplement* can fail to feel irritation at smug disparagement of work done on the other side of the Atlantic or of the Equator. However, we need to keep firmly in mind that publishing and bookselling are businesses, not gentlemanly charities devoted to spreading sweetness and light. What was already true in the time of Gutenberg, Fust and Schoeffer is certainly the case now. Hence it is indispensable to try to approach the question of Australia's British and American connections with as little sentiment as possible.

The underlying reality of the size of the Australian population as compared with that of the United Kingdom or of the United States of America has not changed in relative terms since 1800. In other words Australia – even interpreted as it was in the heyday of the first George Robertson as Australia, New Zealand and the South Pacific – has been and remains a small part of the world audience for books in English. This disadvantage is not affected by the post-1945 changes that have reshaped the local industry to fit in with norms elsewhere.

Before the second half of the twentieth century it is difficult to think of a significant publishing firm in Australia that was not also engaged in wholesale and retail bookselling and perhaps also in printing. The exceptions like E.A. Vidler, active in Melbourne in the 1920s after his job in the publishing department of George Robertson and Company disappeared in 1918, did not provide durable successes. Now specialization is the rule. Angus and Robertson offer the most striking example of the breaking up of three activities seen henceforth as quite separate. Melbourne University Press and the University of Queensland Press are unusual in retaining campus bookshops as well. Some of the other university presses, like the late creation at Sydney in 1964, never had such a link. In 1991 there are literary agents, publishers, editors – many of them working freelance – designers, distributors, booksellers, commercial travellers and all the other distinct occupations that make up the trade. Freed of the necessity to be all-rounders, the industry's leaders still have to confront the problem of retaining their share of the local market and of selling overseas whenever this is appropriate.

Tourists of a bookish kind who have the opportunity to visit several English-speaking countries or even a number of cities situated in culturally distinct regions will know that the *serious* shops they like to frequent will mirror quite effectively the preoccupations of the people they are observing. Such outlets will have, of course, like the airport stalls that are so depressingly uniform across the world in their devotion to the latest paperback bestsellers, the books that everybody is reviewing, talking about and trying hard to have bought. However, they will also have the work of local poets, novelists and playwrights, topical political pamphlets, monographs on the artists of the region, guidebooks and the whole range of national historical writing from specialist treatises to popular essays. It is this second category that Australian publishers can be confident of placing in their own market. Selling it overseas or moving it up to the first category are other matters again, and, since these are quite legitimate business and intellectual aspirations, entrepreneurs and writers themselves must give them some thought.

The separation existed from the beginning in the Australian colonies. Parochial and usually quite practical books and pamphlets were abundantly advertised and, one presumes, efficiently distributed. They had no competition. More ambitious local productions – especially in creative writing – could be expected to encounter some buyer resistance. Efforts were made as early as Henry Savery's novel, *Quintus Servinton* (3 vols. Hobart Town: Henry Melville, 1830 [= 1831]), to distribute a colonial printing in London (Smith, Elder and Co., 1832), but this experiment and the ones made in the 1860s and 1870s by George Robertson through Macmillan and Bentley had limited success. Robertson stressed to later correspondents that his London office was for buying and not for selling, and recommended the services of commission houses like Simpkin, Marshall and Co. instead. Small wonder, then, that authors who saw their public as fundamentally British chose to deal with firms in London. That option continues to exist and to be taken up, notably by some of the most esteemed Australian novelists.

As already noted, the local product has a comparative price advantage in its home market thanks to the profit-taking mechanisms of distribution from Europe and North America. It has been traditional – in justification of high prices in Australian cities – to stress the costs of handling and shipping from British ports as well as wage levels and other factors in the Antipodes themselves. This no doubt needs careful study, but it is ironic to see E.A. Petherick, then Robertson's London manager and later a publisher on his own account, claiming in a long letter to *The Bookseller* in 1874 that his principal was able to overcome all these disabilities in giving colonial retailers the chance to sell at the English published prices. In the late twentieth century it seems that few hardbacks can be offered from London and New York in this way, a circumstance that encourages Australians to confine their bookbuying to works on national or even narrower themes.

The industry is quite well situated to benefit from the handicaps of its overseas rivals. A trade monthly, now called the *Australian Bookseller and Publisher*, has existed since 1921 to announce and advertise local publications. The present *Australian Book Review* has appeared monthly from Melbourne since 1978. Its predecessor of the same name came out in Adelaide from 1961 to 1974. Both have concentrated on reviewing the work of Australian authors, who also receive reasonably favoured treatment from the weekend supplements of newspapers. Radio and television are extensively used to publicize new books. The creation of various prestigious literary awards and prizes has also helped in the advance of works on Australian subjects. Promotion devised with genuine professionalism and the general trend towards study of the national past, among ordinary readers as well as in the programmes of schools and universities, have combined to give the indigenous trade nearly 50 per cent of the market as against 20 per cent in the early 1950s.

The greater resilience shown in this fashion is also reflected in the fortunes of literary and specialized journals. *Southerly* and *Meanjin* have now both passed their fiftieth birthdays, and *Quadrant*, *Westerly* and *Overland* are all survivors from the 1950s. This is not to say that life is easy for publications that have achieved rather more than the standing of 'little magazines'. Subsidies from the Commonwealth Literary Fund and its successor, the Literature Board of the Australia Council, have been crucial in maintaining vehicles for creative writing, criticism and general intellectual discussion that have been influential across the continent. The support of some of the universities and the hard work and cash of editors have also played a role in keeping the journals solvent in ways that would have astonished their mostly ephemeral nineteenth-century predecessors. Overall the twentieth century has added appreciably to the stock of reviews concerned with the humanities and the social sciences. Alongside the organs of state historical societies founded in the early part of the century, *Australian Quarterly*, the *Australasian Journal of Psychology and Philosophy* (*Australian Journal of Philosophy* from 1947) and *Australian Historical Studies* (the latest name of *Historical Studies of Australia and New Zealand*, founded in 1940) have all gone past golden jubilees to inspire the many creations of the post-war period. Various forms of subvention, overt or covert, help to keep such periodicals alive. Some of them, by dint of careful prospection of their basically expert readership, even manage to have larger circulation lists abroad than inside Australia.

Reaching Europe and North America continues to be a major problem. Nearly a century and a half after George Howe's work for the Tahitian Mission the Australian branch of Oxford University Press had astutely recognized the need for English-language textbooks for Papua and New Guinea and had thus begun a considerable involvement with the Pacific area. Selling English courses in Asia and to Asians has become a substantial trade in Australia, with obvious benefits to local publishing. The general northern hemisphere market, on the other hand, seemed to defy the efforts of the younger George Robertson as well. His edition of E.R. Holme's *The American University: An Australian View*, published in 1920, was available in the United Kingdom retail from 'The British Australasian Book-store, 51 High Holborn, London, W.C.1' and wholesale from 'The Australian Book Company, 16 Farringdon Avenue, London, E.C.4', but at the end of his life he seemed to despair of selling Australian books in Britain. Since 1945 other attempts, generally more successful, have been made to secure notice in Europe. Angus and Robertson opened a publishing office in London itself, and other firms organized a presence at fairs in Frankfurt. Even so, and notwithstanding the number of overseas publishers now active in Australia, there remains a sense that the cause of local authors abroad has not been mightily advanced. Recriminations have occasionally been addressed to the Sydney and Melbourne offices of American and British houses because of a believed lack of reciprocity in dealings.

It would be foolish to pass over the simple fact that northern hemisphere publishers, especially those from Britain, are much more interested in selling in Melbourne and Sydney than in promoting Australian books in London or New York. The Australian colonies rivalled North America as the major external market for British books as early as the 1850s and consistently occupied the first position from the 1870s onwards. After the early anarchy that permitted Dowling's

Pickwick Papers, it is clear that British copyright was respected and policed in Australian cities, in particular against the importation of unauthorized American reprints. In this booksellers like the first George Robertson were not only diligent but zealous. Genuine American editions were brought in by them, but they clearly frowned on any illicit traffic in cheap piracies. Even in the twentieth century the trade was long very discreet about the effects of the closed market system being erected behind the barrier of the Copyright Act of 1912 and its successors. Loyalty to the industry overseas was the watchword of public discussion, although difficulties relating to the Net Book Agreement were aired in a pamphlet, *Correspondence between Associated Booksellers of Australia and New Zealand and the Publishers' Association of Great Britain and Ireland, 1924-5* and private opinions were sometimes expressed with vigour and acerbity. In sum the impression given is that the Melbourne and Sydney booksellers attached much more importance to their work as wholesalers and retailers than to any possibilities of placing their own publications outside the country until quite recently.

The movement of foreign firms into Australian publishing can also be perceived as an effort to protect their market share. As soon as it became evident that bookbuyers were hungry for material about their own country and for textbooks written expressly for their own schools and not borrowed from elsewhere, there was apparently no lack of people ready to build local lists. The difficulties and shortages of the Second World War and its aftermath reinforced the growth of national sentiment and stimulated duly licensed reprints of overseas copyright titles. There is evidence that some writers feared a return to normal conditions because they thought it would flood the country with pulp fiction and limit the opportunities for Australians to get themselves published. Similar fears of the effects of an open market have continued to influence the attitude of authors to developments in the trade. Protection, which has also taken the form of a Book-bounty Scheme open to publishers having their works entirely produced inside Australia, is a device that has long been congenial in national tradition.

It was perhaps inevitable that the rise of consumerism since the 1950s would direct attention to the practices of the Australian book trade. The complaints of customers about the difference between northern hemisphere and local prices and about the slow arrival or even the non-importation of many titles have run through most of the post-war decades. The disallowance of resale price maintenance in 1972 and the later recognition of the possibility of separate Australian as opposed to British and Commonwealth rights for American titles have not really ended the sense of grievance. Similar questions have been asked about the sound recording industry and film distribution chains apropos of both pricing and the encouragement of indigenous creative potential. All of this springs in part from an Australian assertiveness whose rebirth is attributed by some observers to the Whitlam Labor Government of the early 1970s. Whatever the origins of the movement, it was clear by the late 1980s that the public wanted answers about the prices and availability of imported books. The relevance of these bookselling matters to the general situation of publishers hardly needs to be underlined.

Two separate reports provided the occasion for a quite furious debate. In September 1988 the Copyright Law Review Committee published *The Import Provisions of the Copyright Act 1968* (Canberra: Australian Government Publishing Service). The gist of its recommendations was that the provisions relating to parallel imports of non-pirated articles should be relaxed if the copyright owner and his or her licensee or agent had not made the title available in Australia 'within a reasonable time'. Reports 24 and 25 of the Prices Surveillance Authority on 31 August and 19 December 1989 (*Inquiry into Book Prices Interim Report* and *Inquiry into Book Prices Final Report*) went much further and proposed free competition and an end to the closed market system. The arguments advanced since then on both sides have gone over many of the issues at the core of the conflict between dependence and independence as options for the Australian book industry. Unfortunately, most of the participants have demonstrated that they have little acquaintance with the complex history of the Antipodean trade and with the see-sawing of overseas and local control of distribution.

The legislative solution foreshadowed by the Australian Government adopts in the main the less radical line espoused by the Copyright Law Review Committee. However, the changes proposed have still to go before Parliament, and there is some disagreement about their likely practical effects on both bookselling and publishing. What is certain is that this is unlikely to be an end to the matter. The tension between different and conflicting interests will continue. In any case reformers and partisans of the status quo have to recognize the extent to which the local industry is already internationalized.

Takeovers, Conglomerates and Independent Small Presses

Who owns the Australian book trade? Who controls it? The questions are neither naive nor flippant. They are, however, difficult to answer because of the rapid changes that have taken and are taking place in international publishing. A country whose total production of books is modest by world standards but nonetheless expanding – 1615 titles in

1974, 4219 in 1987 – becomes by this very fact more interesting to firms looking for businesses to absorb. Thus we now see in Australia both indigenous companies that have been taken over by foreign ones and branches of British and American houses that have themselves become part of larger conglomerates. Alongside them are university presses, native and imported, that have remained independent insofar as they have survived and a growing group of new small publishers of local origin. All of these deserve to be looked at as elements of the industry in 1991.

It should not be forgotten that Australians are also – and still, despite the corporate crashes of the last year or two – players in the multinational game. Indeed, an early start was made with the firm of Gordon and Gotch, founded in Melbourne in 1853 and later active in most parts of what was then the British Empire. The London house eventually became an independent offshoot. The central activity was the distribution of magazines, although many other aspects of the trade have been followed at various stages, including absorption of the Angus and Robertson bookshops in recent times. Now Gordon and Gotch have in their turn been swallowed up, even if they have been allowed to retain a separate corporate identity.

The major Australian presence in the international media is Rupert Murdoch's News group. The proprietor's move to United States citizenship has not changed the perception of many Australians that he is one of them. Certainly he still has commanding local newspaper interests, but through Collins Angus and Robertson Publishers he controls both the oldest established of the British branches in Australia and the premier local firm. It is true that the vicissitudes of Angus and Robertson since a series of takeovers began thirty years ago have turned a company with a strong commitment to quality and scholarly books into one much more concerned with commercial successes in the middle of the range. The backlist is still significant, with a solid representation of classic Australian authors, but it remains to be seen what direction the imprint will now take.

Angus and Robertson had at the time of their own first difficulties in 1960 acquired their old Melbourne rival, the conglomerate Robertson and Mullens, successor of two of the creations of the gold rush era. Rigby of Adelaide was another relic of the same period, yet active as a publisher of general Australiana. It too has fallen victim to a takeover. The same has happened to many of the firms that brought new ideas and initiatives to the publishing scene in the middle or later twentieth century. Diversity and genuine Australian voices are always threatened when publishers like F.W. Cheshire and McPhee Gribble lose their independence, even if the new owners are called Longman and Penguin. Experiments like the McPhee Gribble acquisitions of Australian copyrights of North American literary works can hardly survive when the context of operation is quite different. Yet the inexorable pressures of lack of capital or of inadequate distribution networks bear down on medium-sized publishers.

That the same problems have affected many of the overseas companies working in Australia hardly needs to be said. Each month in the *Australian Bookseller and Publisher* one can read of fresh changes in ownership. Sometimes this involves shifts in policy, sometimes not. The educational bias of certain publishers, especially the American ones, remains in contrast to the orientation to trade books of other firms. In hard and uncertain times the coherence of a list is valuable, as Harlequin Book Distributors, who arrange for the printing and selling of Mills and Boon, Harlequin and Silhouette titles in Australia, would surely agree about their more than one-fifth share of mass market paperback sales. It is all in all salutary to be reminded that Penguin, still so prominent in serious bookshops and having a substantial Australian list, is far from dominant commercially.

The concentration that is so obvious in the major publishers has provoked reactions and created opportunities. Editorial staff discontented with the impersonal character of very large businesses, have moved out into small firms. The latter have seen the possibility of putting in the place of blandness and uniformity individual taste. The monthly lists of 'New Publishers' in the *Australian Bookseller and Publisher* document this trend quite effectively. People are finding special lines, favourite pursuits, niches in the market. Something similar is happening in retail bookselling, and this is all to the new publishers' advantage provided they know how to limit the size of their business and to target their own audience. This side of the industry ranges from highly successful and visible concerns like Lonely Planet and the Fremantle Arts Centre Press to the private presses of printing craftsmen and the 'desktop publishing' operations of a myriad of churches, clubs, associations and university departments. That the products of the last group in particular are poorly distributed and may escape bibliographical control goes without saying, but *this* is the variety, the vitality and perhaps the future of authentic Australian publishing outside the global market with its insistence on world rights for titles designed for a lowest common denominator.

In spite of corporatization and threatened privatization Australia's various government presses continue to have a substantial share of publishing activity. The increasing involvement of the Australian

Broadcasting Corporation in this area is a sign not only of the interdependence of the media, but also of that body's determination to be a free contributor to intelligent discussion of the whole range of issues that should concern the nation. How are the university presses, in theory equally independent and cushioned against market fluctuations, faring in the same task?

Sadly, it must be reported that two of them, Sydney and the Australian National University, have closed and been sold off to foreign interests. Commercial difficulties, due no doubt to the fact that their lists contained many non-Australian titles, were the ostensible reason for this drastic step. The old problem of securing effective publicity and distribution abroad is still with us in the late twentieth century. The future of the University of Western Australia Press was under discussion in 1990. Melbourne University Press and the University of Queensland Press, with a stronger and indeed virtually exclusive interest in the Australian field, have survived. The latter has an important literary list, the former a notable and not unprofitable concern with history and biography. With support from the minor presses and the apparently unequivocal commitment of Oxford and now, more and more, of Cambridge to their Australian presence, there is reason to hope that scholarly publishing will be able to stand out against centralization and the mindless tyranny of the 'bottom line'.

The Role of Publishing in a Poorer Australia?

Whatever the outcome of the copyright debate, it is obvious that Australian publishing will have to cope with the consequences of the country's relative impoverishment. The current recession has hit the industry hard, with bookshops closing and publishers laying off staff. The real danger is that this is more than a passing phase and that reliance on the export of wheat, wool and minerals is leading the country into a long-term decline. Nonetheless, the events of recent years around the world have given us so many surprises that it would be foolhardy to predict where Angus and Robertson and all the others will be in 2001. Hence it is better to end – lamely and timorously – with a question mark.

A Note on Sources

The material presented in this article is based on the reading of a number of secondary works and on personal explorations of a range of primary sources. Reference notes would have to have been extremely numerous to provide precise documentation of all the points made. It was therefore decided to give a relatively brief list of more accessible works where aspects of the argument can be followed up and verified.

Barker, A.W. *'Dear Robertson': Letters to an Australian Publisher*. Sydney: Angus and Robertson Publishers, 1982.

Borchardt, D.H. and Kirsop, W., eds. *The Book in Australia: Essays towards a Cultural and Social History*. Melbourne: Australian Reference Publications, 1988.

Brown, Allan. *Commercial Media in Australia: Economics, Ownership, Technology and Regulation.* St Lucia: University of Queensland Press, 1986.

Eyre, Frank. *Oxford in Australia 1890-1978*. Melbourne: Oxford University Press, 1978.

Hergenhan, Laurie, ed. *The Penguin New Literary History of Australia*. Ringwood, Vic.: Penguin Books, 1988.

Holroyd, John. *George Robertson of Melbourne 1825-1898: Pioneer Bookseller and Publisher*. Melbourne: Robertson and Mullens, 1968.

Page, Roger. *Australian Bookselling*. Melbourne: Hill of Content, 1970.

Rayward, W. Boyd, ed. *Australian Library History in Context. Papers for the Third Forum on Australian Library History, University of New South Wales, 17 and 18 July 1987*. Sydney: University of New South Wales School of Librarianship, 1988.

Richards, Michael. *People, Print and Paper: A Catalogue of a Travelling Exhibition Celebrating the Books of Australia, 1788-1988*. Canberra: National Library of Australia, 1988.

Wilde, William H.; Hooton, Joy; and Andrews, Barry. *The Oxford Companion to Australian Literature*. Melbourne: Oxford University Press, 1985.

4 Government Publishing in Australia

Michael Harrington

This paper discusses publishing activities and trends in the different levels and forms of government in Australia: the Commonwealth, the states and local government; and self-governing and non-self-governing territories. The mode of publishing, including sales and distribution, is discussed, then the major tools for the identification, selection and acquisition of publications.

Governments in Australia have been tardy in introducing freedom of information legislation. The Federal Government did so in 1982, but has been followed by half of the states only. Costs involved may be a factor in its seemingly low use, although it may equally be hypothesized that another factor is apathy on the part of the governed. We vote for our governments – voting is compulsory and no political party wishes to change this. We also abuse them, even if we are not aware that we are blaming the Federal Government for a local or state government action.

It is not suggested that governments in Australia are reluctant to publish the information they possess; they are not. But the volume of publications issued, the number of agencies involved in this activity, their naivety about publishing processes – many think that printing and publishing are synonymous terms – and the range of media available all impede the effective dissemination of this information. There are also other factors: the division of responsibilities between governments; the reluctance of government agencies to use centralized services; and more recently the general acceptance of not only the 'user pays' principle (the user pays at cost recovery rates) but also the commercialization principle (the user pays at rates judged equal to those that the private sector would charge, even if no commercial equivalent exists).

Government in Australia

The Commonwealth of Australia was formed on 1 January 1901 by the federation of the colonies of New South Wales, Victoria, Queensland, South Australia, Western Australia and Tasmania. The Commonwealth of Australia Constitution sets out the structure of the Federal Government and the distribution of power between it and the states. Powers not mentioned in the constitution are exercised exclusively by state governments, all of which were established under the authority of their own constitutions. Local government, the third level of government in Australia, is not recognized in the Commonwealth Constitution – a referendum seeking to change this was defeated in September 1988 – nor in all state constitutions. Local authorities are responsible for municipal matters such as roads, public health, recreational facilities and town planning. They are controlled by state parliaments but have also been receiving direct federal grants since the 1970s.

The Commonwealth Constitution allows the Federal Parliament to make laws for territories acquired or accepted by the Commonwealth. It also provides for the seat of government to be within a territory situated in the state of New South Wales. This became the Australian Capital Territory, which as the Federal Capital Territory (as it was first called) was transferred to the Commonwealth in 1911. A smaller area at Jervis Bay was also transferred to the Commonwealth in 1915, originally to serve as a port for the national capital. The Australian Capital Territory became self-governing in 1989, but the Territory of Jervis Bay remains a direct responsibility of the Federal Government. There are two other self-governing territories: the Northern Territory (since 1978) and Norfolk Island (since 1979). The six other territories – Ashmore and Cartier Islands, Australian Antarctic Territory, Christmas Island, Cocos (Keeling) Islands, Coral Sea Islands, and Heard and McDonald Islands – are administered by the Commonwealth.

Government at the federal, state and self-governing territory levels follows the Westminster model. The relevant constitutions or Acts granting self-government create three governmental branches: a legislature (parliament), which makes laws; an executive, which administers these laws; and a judiciary (law courts), which interprets them.

The Commonwealth Parliament consists of three elements: the Queen, represented by the Governor-General; and two houses, the Senate and the House of Representatives. Administrative services are provided by five parliamentary departments. State parliaments have a similar structure except in Queensland, which is unicameral (has a single house). The legislative assemblies (parliaments) of self-governing territories are also unicameral.

The Governor-General (or the governor of a state) is the head of the executive government, although by convention he or she does not exercise executive power without the advice of his or her ministers. Ministers must be members of parliament (or if they are not at the time of their appointment, they must be elected to parliament within three months).

Ministers are assisted in carrying out their duties by government departments, staffed by public servants. Statutory authorities are another type of executive agency. They are set up by legislation, which defines the characteristics of the agency concerned. It may be a body corporate or unincorporated; it may have the power to hire and fire its own staff, or staff may be appointed under the provisions of the Public Service Act; it may be self-funding or operate on moneys appropriated annually be parliament; it may be called a commission, a board, a tribunal, an authority, a committee or a council; it may undertake research, teaching or training, operate as a business enterprise, regulate specified activities or have quasi-judicial functions.

Non-statutory authorities are set up by ministers, departments and statutory authorities, but not by legislation. They are generally small and most have an advisory function. However, the term can also be used to cover the burgeoning number of government companies. Non-statutory bodies are generally not significant publishers in their own right, notable exceptions being royal commissions and committees of enquiry (a royal commission has the power to command evidence; a committee of enquiry does not).

Law courts in Australia, although the subject of many publications, are not themselves publishers. Law reports are published by authorized (non-government) publishers and are available from them. The SCALE database, produced by the Commonwealth Attorney-General's Department, contains decisions of the High Court of Australia and the Federal Court of Australia, and is available for online access through LAWPAC.

Publishing and Sales

Government publishing in Australia is decentralized. The three tiers of government publish independently of each other. Moreover, each local authority, and many state and federal agencies also run independent publishing and sales and distribution programmes. They all issue publications for a variety of reasons: legal requirements; promotion and advertising; education and training; reporting research undertaken; public information; and even for vanity.

The Commonwealth

The Commonwealth Government used the services of the Victorian Government Printing Office for its publishing requirements immediately after federation, when the seat of government was located in Melbourne. It moved to Canberra in 1927, but the printing office operated as a branch of the Victorian office until the appointment of the first separate Commonwealth Government Printer in 1932.

Criticisms of Commonwealth government printing and publishing started being published in the 1950s, and by the early 1960s the system was a matter of parliamentary concern. The parliament appointed a committee, the Joint Select Committee on Parliamentary and Government Publications, to 'inquire into and report on the printing, publication and distribution of Parliamentary Papers and all Government publications.' The Erwin Report, as the committee's report is popularly known after chairman Dudley Erwin, was published in 1964.[1] It is an important document in any discussion of Commonwealth publishing because its findings and recommendations can be used as standards against which later developments can be judged.

The report documented the then complexities of Commonwealth publishing. There was no single office responsible for publishing documents, setting standards or supplying copies of publications. Arrangements for advising potential readers of documents were so inadequate as to be practically non-existent. Each department was busy doing its own thing; despite public criticism, many felt that they were doing it in the best possible way.

The committee's most important recommendation was that a central publishing office be established to undertake the publishing functions of departments. This office, which the committee recommended should be called the Australian Government Publishing Service (AGPS), would be the sole publisher of all departmental publications. AGPS was established by Cabinet decision in 1969, although it did not become fully operational until its Publishing Branch was set up in July 1970.

The next parliamentary review of Commonwealth publishing and printing was in 1978. The review was undertaken by the Joint Committee on Publications (JCP), itself established as the result of a recommendation of the Erwin Committee to undertake continuing parliamentary review of this area of government activity. The JCP reported that the Erwin Committee's concept as reflected in AGPS was basically sound.[2] The organization's establishment had led to improvements in the standard of Commonwealth government publications and in their availability to the public. However, the committee also found that there was uncertainty about AGPS's authority and responsibilities, and that there was a lack of clear areas of responsibilities for Commonwealth publishing; the JCP itself was unable to obtain access to the text of the Cabinet decision setting up AGPS and defining its role.

As a result of this report, the Commonwealth Charter of Printing and Publishing Responsibilities was drawn up, and tabled in Parliament on 5 March 1984 after its approval by Cabinet.[3] The charter clearly defined the role that AGPS should play in Commonwealth publishing. This was to lay down standards; provide publishing, print procurement and printing services; sell and distribute publications; compile and publish lists of all Commonwealth government publications (at the time of the JCP review, AGPS catalogues listed sale publications only); and claim and protect Crown copyright.

The latest JCP review of Commonwealth publishing and printing took place in 1988. This revealed, as the earlier review had, that agencies required to use AGPS's service were unhappy with the arrangement. Other circumstances had changed considerably between the two reviews, however. AGPS and other government-servicing agencies had been grouped together under the umbrella of the Department of Administrative Services. They were now expected to operate on a commercial basis and demonstrate cost efficiencies. Although the JCP concluded in its report that the number of problems experienced by such agencies had generally been outweighed by the number of tasks that AGPS had successfully handled, one of its recommendations was that printing and publishing should be deregulated and that agencies should be freed from the requirement to use AGPS services for work under the value of A$20,000.[4]

The recommendation was only partially accepted by the government of the day. Government printing has been deregulated since 1 July 1989, and the charter of printing and publishing responsibilities has been amended to incorporate this. Departments and authorities need not now use AGPS for non-core general printing work – non-urgent forms and so on. However, the government considered that deregulating publishing would have severe staffing implications and would seriously curtail AGPS's ability to continue providing a broad range of government information to the general public. As the charter now stands, therefore, AGPS remains the sole supplier of publications work (which includes arranging for their printing) for departments and nonexempt authorities. The decision regarding the deregulation of publishing is to be reviewed at some later date, as yet unannounced.

Australia Government Publishing Service. AGPS is the official publisher and printer of the Commonwealth. It operates as part of the Sales and Services Program of the Department of Administrative Services; other components of this programme carry out building and construction, property management, transport services, removal and storage, and purchasing functions for the Commonwealth. In common with these other elements, AGPS charges for the use of its services at commercial rates in accordance with the principles for the operation of services to government agencies announced by the Minister for Administrative Services in April 1988.[5] It has been required to be self-supporting from income earned from 1 July 1990.

AGPS's traditional clients have been the Commonwealth Parliament, government departments and selected statutory authorities. Commercialization, the expectation that AGPS will be self-supporting, the deregulation of general printing under A$20,000, and the possibility of publishing also being deregulated in the future have meant that AGPS has been permitted to expand its client base. It may now work for other publicly funded agencies, including state, territory, local and foreign governments. In line with this decision, for example, the Commonwealth Government Printing Office has successfully tendered to print legislation and some other official work on behalf of the Australian Capital Territory Administration.

Its Printing Branch, the Government Printing Office, gives priority to federal parliamentary printing requirements and to the urgent and confidential needs of government (known as 'core-work'). It also tenders for other AGPS publications work and for non-core printing jobs. Its services include microfiche and photoreproduction; 'quick print' reprography; high-speed, rapid-turnover imaging from data drawn from either magnetic tape or diskette; and computer-assisted forms design and typesetting.

AGPS is Australia's biggest publishing house, currently producing more than 4000 titles a year. As a government publisher, it differs from private houses in an important aspect: the decision whether or not to publish a work is made by the responsible agency or Minister, not by AGPS. It decides how to publish material rather than what; consequently, it is production-driven rather than by its editorial staff. As part of a print brokerage service, its officers provide technical advice on printing and publishing, give estimates or quotations, arrange for production scheduling and printing (a large proportion of AGPS printing work is contracted to the private sector), coordinate production states and delivery, and maintain quality control, as well as editorial and design services. It also offers marketing, sales and distribution services, print procurement, and the arrangement of printing contracts and specifications.

AGPS operates an Australia-wide and international sales service. Mail sales are based in Canberra, but over-the-counter sales are provided in Commonwealth Government Bookshops in Canberra, in the central business districts of the six state capitals, in the Sydney Suburb of Parramatta, and the Queensland provincial city of Townsville. (The Northern Territory Government Information Service acts as an AGPS agent in Darwin.) Other sales services include the AGPS 'phone sale, which is a 008 (charged at local call rate) telephone service, and facsimile and telex ordering services; electronic ordering on Discovery, the digital data (teletext) network operated by Telecom Australia (the Australian Telecommunications Corporation); and the sale of publications through commercial and other outlets. Future developments include the upgrading of the Discovery book ordering service to full electronic trading. International sales are carried out through selected agents.

AGPS lodges one copy of every work it publishes with the National Library of Australia under the legal deposit provisions of the Commonwealth Copyright Act of 1968. The proper recording of its publications in the national bibliography is thereby assured. It also operates two schemes for the free distribution of its publications to libraries: a library deposit scheme to state reference libraries and to the Northern Territory Library Service; and a free issue scheme to university libraries. Participating libraries are entitled to receive one copy of each title published by AGPS, whether or not it is a sale item. They are expected to make the resulting collection freely available to all library users.

AGPS does not sell every item it publishes. Its Marketing Group determines each publication's sales potential and the sale quantities AGPS will buy – currently, production costs for all titles published are met by the responsible government agency. As part of its book promotion activities, Marketing prepares a bimonthly sales catalogue entitled *New Commonwealth Government Books from AGPS*, and other promotional literature associated with a particular book or subject.

The AGPS Cataloguing Unit prepares three other catalogues: the fortnightly *Commonwealth Publications Official List,* its cumulation, the *Annual Catalogue of Commonwealth Publications*, and the fortnightly *AGPS Catalogue on Microfiche*. The first two are comprehensive in their coverage of AGPS material. Since 1983 they have also included entries for non-AGPS titles when the responsible agencies notify AGPS of their release. Although inferior to the national bibliography in the standard and depth of cataloguing, these represent AGPS's contribution to the bibliographic control of Commonwealth government publications. The *AGPS Catalogue on Microfiche* is a cumulative list of departmental titles published by AGPS since 1976. It excludes all parliamentary titles except parliamentary papers, and all legislative materials. It is expected that the recent acquisition of a more sophisticated computer cataloguing system will bring consequent improvements in the quality, scope, coverage and formats of AGPS bibliographic publications.

AGPS's own publications are compiled by its Official Publications Unit. These include the *Commonwealth of Australia Gazette* (published in eleven series of differing frequency), the *Commonwealth Government Directory* (half-yearly) and its quarterly *Commonwealth Government Directory Update*, the *Ministerial Directory* (half-yearly), the *Ministerial Document Service* (daily), the *Commonwealth Legislation Catalogue* (monthly on microfiche), the *Australian Capital Territory Legislation Catalogue* (quarterly), and the Commonwealth Official Publications Series (monographs dealing with general matters of government and government information). The unit also offers a professional indexing service to AGPS clients, and a search and retrieval service (DataSearch) to supply information tailored to individual requirements from databases it maintains. Both services are available on a fee-for-service basis.

AGPS Press was set up in 1986 and operates as a publishing house within AGPS. It publishes titles of government or government-related interest that have substantial commercial potential, including those submitted by government agencies or those commissioned independently by AGPS. It is also responsible for the development of Commonwealth editorial style. Its major function in that area is the publication of the *Style Manual for Authors, Editors and Printers*, a reference manual of guidelines and conventions, the latest edition of which – the fourth – was published in 1988.

Under a 1985 agreement between the Attorney-General and the Minister for Sport, Recreation and Tourism (the Minister then responsible for AGPS), AGPS administers and protects Crown copyright in all Commonwealth government publications except those administered by the High Court of Australia. This function is undertaken by AGPS Press. Commonwealth government publications are all subject to copyright provisions. Apart from any fair dealing for the purposes of study, research, news reporting or review as permitted under the Commonwealth Copyright Act of 1968, no part may be reproduced without written permission from AGPS (or the High Court). Copyright requests should be directed to the Manager, AGPS Press.

AGPS's most recent venture has been the development of an electronic publishing programme. This is taking three forms: a demand publishing system, the Government Procurement System, and Diskrom Australia.

Demand publishing has three applications. It is used to supply out-of-print titles and it has also been offered as a bureau service providing optical disk storage to clients for little used material. The demand for both of the services has not been great. However, its value is seen in being a means of reducing the costs involved in storing and providing copies of Acts and other forms of legislation in both central office and in Commonwealth Government Bookshops. A pilot project was run in 1991, with full implementation expected in 1992.

The Government Procurement Service comprises four databases: current Federal Government tendering information; historical purchasing information (contracts let); Australian and New Zealand government capital equipment forward procurement plans under A$20 million; and current information relating to the Australian Defence Offsets Program. The service is currently available through Supplinet and will be available through Discovery, both networks run by subsidiaries of Telecom Australia.

Diskrom Australia is a joint venture between AGPS and Computer Law Services Pty Ltd, a private company. Diskrom produces and markets legislation products on CD-ROM. The first of these was called the Corporations Disk, and contained the full text of the newly enacted federal laws and related state codes dealing with companies, together with the text of the relevant Bills, the repealed legislation and related extrinsic material such as explanatory memoranda (issued by a Minister at a Bill's second reading speech and explaining the details of a Bill on a clause-by-clause basis), committee of enquiry reports and so on. Under the provisions of the Commonwealth Acts Interpretation Act of 1901 all such extrinsic material may be used by the courts in interpreting the law. Subsequent releases have included a similar package dealing with taxation law.

Other Commonwealth Government Publishers. Many statutory authorities run independent publishing programmes. The oldest of these is the Commonwealth Scientific and Industrial Research

Organization (CSIRO). CSIRO was set up under an earlier name in 1916 and now operates under the authority of the Science and Industry Research Act of 1949. As part of its statutory functions, it is required to collect, interpret and disseminate information relating to scientific and industrial matters, and to publish scientific and industrial reports, periodicals and papers. Its publishing programme is multi-media and is carried out in its divisions, spread Australia-wide. It maintains a sales office in East Melbourne to cater for wholesale and retail sales.

Titles available for sale from the organization are listed in *CSIRO Publications* and as a Discovery database. *CSIRO Index*, a complete listing of all CSIRO publications and those of its staff, is available on AUSTRALIS and is also published on microfiche. AUSTRALIS itself, an online information retrieval service, is one of the information technology services and products developed by the organization. Research in progress is described as part of annual or biennial reports published by its divisions and in *CSIRO Research in Progress*, another AUSTRALIS database. Research results are reported in divisional publications series and in thirteen scientific research journals published by CSIRO. *CSIRO Films*, a Discovery database, lists films and videos produced by the organization since 1946.

The Australian Bureau of Statistics (ABS) is the national statistical organization. It also runs an independent publishing, sales and distribution programme. It lists all new releases in *Publications Advice* (twice weekly, ABS catalogue number 1105.0), *Publications Issued* (monthly, 1102.0) and *Catalogue of Publications and Products* (annual, 1101.0). The last mentioned is issued at the beginning of the year and some titles listed in it may not be published in the stated twelve-month period.

Other ABS services include the provision of key economic and social statistics on Discovery; AUSSTATS, an online time series data service; and TELSTATS, an electronic mail service delivering commodity-based foreign trade statistics to users. Commercial prices are charged for these services. A telephone recorded message service called Dial-a-Statistic is also available in each capital city and covers major economic statistics. Of particular relevance to libraries is the ABS Library Extension Service, under which ABS staff visit libraries to discuss problems and to undertake training. The service is currently operating in rural New South Wales only.

ABS copies some hard-copy series onto microfiche and sells them in this format. Microfiche, magnetic tape, floppy disk and CD-ROM technology are all used to disseminate data that could not be provided economically in paper form. Microfiche is also used to store and make historical publications available. Its *Catalogue of Official Statistical Publications (Publications Issued by Canberra Office, 1901 to 1984)* (rev. ed. 1112.0) is a complete listing of central office titles available in this format for the post-Federation period. ABS has also microfiched and catalogued all known official statistical records produced by colonial agencies in a set entitled Colonial Microfiche, which is held by the National Library of Australia. The catalogue to this set is entitled *Catalogue of Australian Statistical Publications from 1804 to 1901* (1115.0).

CSIRO and ABS are two important publishers but by no means the only ones publishing independently of AGPS. However, AGPS was never intended to be the sole publisher of Commonwealth government titles. The Erwin Committee did not envisage complete centralization; its main recommendations did not cover statutory authorities staffed independently of the Public Service Act.

The publishing responsibilities of such authorities and their relationship with AGPS are formally defined in the Commonwealth Charter of Printing and Publishing Responsibilities. They are free to operate their own publishing programmes and to decide whether or not to use AGPS resources. They should still comply with AGPS standards, guidelines and procedures for publications required to be tabled in Parliament, and arrange with AGPS for the printing and distribution of the parliamentary paper editions of these works. They should also notify AGPS after the release of their publications and, depending upon their marketability, arrange for AGPS sales. Finally, they should collaborate with the National Library of Australia regarding overseas exchanges.

On the other hand, the charter requires parliamentary and government departments, and statutory authorities staffed under the Public Service Act, to arrange the design, printing, publishing and distribution of publications through AGPS. AGPS should also be notified of the release of any publications not processed through it. The charter stipulates that such agencies should comply with AGPS guidelines, standards and procedures, and collaborate with it in library deposit matters. Government departments and authorities should also submit annual publishing programmes to AGPS and seek advice from it about acquiring in-house printing equipment.

Parliamentary departments may be exempt from using AGPS services by the Presiding Officers (the President of the Senate and the Speaker of the House of Representatives, who act as 'ministers' of the five parliamentary departments). Government departments and authorities may be exempt from using AGPS by agreement between the agency and AGPS. The charter also states that an agency wishing to operate retail outlets should have the approval of the minister responsible for AGPS (the Minister for Administrative Services since 1987).

The Australian Bureau of Statistics is a statutory authority staffed under the Public Service Act, but it has received an exemption from using AGPS. The National Library of Australia, another statutory authority staffed under the Public Service Act, is similarly exempt and operates its own publishing and sales programmes. However, many departments and authorities, although they have no formal exemption from using AGPS's services as required by the charter, ignore its requirements and issue publications independently. It may well be argued that the charter is a paper tiger, since it contains no sanctions that can be brought to bear against agencies deliberately flouting its requirements.

States

State government printing offices are practical printers rather than publishers. Their most important function is to meet the printing requirements of their parliaments and the urgent and security requirements of government departments. Other work is sought to ensure that staff and equipment are fully employed, but must take second place to parliamentary and core work. Government printing offices compete with private printing houses for filler work.

As a result of this arrangement, the range of publications available from government printing offices sales outlets is limited. It includes the major parliamentary series – parliamentary debates (Hansard), the official parliamentary record (the minutes of proceedings, and votes and proceedings), Bills, Acts and parliamentary papers – and official and industrial gazettes (or separately published decisions and awards of industrial tribunals), but very little else. A larger range of publications may be stocked by government information centres, which operate in all states except Queensland, but many executive titles are available directly from the publishing agency only. This means that collecting state government publications can be both labour-intensive and time-consuming.

Requirements tying government agencies to using printing office resources vary from state to state, but with the adoption of commercialization the tendency is to abolish or amend those that exist to allow more freedom. This has been taken furthest in New South Wales, which abolished its printing office in 1990. A small unit was set up in Parliament House to undertake parliamentary printing; all other work, including the printing of legislation for public use, is tendered out. There was an unfavourable reaction from the legal profession, although the situation now seems to have been accepted. Delays reported in receiving copies of parliamentary papers have also been reported from recipient libraries.

All other states have retained their printing offices. However, after partially deregulating government printing and publishing in 1989, the Victorian Government reorganized its former office into four businesses: The Law Printer, the official printer to parliament and for security government works; Corporate Image, specializing in stationery letterheads and so on; Creative Solutions, undertaking general government printing and publishing, and consultancies; and Fast Copy, a quick-print service.

In the states, therefore, government departments and authorities are generally their own publishers, sellers and distributors. Many of them have in-house reproduction facilities or use private services; all carry out other publishing functions such as copy preparation and editing, sales and distribution, and promotion (if it is undertaken at all).

Local Government

Local government authorities use local firms for their printing requirements, although some information – notices about borrowings or of by-laws made, for example, and in some states annual statements of accounts – must be published in the official gazette of the state. The authorities publish annual reports, the preparation of which is a legal requirement. A few publish minutes of council meetings, but most merely make a set of the minutes available to ratepayers at municipal offices. Other publications include information sheets about local services, the occasional local history, and environment and planning reports. Each local authority must be approached direct in order to obtain copies of these.

Territories

Most territorial administrations serve smaller populations than local government authorities do and, like them, are not prolific publishers. For non-self-governing territories, publishing is mainly restricted to legislation and is carried out by AGPS for the Federal Department of the Arts, Sport, the Environment, Tourism and Territories. (The department's Legal Section, not AGPS, should be approached in order to obtain copies of such legislation.) The *Territory of Christmas Island*

Government Gazette, however, is published locally by the Administrator of the Territory.

Norfolk Island publishing – legislation and a gazette – is also carried out locally 'by Authority'. The Northern Territory, however, has followed the pattern set in the states. Its government printing office, established on self-government, is the official printer for the Territory's Legislative Assembly and for the urgent and confidential needs of its executive government. Departments and authorities are, for other titles, their own publishers. The Northern Territory Government Information Centre acts as a central point from which publications may be obtained, but it is not guaranteed to stock a complete range.

The Australian Capital Territory Administration followed tradition to the extent of creating a position of government printer, but this was for legal reasons rather than to head a printing office. Government publishing in the territory is completely decentralized. Legislation, for example, is printed by AGPS and available from its sales outlets, but Bills, Hansard and the minutes of proceedings of the Legislative Assembly are available from the Assembly only. The *Australian Capital Territory Gazette* is available from the Public Affairs Branch of the ACT Government Service. For other publications, the responsible authority must be approached direct.

Bibliographic Control

The National Library of Australia is entitled to receive one legal deposit copy of each work published in Australia that is categorized as library material. The library does not regard government publishers as being bound by this provision: the Copyright Act, in which the deposit provision is contained, binds the Crown but nothing in it renders the Crown liable to be prosecuted for an offence. For Federal Government agencies, the requirement is backed up in the Commonwealth Charter of Printing and Publishing Responsibilities. Similar back-up to each state's legal deposit law exists by way of administrative instructions to government agencies requiring them to lodge copies of publications with the National Library, and with relevant legal deposit libraries in the state. Neither the laws nor the supporting instructions are completely effective: not all government publications are automatically deposited, and not all government publishing officers are even aware that such requirements exist.

Nevertheless, these libraries' collections, and in particular that of the National Library, are the basis of the most comprehensive bibliographies of government publications. *Australian National Bibliography (ANB)* lists all government and non-government works published in the current year and in the preceding two years, and received by the National Library. The same cut-off for listing applies to the library's specialist bibliography, *Australian Government Publications (AGP)*, but because *AGP* is now produced from ABN (Australian Bibliographic Network), receipt by any one of ABN's contributors is all that is necessary for listing. The length of time between books being received and their listing in these bibliographies, and the frequent omission of pricing details in their entries detract from their value for selection and acquisition purposes.

ANB has been published since 1961, and the text from 1972 is available for online access through OZLINE. Entries for government and non-government publications are listed in a single sequence: classified since 1971 and author-title before that. Excluded from listing are pamphlets under five pages; all serial issues except the first, or the first after a changed title; publications that are confidential, security classified or have restricted access, and manuals for internal use within an organization; sales catalogues and other ephemera; maps and films (although maps were included between 1961 and 1967); individual Acts, Bills and all subordinate legislation (but Acts were included between 1961 and 1970); industrial awards and determinations; transcripts of court and tribunal proceedings; and speeches by parliamentarians or extracts from Hansard.

AGP started in 1952 as the *Monthly List of Australian Government Publications*, and changed to its present title in 1955. Until the end of 1960 its contents were substantially included in the *Annual Catalogue of Australian Publications*, which is the preferred source for identification purposes. Its contents from 1983 are available for online access on OZLINE. It has been produced from ABN since 1988, and is published quarterly in microfiche format only, each cumulating earlier issues. It has an author-title and separate subject arrangement. Between 1961 and 1987 it was published in annual hard-copy cumulations and was arranged by jurisdiction and then by responsible authority. It has the same basic exclusions as ABN but it listed Bills and Acts between 1971 and 1987. Local government publications have been listed since 1988 only, as have entries for non-print materials.

The *Annual Catalogue of Australian Publications* was published by the then Commonwealth National Library between 1930 and 1960, and was the national bibliographic record of the time. Government publications were listed in the issues for 1937-1940 and 1945-1960 only. They were grouped in a separate section and arranged by jurisdiction and then by responsible authority. Single issues of Bills, legislation, industrial awards and non-book materials were not listed.

Australian National Bibliography 1901-1950 (Canberra: National Library of Australia, 1988) lists books and pamphlets published in Australia for the period shown in the title. It was compiled from the ABN database and its contents are not restricted to the National Library's holdings. The text of the printed bibliography is also available as part of ABN. It was intended to fill what is commonly known as the 'Ferguson gap', the bibliographic gap between the end of Sir John Ferguson's *Bibliography of Australia 1784-1900* and the start of the *Annual Catalogue of Australian Publications*. There is still a gap for government publications, however, since the last three volumes of the Ferguson bibliography, covering 1851-1900, did not include entries for this material. Specific government publications excluded from *ANB 1901-1950* are legislation and parliamentary papers.

Libraries in the states have also published bibliographies of the publications of their state governments, but only three of these continue: *New South Wales Official Publications Received in the State Library of New South Wales*, *Queensland Government Publications* and *Victorian Government Publications*. The importance of these catalogues has diminished since contributed entries were accepted for listing in *AGP* in 1977 and with the creation of ABN.

The Law Printer in Victoria, the Western Australian Printing Office, the South Australian State Information Centre and the Northern Territory Government Information Centre issue sales catalogues. AGPS catalogues, discussed above, are broader in scope and provide a comprehensive coverage of AGPS titles and selected others. The fortnightly *Commonwealth Publications Official List* is the most important of these from a selection point of view, since it is timely and contains full pricing details for sale publications (although not for 'NS' – non-stock – titles).

Individual government agencies often produce lists of publications issued. Commonwealth agencies are also required to include such a list in their annual reports. The scattered nature of such lists, and the inadequate bibliographic and other details they often contain, however, generally mean that they are used as a last resort in attempting to identify a particular work. There are exceptions: the catalogues produced by the Australian Bureau of Statistics, for example, are more comprehensive than the major bibliographies in their coverage and are the preferred source for identifying ABS titles.

The Future

Commercialization, deregulation and abolition of centralized services are three future directions likely to be taken by government publishing in Australia. Proponents of these actions all claim cost savings. However, for the general collector of government publications, costs are more likely to rise as the number of titles available from central sources is reduced (to nil, if abolition is the course chosen) and hence adding to the labour intensity of the collection process.

Commercialization itself may have a positive effect from the consumer's point of view. In the Commonwealth, for example, it has made the AGPS more market oriented. Its Marketing Group was established to promote products and services as a result of commercialization, and it now employs travelling sales representatives in an attempt to make titles more widely available through commercial outlets. New products and services such as its electronic publishing programme, AGPS Press and the AGPS indexing and other information services are also results of this commercial orientation.

AGPS expects to lose many of its traditional clients if publishing is deregulated, or at least initially. Its catalogues will be less comprehensive for that period, as will the deposit collections received by libraries. It is little compensation to the collector of Commonwealth government publications that AGPS can now accept contract work from non-Commonwealth sources, which it expects will pay its costs while it is wooing back former clients.

It is ironic that the following may describe one possible future for Commonwealth government publishing – to a large extent it has always characterized the present at other levels of government. There will be no single office responsible for publications, for establishing uniformity in printing styles, publishing standards and the manner in which copy should be prepared, and for curbing unnecessary extravagance. There will be no single office to supply copies of publications. There will be inadequate arrangements for advising potential users about publications that are available and how to obtain them. There will be widely differing methods of distribution of publications. This was the past that the Erwin Committee deplored and made recommendations, including the establishment of AGPS, to correct.

Notes

1 Australia. Parliament. Joint Select Committee on Parliamentary and Government Publications, *Parliamentary and Government Publications: Report*. Canberra: Government Printer, 1964 (also published as Parliamentary Paper 32/1964).

2 Australia. Parliament. Joint Committee on Publications, *The Australian Government Publishing Service and Its Role in Commonwealth Printing and Publishing 1964-1978* (Sixth Special Report). Canberra: Australian Government Publishing Service, 1978 (also published as Parliamentary Paper 335/1978).

3 The text was reproduced in Australia. Department of Sport, Recreation and Tourism, *Annual Report 1984-85*. Canberra: Australian Government Publishing Service, 1985 (also published as Parliamentary Paper 424/1985), pp. 170-173. The 1989 revised charter was distributed by AGPS but did not appear in the Department of Administrative Service's annual report for 1989-90.

4 Australia. Parliament. Joint Committee on Publications, *Review of the Auditor-General's Efficiency Audit Report on the AGPS* (Ninth Special Report). Canberra: Australian Government Publishing Service, 1988 (also published as Parliamentary Paper 311/1988). The report reviewed was the Australian Audit Office, *Efficiency Audit Report: Australian Government Publishing Service*. Canberra: Australian Government Publishing Service, 1987 (also published as Parliamentary Paper 334/1987).

5 Reproduced in the Joint Committee on Publications Ninth Special Report, *op. cit.*, and in Australia. Department of Administrative Services, Annual Report 1988-89. Canberra: Australian Government Publishing Service, 1989, pp. 198-200 (also published as Parliamentary Paper 383/1990).

5 Serials Publishing in Australia

Tony Burrows

Australia has produced a wide range of serials in the two centuries since white settlement. This paper looks at the major types of serials published in Australia: newspapers, literary magazines, government and legal serials, women's magazines, radical and satirical periodicals, scholarly and scientific journals. Each of these is considered from an historical perspective, as well as in their current situation. Bibliographic access to Australian serials is also discussed.

For a country with a relatively small population (17 million) and a comparatively short history (just over 200 years of white settlement), Australia has a surprisingly rich and diverse heritage of serials publishing. About 750 periodicals are known to have been published in the nineteenth century, when Australia was no more than a collection of small, isolated colonies, and population growth resulted mainly from discoveries of gold in the second half of the century. At least 4500 newspapers have appeared in Australia during the last 190 years. There have also been numerous literary and cultural magazines which have played a key role in shaping Australia's intellectual life.

Serials publishing in Australia continues to grow and flourish today. Over 1000 magazines are published, as well as more than 700 newspapers. To these can be added the numerous publications of the federal and state governments, many legal serials, and the titles issued by societies and other organizations. Despite a high level of imports of overseas serials – popular magazines and scholarly journals alike – Australia continues to sustain an indigenous serials publishing industry that achieves circulation figures per head of population which are well above average.

The main reason for almost all of these serials, and for their comparatively high circulation, has always been their role in expressing an Australian identity, in enabling their readers to define for themselves what it means to be Australian. This has been especially in evidence in recent years, when 'Australianness' has been discussed and debated more than ever before. Australia's geographical isolation, and its very mixed ethnic and cultural heritage, have made this process of definition crucial in the development of the nation.

Serials are, therefore, an important and pervasive part of Australian life and culture – and have been since the colonial period. Book publishing, in comparison, has been less influential and subject to much greater fluctuations in its fortunes. Yet Australian serials have been comparatively less studied than books. In large part this is due to the predominance of popular serials with a mass audience (including newspapers); 'serious' scholarly journals and the like have always been a minor part of serials publishing, with small circulations, uncertain lives and (in recent years) dependence on government subsidies. But this neglect is beginning to be redressed, with the realization that the study of Australian serials can throw considerable light on the nature of Australian society and on the outlook and interests of all kinds of Australians.

Newspapers

Australia currently produces a large number of newspapers for a country of its population, but most of these are local or regional. There are 188 suburban mastheads, with a circulation of 5 million per week, and over 420 regional and country papers – 165 in New South Wales alone. Australia's sprawling cities and isolated outback towns have encouraged this proliferation of local newspapers, which continues despite the effects of radio and television.

The situation is different, however, when it comes to metropolitan and national papers. There are only four papers which deliberately aim for a national audience. Two of these are financial and economic: the *Australian Financial Review* and the *Daily Commercial News*. The only general national daily is Rupert Murdoch's *The Australian*, a broadsheet launched in 1964, when it was the first new major paper for over twenty years. It appears in all the state capitals simultaneously and has succeeded in providing a national 'quality' perspective, as well as (eventually) making a profit. The fourth national paper is the *Independent Monthly*, launched in 1989 by veteran journalist Max Suich, with backing from the John B. Fairfax company. Despite its tabloid newspaper format, it is a hybrid of a magazine and a newspaper, with a sceptical, critical, independent outlook. Though it has established a niche for itself, its future cannot yet be said to be certain.

The number of metropolitan papers (dailies and Sundays) has been declining steadily for decades, until there are now only twenty-five papers serving Australia's eight states and territories. During 1990 a further three papers ceased or merged. Perth, for example, which is a city of over a million people, now has only a morning daily, *The West Australian*, and a Sunday paper, *The Sunday Times*. Melbourne, with six papers, has the widest selection. The metropolitan papers are mainly tabloids, of varying quality and seriousness, but there are a few 'quality' broadsheets. The most important of these are *The Sydney Morning Herald* and the Melbourne *Age*, both of which originated in the nineteenth century. *The Herald* was Australia's first regular daily, from October 1840 (having first appeared in 1831), while *The Age* goes back to 1854. Despite some fluctuations in quality, both continue to cover a wide range of issues, with some serious analysis and commentary, though their primary focus remains events affecting the cities and states which they serve.

The declining number of metropolitan papers has been paralleled by an increasing concentration of ownership. In May 1988 Rupert Murdoch's News Ltd controlled 61.6 per cent of daily circulation. John Fairfax Ltd, which published *The Age, Australian Financial Review* and *The Sydney Morning Herald*, had 18 per cent. The handful of other owners included Bond Media (7.7 per cent) and Kerry Packer's Australian Consolidated Press (1.4 per cent). Since then Bond Media has sold its interest to an independent company, and the Fairfax company (founded in 1841) has been placed in receivership. Even News Ltd has had to reduce its number of titles through mergers, because of a high level of debt.

The major event of the 1980s was the breaking up of the previously largest company – the Herald and Weekly Times Ltd – which had controlled 43 per cent of daily circulation in the early 1960s. This company was run for many years by Sir Keith Murdoch, and it was, paradoxically, his son Rupert who benefitted most from its demise. The concentration of ownership has also extended to the suburban newspapers, which are now 90 per cent owned by the metropolitan companies. To a somewhat lesser extent the same applies to the regional and country papers.

Australia has a long history of newspaper production and consumption. Over 4500 are known to have been published, more than 3000 of them in New South Wales and Victoria. Beginning with the *Sydney Gazette and New South Wales Advertiser* in 1803, the number of papers increased rapidly during the nineteenth century and spread to all the colonies. By 1909 there were sixty-seven daily papers, representing 15.8 per million people. Britain, in comparison, had five per million people at that time. There were also 182.8 weekly to triweekly papers per million people in Australia, compared with 59.9 in Britain. The first

Sunday papers had not appeared until the 1880s. Most of these nineteenth-century papers were serious but parochial, though there were occasional examples of a sensationalist approach. Ownership was very diffuse and limited to specific papers.

In the twentieth century most of this has changed. The first tabloid – the Melbourne *Sun News-Pictorial* – appeared in 1922, and since then the overall tone of the press has become steadily more sensational and shrill, while remaining very local and parochial. The number of metropolitan and country papers has gradually declined, and the launch of a new title has become an increasingly rare phenomenon. Ownership has become more concentrated in a few large companies. The outlook of the press has been a consistent opposition to socialism, unions and the Labor Party, while various attempts to launch left-wing papers have come to nothing. Newspapers have become heavily dependent on advertising revenue, and are consequently committed to the world of commerce and the consumer society.

An interesting aspect of the Australian press has been the so-called ethnic papers, aimed at the various migrant groups which have played an important part in Australian society. These papers have appeared both in English and in the native languages of their ethnic groups. Their main purpose has been to promote assimilation of migrants into Australian society, while at the same time providing a sense of cohesion within the migrant group. The earliest foreign-language papers were those of the German settlers in South Australia, from 1848, and Scandinavian papers in the Victorian goldfields in the 1850s. In the twentieth century there have been various Italian and Greek papers, as well as numerous papers for Eastern European refugees and migrants after the Second World War. More recently papers have begun to appear for Middle Eastern and South-East Asian ethnic groups. There are now at least 129 ethnic papers being published in Australia.

Though most of these newspapers are non-partisan and try to leave behind the political divisions of their country of origin, there have been some exceptions: a pro-Nazi German weekly in the 1930s, some Italian anti-fascist and left-wing papers, an extreme left-wing Yugoslav paper, and Greek papers on both sides of the political spectrum.

Literary Periodicals

The development of a distinctively Australian literature and culture has been heavily dependent on serials. In the nineteenth century newspapers and general magazines published a large proportion of indigenous literary and critical writings, while books played only a small part.

There was little, if any, distinction between the journalist and the literary author. Poets like Charles Harpur and Henry Kendall published their work in the papers and magazines of the 1860s and 1870s, while such early classics of the Australian novel as Marcus Clarke's *For the Term of His Natural Life* and Rolf Boldrewood's *Robbery under Arms* first appeared in serialized form in monthly magazines of the 1870s and 1880s. At least 449 periodicals with literary features are known to have been published in the nineteenth century, and their contribution to early Australian literature was crucial.

By far the most influential of these was the Sydney *Bulletin*, the weekly magazine which first appeared in 1880. As well as its interest in news, politics and social life – seen from a nationalistic, irreverent, larrikin point of view – *The Bulletin* quickly became a focus for the literary flowering of the 1890s. Among its regular contributors were such seminal figures as Henry Lawson, 'Banjo' Paterson, Steele Rudd, C.J. Dennis and Tom Collins. In 1907 it spawned a monthly literary magazine called *The Lone Hand*, which pursued a policy of 'an Australian sentiment from Australian writers' until its demise in 1921. The influence and originality of *The Bulletin* gradually waned, though in the 1930s it published Vance Palmer, Xavier Herbert, Katharine Susannah Prichard and Dal Stivens. While Douglas Stewart was its literary editor in the 1940s and 1950s most of the major poets were published, but since 1961 *The Bulletin* has been little more than an Australian imitation of the American news magazines and now even includes *Newsweek* as an insert.

Since the 1920s, however, Australian literature has mainly appeared in 'little magazines' and has all but vanished from newspapers and general periodicals. For much of this period literary periodicals have been shaped by their attitude to, on the one hand, European cultural movements – modernism, surrealism, existentialism and the like – and, on the other, *The Bulletin*'s tradition of overtly Australian subjects and themes. The first of these magazines, Norman and Jack Lindsay's *Vision*, which published four issues in 1923-1924, attacked modernism and Australian parochialism alike, in the name of Life and Beauty.

The *Australian Mercury*, though only producing a single issue in 1935, contained an influential manifesto by P.R. ('Inky') Stephensen, calling for an independent Australian literature. Stephensen later edited other small magazines, founded the 'Australia-First Movement' and was interned during the Second World War. Also influential, and more enduring, was the Jindyworobak group of poets, led by Rex Ingamells. They published an annual anthology and several magazines between 1938 and 1953, and called for an Australian culture freed from 'pseudo-

Europeanism'. Their aim was 'to free Australian art from whatever alien influences trammel it.' Australian poets, wrote Ingamells, 'must forget all they have learned of the poetry of their lands.'

One of the magazines which, in contrast, embraced such European trends as modernism and surrealism was *Angry Penguins*, edited by Max Harris between 1940 and 1946. Its efforts to promote Australian (and overseas) literature and art of this kind were seriously undermined by the Ern Malley hoax in 1944. A collection of surrealist poems allegedly written by one Ern Malley, and published with enthusiasm in *Angry Penguins*, was revealed to have been concocted at random by the poets Harold Stewart and James McAuley as a hoax – but not before some of the poems had been the subject of a successful police prosecution for indecency.

Most of Australia's present major literary periodicals were established between thirty and fifty years ago. They are usually published from a university, and focus specifically on Australian culture, leaving overseas culture to overseas periodicals. *Meanjin*, which first appeared in 1940, was edited for many years by Clem Christesen. From its beginnings as a poetry magazine it developed into a wide-ranging literary periodical, and publishes poetry and short fiction as well as providing a forum for intellectual debate within a loose framework of liberal, humanist and somewhat left-wing views. An openly left-wing, and originally Communist, magazine is *Overland*, which began in 1954 under the editorship of Stephen Murray-Smith. Its blend of radicalism, socialist realism and working-class links has been typified by writers like Dorothy Hewett, Frank Hardy and Katharine Susannah Prichard.

Quadrant takes an entirely different line, having been established in 1956, with James McAuley as editor, on the model of the British conservative magazine, *Encounter*. From its emphasis on traditionalist, democratic and liberal values, *Quadrant* has provided a mixture of political and literary material. Other well established periodicals are *Southerly* (from the University of Sydney, since 1939), *Westerly* (from the University of Western Australia, since 1956), the critical journal, *Australian Literary Studies*, and *Poetry Australia*, which has included Les A. Murray among its editors.

In the late 1960s and early 1970s there was a sudden boom in little magazines, especially those publishing poetry. Over 130 are known to have appeared in this period, mostly with short lives and small circulations, and usually reflecting the social change and questioning attitudes characteristic of those years. These magazines were, in the main, not particularly 'Australian' in content, and several of the leading figures involved in them – such as Michael Wilding, Pat Woolley and Kris Hemensly – were from Britain or the United States originally. Among the most memorable, at least for their titles, were *The Ear in a Wheatfield, Celebration: A Journal for the Dark Ages*, and *Etymspheres*, but the most enduring and influential was probably *Tabloid Story*, edited by Wilding, Woolley and Frank Moorhouse. First published in 1972, as an avenue for short stories which were more unconventional and experimental, it was distinguished by its use of a tabloid format, and by the way it always appeared as an insert or supplement to other, 'host' periodicals.

Since this burst of activity died away in the late 1970s there has been a smaller but more lasting group of substantial new literary magazines. Generally more traditional in their approach, they have included *Island Magazine* (from Tasmania), *Australian Short Stories*, and the highly regarded *Scripsi*, which is unusual for its ability to distance itself from Australian cultural politics by taking an international perspective. Several review magazines have appeared, as well as a variety of small, experimental titles – such as *Mattoid* and *Otis Rush*. Ethnic or multicultural literary periodicals have also begun to appear, among them Manfred Jurgensen's *Outrider*, the Jewish *Melbourne Chronicle*, and a bilingual Italian-Australian magazine called *Radici*.

A major feature of the period since 1973 has been the role of the Literary Arts Board (formerly the Literature Board) of the Australia Council in subsidizing literary magazines. This Federal Government agency has made grants totalling more than $3 million to over sixty magazines. The main beneficiaries have been the well established periodicals like *Quadrant* and *Meanjin*, and the Board's decisions when allocating its limited funds have not always been welcomed by the editors of smaller and more unconventional titles. The Board provides small 'project grants' for periodicals with low circulations, and concentrates its continuing, more substantial funding on the larger national publications. These subsidies, which are primarily intended to enable contributors to be paid for their literary works, have become important to the survival of Australia's main literary magazines. For all their importance in promoting and spreading Australian literature and culture, their subscription base is generally very limited.

Government and Legal Serials

Serials published by the Federal Government and the eight state governments are an important and increasingly voluminous part of Australian publishing. Federal publications have, with only a few exceptions, been issued by the Australian Government Publishing

Service (AGPS) since 1970. AGPS has provided a successful centralized and coordinated agency, though its sales and marketing side has not always been particularly efficient. In the late 1980s, however, the Federal Government decided that AGPS should become largely self-financing, and this has affected the kind of material published, as well as driving up prices.

As far as serials are concerned, AGPS publishes the essential record of the Federal Government's activities: Bills, Acts and statutory rules; votes and proceedings of the two houses of Federal Parliament, and its extensive and valuable series of parliamentary papers; and several series of gazettes with announcements of, and advertisements for, governmental business. All of these serials go back well beyond AGPS, in most cases to the foundation of the Commonwealth of Australia in 1901, and were formerly published by the Commonwealth Government Printer. Other serials were previously issued by individual government departments until AGPS was established. AGPS now publishes the annual reports of most departments, agencies and statutory bodies of the Federal Government, which include an increasing number of glossy, commercial-looking publications. Also in the AGPS catalogue is a variety of periodicals, ranging from utilitarian economic analyses to glossier magazines which deal with such topics as culture, foreign affairs and fisheries, and which are partly intended as vehicles for promoting Australia overseas. Among the other serials produced by AGPS are such widely differing items as newsletters of government departments and looseleaf compilations of procedures and regulations.

Not all agencies of the Federal Government are covered by AGPS, however. The major exception in serials publishing is the Australian Bureau of Statistics, formerly the Commonwealth Bureau of Census and Statistics. The Bureau issues a considerable number of statistical periodicals, which cover many aspects of Australian industry and society, from the states' perspective as well as at the national level. Its publications giving the figures for balance of payments, prices and employment levels are regularly headline news, but its whole output is an invaluable source for all sorts of research – over past decades as well as the present. The Bureau has come under increasing pressure from the Federal Government to finance its own activities and the result has been a review of the titles published, with some discontinued and a few launched, and a shift away from mainly free publications to priced ones. The Bureau also issues its material in non-print formats, especially microfiche and magnetic tape.

The serial publications of the state governments are fewer in number and far less well organized, but are still central to the record of activities in each state. In most cases the parliamentary serials and government gazettes are issued by a Government Printer, though New South Wales recently closed down its Government Printer. These publications are among the oldest in Australia, dating from the establishment of colonial administration in the earlier nineteenth century. But other serials – such as annual reports – are usually published by individual departments, and can be difficult to trace and obtain. Magazine-type periodicals are seldom published by state governments, and their publications tend to be utilitarian and heavily subsidized.

Legal publishing in Australia, by comparison, is thoroughly commercial, and priced accordingly. The official reports of cases in the Australian system of state and federal courts have been issued for many years by Butterworths and the Law Book Company, while looseleaf services – which have been growing rapidly in number – are primarily published by CCH Australia. Scholarly legal journals are largely the province of university law schools, which exist in most of the universities and which usually issue their own journal. There is something of a boom in legal periodicals at present, with several new journals appearing, some from the Law Book Company, as well as various specific newsletters published by small and specialized legal publishing companies.

Other Serials

As well as these literary, governmental and legal serials, Australia has always had a disproportionately large number of other magazines and journals, both general and specialized. At least 750 are known to have been published in the nineteenth century, though most of these had short and financially precarious lives. They were usually based on, and competed with, British and American magazines, and suffered from poor distribution and a lack of suitable equipment. Their production costs were high, but revenue from advertising was difficult to attract. In the later nineteenth century magazines resorted to such measures as competitions, prizes and insurance coupons to encourage subscribers. After 1850 serial publishing became gradually more sophisticated, with the emergence of illustrated magazines and a shift to weekly rather than quarterly publication. These nineteenth-century publications were usually general in their coverage, but more specialized titles began to appear in the latter part of the century, especially those with a sporting, theatrical, religious or financial focus. Their Australian content became much more pronounced, while their dependence on material reprinted from overseas magazines gave way to original local contributions.

The twentieth century has seen the development of a wide range of specialized periodicals, especially after about 1920. There has been an increasing number of glossy, commercial magazines, often modelled on British or American originals. At present over 1000 magazines are published in Australia – at least sixty-four dealing with sports and leisure, forty-six business, thirty-seven with motoring, and twenty-eight women's magazines. With a 20 per cent increase between 1985 and 1990 in the numbers of copies sold, Australian magazine publishing seems to be experiencing a period of unprecedented growth.

These commercial magazines are also increasingly concentrated in the hands of a few major companies. The first of these magazine publishing groups was K.G. Murray, which owned as many as twenty titles in the period between 1930 and 1960, and also published Frank Greenop's definitive *History of Magazine Publishing in Australia* in 1947. The Murray group lasted until 1973, when it was absorbed by Australian Consolidated Press (ACP). Now owned by Kerry Packer, ACP publishes many of Australia's best-selling magazines, having also taken over Modern Magazines in 1978 and the Fairfax Company's magazines in 1988. Though it produces *The Bulletin*, ACP's main strengths are women's magazines (*Australian Women's Weekly*, *Woman's Day* and Australian editions of *Cosmopolitan* and *Good Housekeeping*) and business magazines (*Australian Business*, *Business Review Weekly* and *Personal Investment*). The only major rival to ACP is Rupert Murdoch's News Ltd, which absorbed the magazines published by Herald and Weekly Times Ltd in 1988. Apart from *TV Week*, these are mainly women's or house and garden magazines, such as *New Idea*, *Family Circle*, *Australian Home Beautiful* and *Better Homes and Gardens*.

Women's magazines, in particular, have been an important part of Australian popular culture, beginning with several titles in the later nineteenth century, such as *Dawn*, edited by Louisa Lawson and published between 1888 and 1905. Among the longer lasting have been *New Idea*, a weekly first issued in 1904 and currently selling around 1 million copies, *Woman's Day* (derived from various predecessors which first appeared in 1906), and the *Australian Women's Mirror*, which appeared between 1924 and 1961 as an offshoot of *The Bulletin*. All the women's magazines have much the same content: fashion, cookery, homes and gardens, and news and gossip about people from the world of entertainment.

The most influential and best-loved of these magazines, however, is the Australian *Women's Weekly*. Founded in 1933 by Sir Frank Packer (father of Kerry) and the politician and trade unionist E.G. Theodore, the *Weekly* offered a successful blend of royalist sentiment, fascination with Hollywood stars, and advice for the ideal housewife on fashion, cookery, homes and gardens, and motherhood. With time, it has come to include more news and a cautious exploration of the new social trends and topics of the changed climate of the 1960s and later. Under a succession of talented editors (usually women), the *Weekly* increased its circulation and maintained its middle-class outlook, and has become an Australian institution, much parodied and mocked, but a seemingly permanent fixture. More recently, worries over slipping circulation figures and profits resulted in its becoming a monthly, though without a change in name. Its best-known recent editor has been Ita Buttrose, who had also edited magazines like *Cleo* and *Cosmopolitan*, directed at a younger, more 'liberated' female audience. Her latest venture, launched in 1989, is the modestly titled *Ita*, which caters for the interests of the middle-aged career woman – 'the woman who wasn't born yesterday'. As well as the traditional preoccupations (fashion, beauty, food and children – now young adults), it also covers finance, fitness, careers and personal development.

The opposite side of the coin, perhaps, is represented by the periodicals which emerged from the women's movement. The earliest feminist magazines appeared in the late 1960s, though much earlier publications have been claimed as precursors, especially Louisa Lawson's *Dawn*, which was edited and written entirely by women. Most of the publications inspired by the women's movement, such as *Mejane* and *Vashti's Voice*, did not survive the 1970s, but there have been some notable exceptions. *Refractory Girl* and *Hecate* are still being published, and their influence has been significant. The latter has received continuing grants from the Australia Council. While new feminist periodicals continued to appear in the 1980s, the total circulation of this type of publication remains very small in comparison with the commercial and conventional women's magazines.

Australia has a long history of radical periodicals, though none of these could be regarded as particularly influential. *The Bulletin*, in its earliest years, was overtly anti-establishment and populist, but it had some more radical contemporaries, such as William Lane's *The Worker* (published between 1890 and 1974) and *The Australian Worker*. Henry Lawson was a frequent contributor to the latter. Important socialist papers have included *Tocsin*, later renamed *Labor Call* and *Labor*, which appeared from 1897 to 1961, and *The Socialist*, first issued in 1906 by the Victorian Socialist Party. The Australian branch of Industrial Workers of the World published *Direct Action* during the First World War.

In the 1930s and 1940s the Communist Party of Australia was active in publishing. Its best-known periodicals were the *Communist Review* (which became the *Australian Left Review* in 1967) and *Australian New Writing*, first published in 1943 under the editorship of Katharine Susannah Prichard and Bernard Smith. The literary magazine, *Overland*, appeared in 1954 under Communist patronage, but its editor, Stephen Murray-Smith, broke with the Party a few years later.

By the 1960s radical periodicals tended to be associated with the universities and generally reflected the views of the New Left. The Marxist review, *Arena*, has appeared since 1963, and the socialist paper, *Direct Action*, since 1970. The student press became particularly active in the late 1960s and 1970s, with titles like *National U, Honi Soit* and *Tharunka*. Nevertheless, the student and radical audience remained small, though very vocal.

More influential, and with a wider audience, was the succession of critical and sceptical papers and magazines which appeared from the late 1950s. Their forerunner was the short-lived *Tomorrow*, edited by Max Harris, with only ten issues in 1946. Tom Fitzgerald's fortnightly magazine, *Nation*, was the most important of these. After appearing between 1958 and 1972, it merged with the *Sunday Review* to form *Nation Review*. This was later followed by the *National Times*, a paper which then became the *Times on Sunday*, before closing down. These papers were noted for their caustic and critical commentaries on politics, Australian and international, as well as their interest in social and cultural questions, seen usually from a 'liberal left' point of view. Their tone tended to be intellectual and sceptical. Current periodicals in the same vein are *Australian Society*, a monthly modelled on Britain's *New Society, The Independent Monthly*, a magazine in tabloid format, and *The Eye*.

Many of these have included a strong element of satire, but there has also been a history of specifically satirical magazines. This 'larrikin' tradition reaches back into the nineteenth century, with the *Melbourne Punch* (published from 1855 to 1925) and its less successful rivals. *The Bulletin* was a seminal influence here too, since it contained a considerable amount of satirical material, at least at the beginning. In the twentieth century satire was represented by the soldiers' magazines of the First World War and the long-running popular paper, *Smith's Weekly*. But the most notorious satirical paper was *Oz*, edited by Richard Neville and Richard Walsh. *Oz* was a characteristic product of the 1960s, lampooning such institutions as the Queen, the church and and the Returned Services League, and promoting sexual permissiveness and freedom from censorship. The editors were successfully prosecuted for obscenity and libel. Another distinctive feature of *Oz* was the artwork of Martin Sharp, with its heavy use of collage and Dadaist drawings. Satire continues at present, rather tenuously, with Queensland's *Cane Toad Times*, while another Queensland paper, *Matilda*, fell foul of Australia's laws on defamation and libel in 1986.

As well as all these satirical, radical and feminist periodicals, Australia has produced a wide range of scholarly and scientific journals. Probably the most prolific area is, perhaps unsurprisingly, historical studies, where there are periodicals published by the state historical associations and the Royal Australian Historical Society – most originating in the later nineteenth century – as well as other journals usually connected with the universities, such as *Australian Historical Studies, Journal of Pacific History, Labour History* and *Australian Economic History Review*. In the other arts and social sciences there is normally at least one scholarly journal for each broad area, published either through an association or through a university. Current important examples include *Australasian Journal of Philosophy, AUMLA, Australian Aboriginal Studies, Australian and New Zealand Journal of Sociology, Australian Psychologist, Economic Record* and *Oceania*. Almost invariably, these journals have an Australasian focus, and most began in the 1960s, a period of rapid expansion in university education and research.

In the sciences the oldest periodicals are those published by scientific societies, such as the *Papers and Proceedings of the Royal Society of Tasmania*, founded in 1849, and the *Proceedings of the Linnean Society of New South Wales*, founded in 1876. The most important publications, though, are the Australian Journals of Scientific Research, published by the Commonwealth Scientific and Industrial Research Organization (CSIRO), a body funded by the Federal Government. There are currently thirteen journals, covering most major scientific disciplines (physics, chemistry, botany and so on). Most have a substantial international reputation and first appeared in 1948. In recent years they have been put on a commercial footing, having previously been distributed by gift or exchange. There is also a considerable number of more popular scientific magazines and newsletters. Among these are the glossy *Australian Natural History* and *Search*, the fortnightly magazine of the Australian and New Zealand Association for the Advancement of Science. The weekly *New Scientist* publishes an Australian edition, with a small but growing Australian content.

A survey in 1987 of Australia's scientific and social science journals showed that, of a sample of 133, about 75 per cent were running at a loss. Their average print run was about 2000 and their number of subscriptions was steady or growing gradually. Few had a substantial income from advertising revenue, and most had part-time amateur editors. They are usually published by societies or universities and kept going by subsidies and by a significant amount to unpaid labour. There is little evidence of serious attention to financial management, marketing and distribution, or of strategies for the future. Though these journals often produce material of high quality, and usually enable publication of Australasian research which (at least in the social sciences) would be unlikely to appear in an overseas periodical, their future appears tenuous in quite a few cases. At present Australia manages to support a comparatively large number of scholarly journals, but changing economic conditions may well prune this list considerably.

Bibliographic Access

The standard list of current Australian periodicals is *Australian Periodicals in Print,* issued annually by D.W. Thorpe in Melbourne. It claims to cover all periodicals, magazines, directories, yearbooks and newspapers, but is far from complete, perhaps because of its reliance on questionnaires to publishers. From 1981 to 1986 it was known as *Australian Serials in Print*. Before that the National Library of Australia published *Current Australian Serials*, which appeared in nine editions between 1963 and 1975. It excluded newspapers and annual reports.

Federal and state government serials are listed in *Australian Government Publications*, published by the National Library since 1952 and available only on microfiche since 1988. A useful source for current newspapers and commercial magazines is the *Press, Radio and TV Guide: Australia, New Zealand and the Pacific Islands*. The definitive list of newspapers, up to 1985, is *Newspapers in Australian Libraries: A Union List, Part 2, Australian Newspapers*, the fourth edition of which was published by the National Library in 1985. For the nineteenth century there is a checklist of known periodicals (excluding annuals and newspapers), compiled by Alfred Pong. Subject lists of current periodicals appear in the *Australian and New Zealand Journal of Serials Librarianship*.

The only source which aims to provide an exhaustive list of Australian serials is *NUCOS*, the *National Union Catalogue of Serials*, published on microfiche by the National Library. *NUCOS* is derived from the National Bibliographic Database (NBD), maintained through the Australian Bibliographic Network (ABN). It lists all serials held by Australian libraries, so specifically Australian serials can be hard to trace. Nor is there any subject access to *NUCOS*, though this is available online to ABN. Considerable efforts have been made to increase the NBD's retrospective coverage of Australian serials, but this is not yet complete. Eventually, however, *NUCOS* and the NBD should record all Australian serials. Until then bibliographic access to current and past Australian serials will remain fragmented and patchy.

References

Australian and New Zealand Journal of Serials Librarianship 1, 1- . New York: Haworth Press, 1990- .

Bennett, Bruce, ed. *Cross Currents: Magazines and Newspapers in Australian Literature*. Melbourne: Longman Cheshire, 1981.

Bowman, David. *The Captive Press*. Ringwood, Vic.: Penguin, 1988.

Denholm, Michael. *Small Press Publishing in Australia: The Early 1970s*. North Sydney: Second Back Row Press, 1979.

Denholm, Michael. 'The Little Magazine in the Twentieth Century,' in *The Book in Australia: Essays towards a Cultural and Social History*, ed. D.H. Borchardt and W. Kirsop. Melbourne: Australian Reference Publications, 1988, pp. 88-95.

Gilson, Miriam and Zubrzycki, Jerzy. *The Foreign-language Press in Australia*. Canberra: Australian National University Press, 1967.

Greenop, Frank S. *History of Magazine Publishing in Australia*. Sydney: K.G. Murray, 1947.

Inglis, K.S. 'The Daily Papers,' in *Australian Civilization*, ed. Peter Coleman. Melbourne: Cheshire, 1962, pp. 145-175.

Judge, Peter. 'Natural and Social Science Journals: A Situation Report from Australia and New Zealand,' *Search* 18 (1987): 303-306.

Lindesay, Vane. *The Way We Were: Australian Popular Magazines 1856-1969*. Melbourne: Oxford University Press, 1983.

Mayer, Henry. *The Press in Australia*. Melbourne: Lansdowne Press, 1964, repr. 1968.

O'Brien, Denis. *The Weekly*. Ringwood, Vic.: Penguin, 1982.

Pong, Alfred. *Checklist of Nineteenth Century Australian Periodicals*. Bundoora, Vic.: La Trobe University, Borchardt Library, 1985.

Rolfe, Patricia. *The Journalistic Javelin: An Illustrated History of The Bulletin*. Sydney: Wildcat Press, 1979.

Souter, Gavin. *Heralds and Angels: The House of Fairfax 1841-1900*. Carlton, Vic.: Melbourne University Press, 1991.

Strahan, Lynne. *Just City and the Mirrors: Meanjin Quarterly and the Intellectual Front, 1940-1965*. Melbourne: Oxford University Press, 1984.

Stuart, Lurline. 'Colonial Periodicals: Patterns of Failure,' *Bibliographical Society of Australia and New Zealand Bulletin* 13 (1989): 1-10.

Stuart, Lurline. *Nineteenth Century Australian Periodicals: An Annotated Bibliography*. Sydney: Hale and Iremonger, 1979.

Tregenza, J. *Australian Little Magazines 1923-1954* (Adelaide: Libraries Board of South Australia, 1964).

Walker, R.B. *The Newspaper Press in New South Wales, 1803-1920*. Sydney: Sydney University Press, 1976.

Walker, R.B. *Yesterday's News: A History of the Newspaper Press in New South Wales from 1920 to 1945*. Sydney: Sydney University Press, 1980.

Walsh, Richard. 'Periodicals,' in *The Australian Encyclopaedia*. 5th ed. Vol. 6. Terrey Hills, NSW: Australian Geographic, 1988, pp. 2262-2268.

Webby, Elizabeth. 'Journals in the Nineteenth Century,' in *The Book in Australia: Essays towards a Cultural and Social History*, ed. D.H. Borchardt and W. Kirsop. Melbourne: Australian Reference Publications, 1988, pp. 43-65.

6 An Introduction to Australian Reference Publishing

John Mills

The role of commercial and non-commercial, other than government, reference publishing in Australia is outlined. The contribution of the various publishers to production of bibliographic control titles, ready reference titles and indexing, abstracting services and databases is examined. The essential Australian reference sources are identified, and the special features of Australian reference publishing are discussed.

The publishing of reference books in Australia is characterized by a large number of producers and a small domestic and overseas market. The largest publisher in Australia is government, discussed elsewhere in this volume, characterized by a combination of local government, state government and federal government bodies producing a range of reference material. It is not easy to categorize the other publishers of reference material, as they range from the semi-government authorities such as the National Library of Australia and the various state libraries, to professional associations such as the Australian Library and Information Association, to non-library affiliated institutions which include commercial enterprises, professional associations and societies and small press operators. It is to these 'other' publishers that this paper is addressed. Reference publishing in Australia by these active publishers is approached here in relation to bibliographic control, ready reference, indexing, abstracting services and databases.

Bibliographic Control

Current National Bibliography

The National Library of Australia (NLA) is the foremost publisher in Australia of the tools of bibliographic control. With its *Australian National Bibliography (ANB)* books and pamphlets published in Australia and overseas publications by Australians or with Australian subject content are recorded. In addition, government publications, with the exception of individual Acts, Bills and Ordinances, are listed, as are new periodical titles and those issued with changes in bibliographical details. *ANB* is incorporated into ABN, the Australian Bibliographic Network, a cooperative online shared cataloguing network and a gateway to many other databases hosted or produced by the National Library of Australia.

Australian Government Publications (AGP), published quarterly by the NLA, tends to include those titles not included in *ANB*, although considerable duplication with *ANB* does occur. *AGP* lists printed material issued by agencies of the Commonwealth of Australia and its overseas Territories, the states of Australia and the Northern Territory received in the National Library. Entries are also taken from information contributed by the State Library of Tasmania, the State Library of Victoria and the J.S. Battye Library of West Australian History. Some local government publications and non-print materials are also listed. The various publication catalogues produced by the Australian Government Publishing Service, especially *New Commonwealth Government Books from AGPS*, which is the printing, publishing and distribution centre for the publications of the Commonwealth Parliament and Commonwealth government departments and statutory authorities, are also important in tracing the output of the Commonwealth. State government publications enjoy less bibliographic control in terms of comprehensive state oriented catalogues, although some control is in evidence.[1]

Two important semi-government authorities producing a considerable amount of reference material are the Australian Bureau of Statistics and the Commonwealth Scientific and Industrial Research Organization. The Australian Bureau of Statistics (ABS) is the central statistical authority for the Commonwealth Government and provides statistical services for the state governments. Through its *Catalogue of Publications and Products* the ABS provides a guide to its publications; access to ABS data can also be obtained via other means such as the *AUSSTATS* service.[2]

The Commonwealth Scientific and Industrial Research Organization (CSIRO), as the largest scientific research organization in Australia, is an extremely important collector, interpreter and disseminator of scientific and technical information and publisher of scientific and technical reports, periodicals and papers. To maintain bibliographical control of the immense publication programme, CSIRO relies on its database system, AUSTRALIS, and on CLINES – the CSIRO Library Network – which links the services, collections and functions of CSIRO libraries on a single database. AUSTRALIS contains several CSIRO databases, *CSIRO Index*, *CSIRO Films*, in addition to other non-CSIRO generated material.

Bibliographic control of non-book material is generally poor in Australia, although the NLA-produced *Australian Maps* covers maps produced in Australia. Maps also find their way into *Australian Government Publications* and into some of the state government generated lists.

Retrospective National Bibliography

The National Library of Australia is also the major publisher involved in retrospective national bibliography publishing in Australia. Until 1900 Australia is well covered bibliographically with Ferguson's *Bibliography of Australia*. There is then a gap until 1937, when the first *Annual Catalogue of Australian Publications* was issued by the Commonwealth National Library. This publication continued until 1960, when it was superseded by the *Australian National Bibliography*. Additionally, *Books Published in Australia*, a monthly list, supplemented the *Annual Catalogue* from 1946; and from 1952 a second monthly publication, *Australian Government Publications*, supplemented the *Annual Catalogue*. Both were cumulated annually in the *Annual Catalogue*.

Ferguson's monumental work covers publications in and about Australian before 1850, but excludes fiction and certain other categories published between 1850 and 1900. Ferguson and the *Annual Catalogue* were until recently the major retrospective national bibliographies in Australia. To a certain extent current national bibliographies such as *ANB* are also retrospective in that they provide a permanent record of what has been produced over the past decades.

Coverage by the *Annual Catalogue* was considered imperfect, especially with the extensive Ferguson coverage of pre-1900 publications. To cover this and the post-1900 gap, the National Library produced a retrospective national bibliography, the *Australian National Bibliography 1901-1950*, filling the gap between Ferguson's *Bibliography of Australia* and the current *Australian National Bibliography*.

Current Trade Bibliography

Trade bibliography publishing in Australia is dominated by the Melbourne based publisher, D.W. Thorpe, a division of the international Butterworths Pty Ltd. The standard guide to Australian book publishing is their *Australian Books in Print*, published annually and providing title, author and keyword access; a companion volume is *Subject Guide to Australian Books in Print*. The most complete list of periodicals in print is also provided by Thorpe in *Australian Periodicals in Print*. The monthly periodical, *Australian Bookseller and Publisher*, does for the Australian book trade what *The Bookseller* and *Publishers Weekly* do for the British and US markets respectively. The recently begun *Guide to New Australian Books*, an annotated bimonthly bibliography of new Australian books, promises to be a key selection source covering text, reference, children's academic and general books. Of all non-book material perhaps film and video is the best represented in terms of listings. One of the most useful catalogues is *Australian Catalogue of New Films and Videos*; Australian and overseas titles in 35mm, 16mm and all video formats are included, but Super 8 titles are omitted. The catalogues/lists issued by the major producers and reviews of material in subject periodicals are other sources for information.

Other Important Bibliographic Control Titles

Many databases are available in Australia. Those seeking information on these and on database vendors are fortunate in being able to access the following commercial guides: the *Recipe Book of Online Searching* and the *Directory of Australian and New Zealand Databases*. The *Recipe Book of Online Searching* outlines the providers of online information services in Australia, both Australian and overseas vendors, and gives relevant contact information, databases available and general service details and a summary of enquiry procedures conditions. The *Directory of Australian and New Zealand Databases* complements the *Recipe Book...* by providing details on the individual databases provided by the vendors; a subject index to the databases listed enables the user to find relevant databases. These titles are essential guides to the databases available in Australia and to their efficient and effective use. The *Recipe Book...* is produced by Online Information Resources Pty Ltd and the *Directory...* by the Australian Database Development Association.

Theses (honours, masters levels and above) are covered in *Union List of Higher Degree Theses in Australia*, and newspapers are listed in the *NUCOS (National Union Catalogue of Serials)* available via ABN or in the print equivalent, *Newspapers in Australian Libraries*.

Many union catalogues and union lists exist, providing locations for listed items, but the Australian Bibliographic Network (ABN), previously discussed, *National Union Catalogue of Serials (NUCOS)*, *NUC:D (National Union Catalogue of Library Materials for People with Disabilities)*, covering braille and audio books and serials and large print serials, and *NUC:N (National Union Catalogue of Non-Book*

Materials), all available via ABN and produced by the National Library of Australia, are perhaps the most important.

Guides to Reference Sources

In the production of guides to reference books the most ambitious attempt is *Australians: A Guide to Sources* which is one volume of the bicentennial series, *Australians: A Historical Library*. Under the guiding hands of D.H. Borchardt *et al.* we are led through the printed literature of Australia in over forty subject categories. Although the literature is approached from a historical perspective and only printed material is generally considered, it is an essential reference tool. Borchardt, perhaps deserving of the title 'father of Australian bibliography', was also responsible for *Australian Bibliography: A Guide to Printed Sources of Information*, published by Pergamon Press in 1976. This is the forerunner of several other more specific subject guides published by Pergamon Press: Sheehan's *A Guide to Sources of Information on Australian Business*, Choate's *A Guide to Sources of Information on the Arts in Australia*, Hagger's *A Guide to Australian Economic and Social Statistics*, Cook, Lane and Piggott's *A Guide to Commonwealth Government Information Sources* and Jones' *A Guide to Sources of Information on Australian Industrial Relations*. However, these guides do become dated quickly and the titles listed out-of-print, so the selector needs to be wary.

The Australian Library and Information Association (ALIA) has also entered the guide to literature area with its series on Australian reference books. Radford's *Guide to Australian Reference Books: Humanities* appeared in 1983 and Brady's *Guide to Australian Reference Books: Social Sciences* in 1991. Many other guides have been produced; two that do not attempt completeness but should be mentioned are *Australian Books: A Select List of Recent Publications and Standard Works in Print*, produced annually by the National Library of Australia, and Mills and Richardson's *Information Resources and Services in Australia* which is an attempt to identify major reference resources in over forty subject areas.[3]

Library directories have remained the province of the Australian Library and Information Association and Auslib Press. The most important titles are *Directory of Australian Academic and Research Libraries*, *Directory of Special Libraries in Australia*, *Australian Libraries: The Essential Directory* and *Directory of Australian Public Libraries*.

Reviews of Reference Titles

Reviews of new Australian reference titles are not easy to find; no one source can be said to be totally appropriate. The standard source for reviewing new Australian books is *Australian Book Review*; this appears monthly and is produced by the National Book Council. *InCite*, the fortnightly newsletter of the Australian Library and Information Association, is perhaps the most valuable source alerting readers to new Australian reference titles. However, the reviews in this title tend to be statements of content rather than evaluative reviews. Daily newspapers also provide some reviews, and the periodical indexing services index some of the reviews appearing in numerous periodical titles. Other library science periodicals, especially *Australian Library Journal* and *Australian Library Review*, include reviews. The trade periodical, *Australian Bookseller and Publisher*, can also be relied upon to alert its readers to new reference titles, if not to include reviews of them.

Ready Reference Sources

When discussing the publishing of ready reference titles, one is immediately faced with the problem of defining 'reference title'. The traditional definition, a work not intended to be read from cover to cover but consulted for a particular fact or item of information, reduces the number of titles produced in Australia that could be considered as reference. We are left with the standard representation of encyclopedias, dictionaries, yearbooks and so on. However, if the definition is widened to include works that are valuable for specific pieces of information not easily found elsewhere, then many more titles could be considered as reference. This paper takes the latter definition, both to enable discussion of a wider range of titles that could be considered of reference value and to extend the very small list of what may be considered as 'pure' reference titles. That Australia produces so few 'pure' reference titles is not so much a function of its size as of its reliance on results of scholarship produced elsewhere and its paranoia that anything produced in Australia must be of inferior quality to that produced elsewhere. The celebration of Australia's Bicentenary broke this paranoia to some extent, with the promotion of Australian studies and the production of many new reference titles, but it still exists. While an Australianized *Encyclopedia Britannica* may not be needed, more reference titles that consider the Australian environment and local applications are needed.

This section has identified a number of important Australian reference titles in use; for more detailed information on the range available, readers should refer to one or more of the titles mentioned above.

Encyclopedias and Dictionaries

While the Australasia supplement to *World Book Encyclopaedia* is useful for detailed miscellaneous information on Australia, the *Australian Encyclopaedia* is needed for detailed information. Now in its fifth edition, this is a comprehensive guide to Australian life, history, personalities and places. Several single-volume encyclopedias also exist which, while in no way replacing the multi-volume *Australian Encyclopaedia,* often provide more up-to-date information. These include the recently published *The Penguin Australian Encyclopaedia, The Concise Encyclopaedia of Australia, The Concise Encyclopaedia of Australia and New Zealand* and *The Concise Australian Reference Book.*

The unique features of Australian English have meant that titles on Australian word usage have been available for some time. *Morris's Dictionary of Australian Words, Names and Phrases* (first published as *Austral English* in 1898), Baker's *The Australian Language* and *Dictionary of Australian Slang* have recently been joined by the comprehensive *Australian National Dictionary*, a dictionary devoted to explaining the words making up Australian English and published by Oxford University Press. With rather less detail than the *Australian National Dictionary* but the same store of words is *Australian Words and Their Origins.*

General dictionaries such as those in the Oxford and Webster series have to date been relied upon to provide definitions, pronunciation and word meanings and usage; these were joined in the 1980s by the *Macquarie Dictionary*, said to be the first dictionary compiled for Australian use of the English language. For Aboriginal words, Reed's *Aboriginal Words of Australia* can be helpful, although the sheer number of Aboriginal languages means that the serious researcher must seek expert advice in this area.

Biographical Sources

The most current guide to living Australians which gives brief biographical information is the *Who's Who in Australia*, published every three years and containing short biographical information on Australians from all walks of life. *Debrett's Handbook of Australia* can also be referred to for similar information, as can the *Australian Encyclopaedia.*

For non-current biographical information, the *Australian Dictionary of Biography* is the essential title. Published by Melbourne University Press, the *ADB*, as it is commonly known, includes detailed biographical information and a list of further reading. In twelve volumes up to 1939, persons are included because of their importance to Australian development.

Almanacs and Handbooks

The closest Australia has to an almanac is *The Australian Almanac*; it covers a wide variety of sporting and miscellaneous information with a chronology of Australian and world events and a section on overseas countries. However, other titles also go some way to providing historical facts and figures and records. These include Jack Wilkinson's *The Fantastic Book of Australian Facts, The Macquarie Book of Events*, Barker's *When Was That?: Chronology of Australia from 1788* and Robin Brown's *Collins Milestones in Australian History.* Robertson's *The Guinness Book of Australian Firsts* and *The Guinness Book of Records* with its Australian supplement provide useful information on Australian records.

Yearbooks

Perhaps collectively, the yearbooks produced by the Australian Bureau of Statistics are the most important sources for information on Australia and each of its states and territories. Produced more or less on an annual basis, these titles are among the most valuable published by the Australian Government Publishing Service. At first glance these yearbooks appear a rather dry collection of statistics, but closer inspection reveals data on climate, education, social welfare and many other areas.

Through the Australian Bureau of Statistics (ABS), state oriented yearbooks are produced by each state office of the ABS and a national yearbook by the central ABS office in Canberra; pocket yearbooks are also produced with a summary of the statistics and information appearing in the yearbooks. The national yearbook has been produced since 1901 and is called *Year Book Australia,* while there also exist the *Victorian Year Book, Western Australian Year Book, Tasmanian Year Book, South Australian Year Book, New South Wales Year Book* and *Queensland Year Book.* A yearbook is not produced in the Northern Territory or the Australian Capital Territory, however the *Northern Territory Statistical Summary* and *Australian Capital Territory Statistical Summary* fulfil the role of a yearbook to some extent.

Less statistical in orientation and perhaps more popular is the annual *Australia Handbook,* by the Australian Information Service and published by the Australian Government Publishing Service. Two commercially produced yearbook-type publications are the *Concise Australian Reference Book* and the *Pacific Islands Year Book.*

A number of publications include the word 'yearbook' in their title, especially those dealing with a particular industry or learned society, religious body or association. Many of these can be traced by using Reid's *Directory of Australian Directories* or by checking the *Directory of Australian Associations* for addresses.

Geographical Sources

The bases for compilation of atlases, maps, gazetteers and to a lesser extent travel guides are the maps and information generated by the various government mapping authorities; the main producer on an Australia-wide basis is the Commonwealth government agency, Australian Surveying and Land Information Group (AUSLIG).

Atlases. The standard atlas for Australia is the *Reader's Digest Atlas of Australia*; for the states some government produced atlases exist, although they are of less importance than the commercially produced *Reader's Digest Atlas of Australia.* The state oriented atlases tend to emphasize more than geographic mapping, with additional information on population density, earthquake location, boundary changes and so on. The state atlases are *Atlas of Victoria, Atlas of Tasmania, Atlas of Northern Australia, Atlas of South Australia, Atlas of New South Wales* and *Western Australia: An Atlas of Human Endeavour 1829-1979.*

Gazetteers. When one discusses gazetteers in Australia, those produced by government mapping agencies need to be separated from those commercially produced titles. The reason is that government produced titles do little more than provide the name of a place or feature and its latitude and longitude. While comprehensive in their listing, e.g. *Master Names File* produced by AUSLIG, commercially produced gazetteers are fairly selective in places and features included but more detailed in the information provided. Titles include *The Penguin Macquarie Dictionary of People and Places,* the Kennedy's *Australian Place Names* and Wilson's *A-Z of Australian Towns and Cities.* There is also a series of commercial directories covering Australia that provides quite detailed information on many large and small towns, in addition to general commercial information listing companies and their addresses. These directories are called *Universal Business Directories* and are produced on a regional basis.

Travel Guides and Road Maps. Providing information on towns and cities in addition to tourist information are various of commercially produced travel guides/atlases. A major producer of such guides is Universal Press, the producers and publishers of the *Universal Business Directories* discussed above; they produce *Gregory's* and *Robinson's* guides. Hence we have, for example, *Gregory's Australian Book of the Road*, *Gregory's Touring Australia*, *Robinson's Road Atlas of Australia*. Also in existence are *Explore Australia*, revised regularly, *Reader's Digest Motoring Guide to Australia* and *Touring Atlas of Australia.*

Indexing, Abstracting Services and Databases

Government in Australia is a major supporter of the production of indexing, abstracting services and databases. While many titles are produced by government departments at a Commonwealth and state level, others are produced by semi-government authorities and by institutions that receive government funding. Additionally, the business community, through press agencies mainly, professional associations and non-profit organizations are other producers.

While many titles are available in print and online formats,[4] others are only available in one or the other format. Increasingly, titles are also becoming available on CD-ROM, a recent example being AUSTROM – Australian Social Science and Education Information on CD/ROM; this is produced by INFORMIT in Melbourne. The following databases are available on this CD-ROM: *CINCH (Australian Criminology Database), APAIS (Australian Public Affairs Information Service), AEI (Australian Education Index), ARCH (Australian Architecture Database), ASCIS (Curriculum Resources Abstracts), AUSPORT (Australian Sport Database), EDLINE, FAMILY (Australian Family and Society Abstracts), IRAB (Index to Reviews of Australian Books), LEISURE* which covers tourism and leisure, *WESTDOC*, which contains regional and multidisciplinary bibliographic information relating to the Western Region of Melbourne, *Pinpointer* (covering leisure and consumer areas) and *Home Economics Index.*

The fact that several of Australia's major databases, most of which are also available in print or microfiche formats, can fit into one CD-ROM disk is both a statement on the size of Australian services and an indication that in the social sciences and education researchers have at their fingertips essential titles. This is not to suggest that few other important services exist. *Guidelines* provides for current and popular information over a range of subject areas, and *AUSTLIT: Australian Literary Database* is a valuable source for information on Australian literature.

Indexing/abstracting services and databases covering science and technology in Australia tend to concentrate on specific subjects and to be produced by government departments or organizations; there is no general indexing covering science and technology. *ABOA: Australian Bibliography of Agriculture, AESIS: Australian Earth Sciences Information System* and those produced by the Commonwealth Scientific and Industrial Research Organization (CSIRO), especially its own index of its publications, *CSIRO Index*, are important. The CSIRO's online system, AUSTRALIS, also has available many science and technology oriented databases.

Other services worthy of mention are the *Australasian Medical Index (AMI)*, comprising Australian and New Zealand journal literature not covered by MEDLINE, and the *Australian Business Index*, an up-to-date guide to the current situation, changes and problems affecting business in Australia.

The public availability of online newspaper indexes in the latter half of the 1980s added significantly to access to the contents of newspapers. Among the dailies now available are *The Australian Financial Review, Sydney Morning Herald* on the AUSINET system, the *Courier Mail* (Brisbane) on the QNIS system, *The Adelaide Advertiser* and *The Mercury* (Hobart) on the Press Com system.

Conclusion

While reference publishing in Australia is certainly alive and well, its immediate future is not bright. Falling demand for titles, caused by declining acquisitions budgets coupled with rising book prices, already high by comparison with overseas, sees publishers attempting to cut costs and be more circumspect about publishing titles. The rising emphasis upon marketing also favours the bigger players who are more able to compete aggressively. Small press publishing, although not a large player in the reference publishing area, is nevertheless under threat. The introduction of online and CD-ROM reference databases has seen new players enter the area, and they are claiming their market share. Further rationalization of reference publishing can be expected to occur with the reduction in funding for semi-government enterprises and the decline in profits for commercial enterprises. Production on a cost recovery basis in the non-commercial and semi-government areas will not be easily achieved in the immediate future. Growth sectors, notably in law and business, may, however, continue to expand as online connection to information becomes more commonplace and the only means of access.

Notes

1 Some states also produce their own guides to locally produced government and often other publications; a good example is *Legal Deposit Publications in Western Australia,* which lists any book that 'is first sold, published or offered for sale within Western Australia.... The Act defines a book as meaning and including '...every volume, part or division of a volume, newspaper, pamphlet, sheet of letterpress, sheet of music, map, chart, or plan, separately published.' Titles for other states which tend to concentrate on government publications are *Publications Available from the State Information Centre* [SA], *Queensland Government Publications, Catalogue of Publications* [NT], *New South Wales Official Publications Received in the State Library of New South Wales* and *Victorian Government Publications.* Tasmania does not produce a guide to its state government publications, although publications received under legal deposit in the State Library of Tasmania are entered onto ABN. An accessions list of material received in the Mortlock Library of South Australiana called *Mortlock Miscellany* is also produced. State government printing offices, which are responsible for much of the publishing output of state governments, produce lists of their publications from time to time. For local government publications there is now a guide in *AGP,* but the task of even tracing what is produced is enormous, given the nature of local government.

2 Access to ABS data can also be obtained via Telecom's Discovery (formerly Viatel) service and via *AUSSTATS*, the online Australian Bureau of Statistics database; Discovery has a selection of major economic and social statistics updated daily, while *AUSSTATS* is more for the statistics specialist and analyst, allowing statistical analysis of the wide range of data included. An especially important statistics collection is *CData 86 - Population Census on Compact Disk,* containing the 1981 and 1986 population census summary information. Special software known as Supermap enables one to retrieve, manipulate and map the Census data.

3 Other guides that have proved invaluable to researchers in Australia include Mayer, Bettison and Keene's *A Research Guide to Australian Politics and Cognate Subjects (ARGAP)*, Mayer and Kirby's *A Second Research Guide to Australian Politics and*

Cognate Subjects (ARGAP 2). In the area of law the useful *Legal Research Materials and Methods* by Campbell *et al.* stands out. In the literature area there are many useful guides, notably Lock and Lawson's *Australian Literature: A Reference Guide*, Day's *Modern Australian Prose 1901-1975: A Guide to Information Sources*, Andrews and Wilde's *Australian Literature to 1900: A Guide to Information Sources* and Jaffa's *Modern Australian Poetry 1920-1970: A Guide to Information Sources*.

4 A good example are the services available on OZLINE, an online retrieval service offered by the National Library of Australia. It is possible to access online *APAIS*, *Australian Government Publications* until December 1987, *Australian National Bibliography*, *MAIS*: *Multicultural Australia Information System*, *CINCH: The Australian Criminology Database*, *FAMILY* (print version: *Australian Family and Society Abstracts*), *AUSPORT* (print version: *Australian Sport Index*), *AHRR*: *Australian Historic Records Register* (also available in microfiche). All with the exception of *MAIS* are available in print and/or microfiche.

References

ABOA: Australian Bibliography of Agriculture. Available online on AUSTRALIS, 1975- .

Adelaide Advertiser. Available online on the Press Com system.

AEI (Australian Education Index). See *Australian Education Index*.

AESIS: Australian Earth Sciences Information System. Available online on INFO-ONE International, 1976- . Also available printed as *AESIS Quarterly*, q.v.

AESIS Quarterly: Australian Earth Sciences Information System. Glenside, SA: Australian Mineral Foundation, 1976- ; quarterly.

AHRR: Australian Historic Records Register. Available on OZLINE as discussed in Note 4, and also on microfiche from the National Library of Australia.

Andrews, Barry G. and Wilde, W.H. *Australian Literature to 1900: A Guide to Information Sources*. Detroit, Mich.: Gale Research, 1980.

Annual Catalogue of Australian Publications. Nos 1-25, 1936-1960. Canberra: National Library, 1937-1960.

APAIS: Australian Public Affairs Information Service. A Subject Index to Current Literature. Canberra: National Library of Australia, 1972- ; monthly. Available online on OZLINE and on the AUSTROM disk.

ARCH: Australian Architecture Database. Available online on AUSINET, 1980- . Available in microfiche as *AAPI: Australian Architectural Periodicals Index*.

ASCIS: Australian Schools Cataloguing Information Service, a bibliographic utility and an information service for schools, offered by Curriculum Corporation. Available on AUSINET, 1970- , and partially on AUSTROM as ASCIS (Curriculum Resources Abstracts).

Atlas of New South Wales. Bathurst, NSW: Central Mapping Authority of New South Wales, 1987.

Atlas of Northern Australia. Darwin: Professional Services Branch, Northern Territory Department of Education, 1982.

Atlas of South Australia, ed. by Trevor Griffin and Murray McCaskill. Adelaide: Government Printing Division in Association with Wakefield Press on behalf of the SA Jubilee 150 Board, 1986.

Atlas of Tasmania, ed by J.L. Davies. Hobart: Lands and Surveys Department, 1965.

Atlas of Victoria, ed. by J.S. Duncan. Melbourne: Victorian Government Printing Office on behalf of the Government of Victoria, 1982.

AUSPORT. Available on AUSTROM database and in print as *Australian Sport Index*, q.v. and online on OZLINE as *AUSPORT*.

AUSSTATS. Available online through the Australian Bureau of Statistics.

AUSTLIT: *Australian Literary Database*. Available online direct from producer, Australian Defence Force Academy Library, Canberra, ACT, 1988- .

Australasian Medical Index (AMI). Available online on the Australian MEDLINE Network, 1980- .

Australia Handbook. Australian Information Service. Canberra: Australian Government Publishing Service, 1961- ; annual.

Australian Almanac 1989. North Ryde, NSW: Angus and Robertson, 1988.

Australian Book Review. Melbourne: National Book Council, 1962-1978; New Series, 1978- ; 10 issues per year.

Australian Books: A Select List of Recent Publications and Standard Works in Print. Canberra: National Library of Australia, 1950- ; annual. Supersedes *Select List of Representative Works Dealing with Australia 1933-1948*.

Australian Books in Print. Melbourne: D.W. Thorpe, 1981- ; annual. Also available online on AUSINET.

Australian Bookseller and Publisher. Melbourne: D.W. Thorpe, 1976/77?- ; monthly (December-January issues are combined).

Australian Business Index. Milsons Point, NSW: Australian Business Index, 1981- ; monthly. Available in print 1981- ; available on microfiche 1984- ; available online on AUSINET as *Australian Business Index (ABIX)*, 1981- .

Australian Capital Territory Statistical Summary. Belconnen, ACT: Australian Bureau of Statistics, 1963- ; annual.

Australian Catalogue of New Films and Videos. Albert Park, Vic.: Australian Catalogue Publishing, 1989-1990- ; annual.

Australian Dictionary of Biography. Gen. eds: Douglas Pike, Bede Nairn and Geoffrey Serle. Vols 1-12. Carlton, Vic.: Melbourne University Press, 1966-1990.

Australian Education Index. Hawthorn, Vic.: Australian Council for Educational Research, 1958- ; quarterly. Available online on AUSINET and on the AUSTROM disk as *AEI (Australian Education Index)*.

Australian Encyclopaedia. 5th ed. 9 vols. Terrey Hills, NSW: Australian Geographic, 1988.

Australian Family and Society Abstracts. Melbourne: Institute of Family Studies, 1988- ; annual. Continues *Family* 1984-1988. Available online on AUSTRALIS, OZLINE and LINK as *Family* covering 1980- ; also on AUSTROM disk.

Australian Financial Review. Available online on the AUSINET system.

Australian Government Publications. Canberra: National Library of Australia, 1962- ; quarterly with annual cumulations. Also issued monthly 1952-1960 and cumulated in the Commonwealth National Library's *Annual Catalogue of Australian Publications*. Available on OZLINE until 1987.

Australian Leisure Index (ALI). Footscray, Vic.: Australian Clearing House for Publications in Recreation, Sport and Tourism, 1982-1988 ; annual. Available online on AUSTRALIS as *Leisure (LEIS)*, 1982- . From 1989 only as *Australian Tourism Index*, q.v.

Australian Libraries: The Essential Directory. Blackwood, SA: Auslib Press, 1988. (Second edition due late 1990.)

Australian Library Journal. Sydney: Library Association of Australia, 1951- .

Australian Library Review. Wagga Wagga, NSW: Centre for Information Studies, Charles Sturt University-Riverina, 1984- . Title change with Volume 7, 1, 1990 from *Riverina Library Review*.

Australian Maps. Canberra: National Library of Australia, 1964- ; annual.

Australian National Bibliography. Canberra: National Library of Australia, 1961- ; monthly with annual and three-monthly (microfiche) cumulations. Also available online on OZLINE.

Australian National Bibliography 1901-1950. 4 vols. Canberra: National Library of Australia, 1988.

Australian National Dictionary, ed. by W.S. Ramson *et al*. Melbourne: Oxford University Press, 1988.

Australian Periodicals in Print. Melbourne: D.W. Thorpe, 1987- ; annual.

Australian Sport Index. Canberra: National Sport Information Centre, 1989- ; annual. Also on disk and online as *AUSPORT*, q.v.

Australian Tourism Index. Footscray (Vic.): Victoria University of Technology, 1989- . Annual. Formerly produced by Footscray Institute of Technology, now part of Victoria University of Technology.

Australian Words and Their Origins, ed. by Joan Hughes. Melbourne: Oxford University Press, 1989.

Australians: A Guide to Sources. See *Australians: A Historical Library*.

Australians: A Historical Atlas. See *Australians: A Historical Library*

Australians: A Historical Dictionary. See *Australians: A Historical Library*.

Australians: A Historical Library. 11 vols: Vol. 1 Australians to 1788; Vol. 2 Australians 1838; Vol. 3 Australians 1888; Vol. 4 Australians 1938; Vol. 5 Australians from 1939; Vol. 6 Australians: Historical Statistics; Vol. 7 Australians: A Guide to Sources; Vol. 8 Australians: A Historical Dictionary; Vol. 9 Australians: Events and Places; Vol. 10 Australians: A Historical Atlas; Vol. 11 Australians: The Guide and Index. Broadway, NSW: Fairfax, Syme and Weldon, 1987.

Baker, Sidney J. *The Australian Language: An Examination of the English Language and Speech as Used in Australia from Convict Days to the Present, with Special Reference to the Growth of Indigenous Idiom and Its Use by Australian Writers*. Rev. ed. Melbourne: Sun Books, 1981.

Baker, Sidney J. *A Dictionary of Australian Slang*. South Yarra, Vic.: Lloyd O'Neil, 1986 (c.1982).

Barker, Anthony. *When Was That?: Chronology of Australia from 1788*. Sydney: John Ferguson, 1988.

Books Published in Australia, 1946-1960. National Library of Australia. Canberra: National Library of Australia, 1946-1961.

Borchardt, Dietrich Hans. *Australian Bibliography: A Guide to Printed Sources of Information*. 3rd ed. Rushcutters Bay, NSW: Pergamon Press, 1976.

Brady, Barbara. *Guide to Australian Reference Books: Social Sciences*. Sydney: ALIA, 1991.

Brown, Robin. *Collins Milestones in Australian History: 1788 to the Present*. Sydney: Collins, 1986.

Campbell, Enid, *et al*. *Legal Research Materials and Methods*. 3rd ed. Sydney: Law Book Company, 1988.

Catalogue of Publications. Darwin: Northern Territory Government Information Centre, [1983]- .

Catalogue of Publications and Products. Canberra: Australian Bureau of Statistics, 1989- ; annual.

CData 86: Australian Bureau of Statistics 1981, 1986. Population Censuses Summary Data [CD-ROM]. Hawthorn East, Vic.: Space-Time Research, 1988.

Choate, Roy. *A Guide to Sources of Information on the Arts in Australia.* Sydney: Pergamon, 1983.

CINCH: The Australian Criminology Database. Available online on OZLINE, 1928 (selectively)- . Available on AUSTROM.

Concise Australian Reference Book. Sydney: Fairfax Library in association with Daniel O'Keefe Publishing, 1989.

Concise Encyclopaedia of Australia. 2nd ed. Sydney: Collins, 1988.

Concise Encyclopaedia of Australia and New Zealand. Rev. ed. Sydney: Crowell International, 1987.

Cook, John; Lane, Nancy; and Piggott, Michael. *A Guide to Commonwealth Government Information Sources.* Sydney: Pergamon Press, 1988.

Courier Mail. Available online on the QNIS system.

CSIRO Films. Available online on AUSTRALIS, 1946- .

CSIRO Index. East Melbourne: CSIRO Central Information, Library and Editorial Section, 1975- ; annual. Paper 1975-1978 (Vols 1-4), microfiche 1979-1987 (Vol. 5, 1979-Vol. 13, 1987). Available online on AUSTRALIS, 1969- .

Day, A. Grove. *Modern Australian Prose 1901-1975: A Guide to Information Sources.* Detroit, Mich.: Gale Research, 1980.

Debrett's Handbook of Australia. 3rd ed. Sydney: Debrett's Peerage (Australasia) and Collins, 1987.

Directory of Australian Academic and Research Libraries. Blackwood, SA: Auslib Press, 1989.

Directory of Australian Associations. Melbourne: Information Australia, 1987; looseleaf updates.

Directory of Australian and New Zealand Databases. 3rd ed. Ed. by Sherrey Quinn. Hawthorn, Vic.: Australian Database Development Association, 1988. Available online on AUSINET.

Directory of Australian Public Libraries. 2nd. ed. Ed. by Alan L. Bundy and Judith Bundy. Adelaide: Auslib Press, 1987. (3rd ed. due late 1990)

Directory of Special Libraries in Australia. 7th ed. Sydney: Australian Library and Information Association, 1988.

EDLINE. Available online on AUSINET, 1980- and on AUSTROM disk.

Explore Australia: The Complete Touring Companion. 9th ed. Ringwood, Vic.: Viking O'Neil Australia, 1990.

FAMILY Database. Available online on AUSTRALIS, OZLINE and LINK, covering 1980- ; on the AUSTROM disk, and annually in print form as *Australian Family and Society Abstracts*, q.v.

Ferguson, John Alexander. *Bibliography of Australia.* 7 vols. Sydney: Angus and Robertson, 1941-1965.

Ferguson, John Alexander. *Bibliography of Australia: Addenda 1784-1850.* 4 vols. Canberra: National Library of Australia, 1986.

Gregory's Australian Book of the Road. Macquarie Park, NSW: Gregory's, 1988.

Gregory's Touring Australia. 2nd ed. Macquarie Park, NSW: Gregory's, 1987.

Guide to New Australian Books. Port Melbourne: D.W. Thorpe in association with National Centre for Australian Studies, August 1990- ; bimonthly.

Guidelines: A Subject Guide for Australian Libraries. Mt Waverley, Vic.: Bibliographic Services, 1969- ; nine per annum.

Guinness Book of Records. Enfield, Middlesex: Guinness Book of Records, 1955- ; annual. Includes an Australian supplement.

Hagger, A.J.A. *A Guide to Australian Economic and Social Statistics.* Sydney: Pergamon Press, 1983.

Home Economics Index. Available in print (Armadale, Vic.: Victoria College, Rusden, Armadale, Campus Library, 1980- ; annual) and on AUSTROM.

InCite: Newsletter of the Australian Library and Information Association. Sydney: Australian Library and Information Association, 1980- ; fortnightly.

IRAB (Index to Reviews of Australian Books). Available as a trial database on AUSTROM.

Jaffa, Herbert C. *Modern Australian Poetry, 1920-1970: A Guide to Information Sources.* Detroit, Mich.: Gale Research, 1979.

Jones, Gregory P. *A Guide to Sources of Information on Australian Industrial Relations.* Sydney: Pergamon Press, 1988.

Kennedy, Brian and Kennedy, Barbara. *Australian Place Names.* Rydalmere, NSW: Hodder and Stoughton, 1989.

Legal Deposit Publications in Western Australia. Perth: State Library Service of Western Australia, 1985- ; quarterly.

Leisure. Database available on AUSTRALIS as *Leisure (LEIS)* and annually in print form until 1988 as *Australian Leisure Index,* q.v. From 1989 known as *Australian Tourism Index*, q.v. and covering only tourism and related areas.

Lock, Fred, and Lawson, Alan. *Australian Literature: A Reference Guide.* 2nd ed. Melbourne: Oxford University Press, 1980.

Macquarie Book of Events, ed. by Bryce Fraser. Sydney: Macquarie Library, 1983.

Macquarie Dictionary. 2nd rev. ed. Chatswood, NSW: Macquarie Library, 1987.

MAIS: Multicultural Australia Information System. Available online on OZLINE, 1988- .

Master Names File. Canberra: AUSLIG (Australian Surveying and Land Group), annual. Microfiche from computer database.

Mayer, Henry and Kirby, Liz. *A Second Research Guide to Australian Politics and Cognate Subjects (ARGAP 2)*. Melbourne: Longman Cheshire, 1984.

Mayer, Henry; Bettison, Margaret; and Keene, Judy. *A Research Guide to Australian Politics and Cognate Subjects (ARGAP)*. Melbourne: Cheshire, 1976.

Mercury. Available online on the Press Com system.

Mills, J.J. and Richardson, Joanna. *Information Resources and Services in Australia*. 2nd ed. Wagga Wagga, NSW: Centre for Information Studies, 1992.

Morris, Edward E. *Morris's Dictionary of Australian Words, Names and Phrases*. Melbourne: Currey O'Neil, 1982. First published in 1898 as *Austral English*.

Mortlock Miscellany: select list of acquisitions. Adelaide: Mortlock Library of South Australiana, 1988 -.

New Commonwealth Government Books from AGPS. Canberra: Australian Government Publishing Service, 1987- ; bimonthly.

New South Wales Official Publications Received in the State Library of New South Wales. Sydney: State Library of New South Wales, 1975- ; monthly. Continues *New South Wales Official Publications*.

New South Wales Year Book. Australian Bureau of Statistics. Canberra: Australian Government Publishing Service, 1904-1905- ; annual.

Newspapers in Australian Libraries: A Union List. 4th ed. 2 vols. Canberra: National Library of Australia, 1984-1985. Part 1 Overseas newspapers; Part 2 Australian newspapers.

Northern Territory Statistical Summary. Australian Bureau of Statistics. Canberra: Australian Government Publishing Service, 1960- ; annual.

NUC:D (National Union Catalogue of Library Materials for People with Disabilities). Canberra: National Library of Australia, March 1989- ; quarterly, microfiche.

NUC:N (National Union Catalogue: Non-Book Materials). Canberra: National Library of Australia, 1988; microfiche, trial edition.

NUCOS (National Union Catalogue of Serials). Canberra: National Library of Australia, March 1984- ; microfiche. Also available on ABN.

Pacific Islands Year Book. Sydney: Pacific Publications, 1972- ; annual. Continues *Pacific Islands Year Book and Who's Who.*

Penguin Australian Encyclopaedia. Ringwood (Vic.): Penguin, 1990.

Penguin Macquarie Dictionary of People and Places: A Handy Guide to Who and Where. Ringwood, Vic.: Penguin Books Australia, 1986.

Pinpointer: Australian Index to Leisure; Activities and Consumer Reports. Adelaide: Libraries Board of South Australia, 1963- ; bimonthly. On microfiche since 1988 and on AUSTROM. Subtitle changes.

Publications Available from the State Information Centre [SA]. Adelaide: State Information Centre, 1988- ; quarterly.

Publishers Weekly. New York: R.R. Bowker, 1872-

Queensland Government Publications. Brisbane: Library Board of Queensland, 1977- .

Queensland Year Book. Australian Bureau of Statistics. Canberra: Australian Government Publishing Service, 1937- ; annual.

Radford, W. *Guide to Australian Reference Books: Humanities.* Ultimo, NSW: Library Association of Australia, 1983.

Reader's Digest Atlas of Australia. Surry Hills, NSW: Reader's Digest, 1977.

Reader's Digest Motoring Guide to Australia. 2nd ed. Sydney: Reader's Digest, 1988.

Recipe Book of Online Searching. 10th ed. Ed. by Sherrey Quinn. Doncaster, Vic.: Online Information Resources Pty Ltd, 1989/90; looseleaf updates.

Reed, A.W. *Aboriginal Words of Australia.* Frenchs Forest, NSW: Reed, 1969.

Reid, Ralph S. *Directory of Australian Directories.* Sydney: Library Association of Australia, 1987.

Robertson, Patrick. *Guinness Book of Australian Firsts.* Sydney: Collins Australia, 1987.

Robinson's Road Atlas of Australia. Macquarie Park, NSW: Universal Press, 1989.

Sheehan, Joy. *A Guide to Sources of Information on Australian Business.* Sydney: Pergamon Press, 1983.

South Australian Year Book. Australian Bureau of Statistics. Canberra: Australian Government Publishing Service, 1966- ; annual.

Subject Guide to Australian Books in Print. Melbourne: D.W. Thorpe, 1988- ; annual. Formerly *Australian Books in Print by Subject.*

Sydney Morning Herald. Available online on AUSINET, 1989- .

Tasmanian Year Book. Australian Bureau of Statistics. Canberra: Australian Government Publishing Service, 1967- ; annual.

Touring Atlas of Australia. 3rd ed. Ringwood, Vic.: Penguin Books Australia, 1989.

Union List of Higher Degree Theses in Australian Libraries: Cumulative Edition to 1965. Hobart: University of Tasmania Library, 1967; updated by annual supplements, title varies.

Universal Business Directories. *Business Directory of....* Place of publication varies; available for major cities and large centres of Australia; updated regularly.

Victorian Government Publications. Melbourne: Library Council of Victoria, 1976-.

Victorian Year Book. Australian Bureau of Statistics. Canberra: Australian Government Publishing Service, 1873- ; annual.

WESTDOC. Available on AUSTROM.

Western Australia: An Atlas of Human Endeavour 1829-1979. 2nd ed. Perth: Lands and Survey Department, 1986.

Western Australian Year Book. Australian Bureau of Statistics. Canberra: Australian Government Publishing Service, 1957- ; annual.

Who's Who in Australia. 26th ed. Melbourne: Herald and Weekly Times, 1988.

Wilkinson, Jack. *The Fantastic Book of Australian Facts*. South Yarra, Vic.: Currey O'Neil, 1983.

Wilson, Robert. *A-Z of Australian Towns and Cities*. Sydney: Weldon, 1989.

Year Book Australia. Belconnen, ACT: Australian Bureau of Statistics, 1901-1907- ; annual.

7 Happy but Not Rich! Self-Publishing Australiana

Wendy Lowenstein

A range of Australiana has been self-published in recent years. By means of seven case studies this paper illustrates the variety, the successes, the problems, the financial rewards and the satisfactions and frustrations of self-publishing in this field.

Many famous writers have published their own books, including Charlotte Brontë, James Joyce, Alfred Lord Tennyson, Robbie Burns and Upton Sinclair. Some earlier self-published Australian classics are still profitably in print. During the late nineteenth century Melbourne bookseller Edward Cole self-published a number of popular books. Of these, *Cole's Funny Picture Book* and *Cole's Fun Doctor* were most successful, with sales running into hundreds of thousands. During the 1930s depression Frank Dalby Davison self-published another classic, *Man Shy*, the story of a herd of wild cattle displaced by settlement. Davison had some copies bound in wallpaper and peddled it from door to door himself. In 1950 Frank Hardy's famous novel of the Melbourne underworld, *Power without Glory*, was self-published, with strong support from the left-wing movement, which also promoted it strongly. An under-the-counter item at first, it became a record-breaking seller after its author was tried and acquitted on a charge of criminal libel. It later became a successful TV mini-series. The Cole family kept Edward Cole's books profitably in print for many years, while Dalby Davison and Hardy both turned to commercial publication when available, but many writers continue to prefer to publish their own work.

A broad range of Australiana has attracted and often been profitable to self-publishers during the last forty years. At least one long-established self-publisher in our sample (see Appendix) earns a good living at it, and others admit to significant profits. Most likely to self-publish successfully are those whose self-publishing dovetails with a hobby or business. There is room in the self-publishing field for those who have only one book to write, those who want to make a living on their own terms, those pleased to make moderate profits, as well as those content to have their work published and recover their money, and, of course, for those professional writers who perceive a neglected market and set out to research, write and publish for it. There is room too for those who can afford to make a tax loss.

Self-publishers actively publishing Australiana today embrace a whole range of experience, interests, output and technical competence. While some use professional typesetters, designers and book printers, others have their own printing press and/or do their own typesetting, design, layout and all, and even have their own binding facilities. If a 'proper' book is not demanded, low-tech alternatives are employed.

Some self-publishers produce only one book – memoirs, family history, local history, or something that filled a market niche and, like Maureen Wright's *Murray River Charts*, continues in demand. The tendency of the established author-publisher is to move between the worlds of commercial and self-publication, to publish larger, long-run books through the trade, and publish others themselves, perhaps short-run or out-of-the-way titles, alone or even under the umbrella of a club, society or interest group. Publishing by professional and other non-trade bodies is increasing, and may allow for a joint-venture publishing agreement which allows an author a much more flexible and participatory role than do mainstream publishers.

The most successful self-published publications are often taken up by a commercial publisher, the trade being much more ready to take over a proven success than risk capital in a new idea. Self-publishers like Bill Hornadge are also often ready to unload these earlier successes because most are writers and only incidentally publishers, and find that keeping several titles in print, and distributing them too, consumes capital and writing time. Projects highly successful in the hands of their authors, however, often flop with a publishing house which fails to understand the market. Also, books abandoned by commercial publishing houses often then prove extremely successful and profitable to their authors, especially if they can acquire artwork or film.

Self-Publishing Has Kept Me Happy If Not Rich

Probably the most important, and certainly the most prolific, versatile and consistent self-publisher of Australiana today is artist Ron Edwards of Kuranda, North Queensland. 'Commercial publishing gives you money without worry, but self-publishing allows you to speak to people out there without any pedantic bastard trying to get in the way. Whether or not what you say is important, you have the freedom to say it!'

Then 20 years old, Edwards published his first work in 1950. After art school he acquired a screw-type hand press, moved to a galley press, then a big hand press and an Arab platen. He has since published more than 100 titles. Many are handsomely illustrated collectors' items. All are unique. A North Queensland eccentric, and 'the norther they go the eccentricker they get', as a former Oxley librarian once said after trying to persuade him to conform with the library deposit laws, Ron Edwards is versatile, single-minded, enormously hardworking and a law unto himself. From the start he has earned a sufficient living for his family mainly by self-publishing, with forays into painting or commercial publishing. After art school he established his Galley Press in Melbourne, and his interest being fine printing and black and white illustration, produced limited editions of poetry embellished with wood or lino-cuts and designed for collectors. Type was handset. Moving to Ferntree Gully outside Melbourne, he established Rams Skull Press. In 1951 he discovered Australian folklore, which has become his passion, and with poet John Manifold published *Bandicoot Ballads*, a collection of fold song broadsheets. A series of limited edition folklore chap-books followed, with texts by Hugh Anderson, Russel Ward and John Manifold, and his own first *Overlander Songbook* (1956). This early work, part of the Australian folk revival and a flourishing period of literary nationalism, occupied and sustained Edwards and his family throughout the 1950s.

In 1960, after selling up presses and type, the Edwards family moved to Freshwater near Cairns, North Queensland, where Edwards built home and gallery, while working as a landscape painter, with his wife Anne running gallery and business side. Immersed in collecting the wealth of folk songs he found on the northern pastoral frontier, Edwards decided that making this material accessible was more important than printing beautiful books. In 1966 he started publishing his own collected material in *Northern Folk*, a small, unpretentious, black and white magazine. Produced under the aegis of the Cairns Folk Club, but in fact self-published, it was commercially printed. Music was hand-drawn, and pages decorated with fine pen and ink drawings. Torres Strait Islander and Aboriginal songs, previously not collected, were published for the first time. Rams Skull also published similar small collections of Australian folk songs and ballads designated as *The Overland Songbook* parts 2, 3, 4, 5 (paper-covered, 24 pages, 50 cents). At this time Edwards started using and re-using text, music, material, illustration and artwork for different markets, a practice which has allowed him to prosper as a thoroughly idiosyncratic self-publisher. 'I'm never bored by this. I love moving things around. One day it'll all make the pattern I'm seeking.'

Nothing has ever been wasted. Songs and ballads published in the small 1960s publications were collected, augmented and commercially published by Rigby as a larger *Overlander Songbook* (1971, 235 pages) and eventually as the *Big Book of Australian Folk Song* (1976, 507 pages). (He hopes to live long enough to publish a 2000-page book of folk songs.) Meantime he researched, wrote and illustrated Bushcrafts 1 and 2 (*Australian Traditional Bush Crafts* [1975] and *The Skills of the Australian Bushman* [1979]) for Rigby.

Edwards' illustration often romanticizes the pastoral industry; his writings, however, never shirk the realities, crudity, racism and sexism of the frontier. His *Australian Bawdy Ballads* (Folklore Occasional Paper, 1971) reeks of the hatred of pastoral workers for black women. Edwards believes that, humiliated by their sexual dependence on women whom they regard as belonging to an inferior race, the men of the frontier have taken their revenge in these crude stories, ballads and songs.

During the 1980s Edwards abandoned commercial publishing, regained the film and rights of some books and has since kept Bushcrafts 1 and 2 profitably in print. He has also written, illustrated and self-published *Bushcraft 3* (1987, 164 pages, 6000 copies). This one-man dynamo now uses a wordprocessor and desktop publishing program and has a small but well equipped printery, employs a keyboard operator, and produces his smaller publications in runs sometimes as low as ten copies.

Bush leathercraft, saddle-making and repairs, leatherworking techniques and horse gear all featured in the Bushcraft series. Edwards has since expanded this area into twelve booklets. Sold Australia-wide through a distributor, the booklets were highly successful. For example, *Stockman's Plaited Belts* (1982, 500 copies, $3.50) has been reprinted seven times and sold 20,000 copies. In 1984 these booklets were compiled, each becoming one chapter of *Bush Leatherwork* (1985, 260 pages), his easiest and most profitable book ever, having sold already 8000 copies. More booklets on saddlery and leatherwork followed and were compiled into *More Bush Leatherwork* (1989, $25.00).

Ron Edwards travels widely in the north, has built three family homes plus sundry studios, workshops and galleries, and become an authority on Australian bushcrafts and northern folklore and song. He has also spent much time in Japan and China, and produces illustrated booklets about his travels, and books on Chinese mud-brick building techniques.

His Occasional Folk Lore series now consists of seventeen papers by a variety of authors.

Nothing is hard about self-publishing, he says, although distribution is a problem, which he blames on isolation. But one wonders. Bill Hornadge finds similar isolation no handicap. 'Good promotion', Edwards asserts, 'is essential. I wish I did some! I should send out review copies but by then I'm working on the next book and never get around to it.' He mails his catalogue only on request. Not all his self-published books have been profitable – he decides on print runs by guesswork, sometimes guesses wrong, and publishes what interests him, commercial or not. His definitive *Australian Folk Song Index* (400 pages, $60.00) has sold only a handful, and has lost $18,000.

Edwards' advice to self-publishers is: 'Forget the money! A bushman I knew wanted to publish his autobiography. But he wouldn't do it unless he was sure of getting his money back. Then he went on a holiday to Hong Kong. I said, "But did you get your money back?" "Of course not", he said, if you don't expect to get your money back for a holiday, why expect to get it back for publishing your own writing which will give you much greater pleasure?'

Don't Hold Your Breath Waiting for the First Million to Roll In

While some writers like Edwards find room on the frontiers of the self-publishing world, blithely following their own star, others look for market niches ignored by the big publishers, writing and publishing for small markets which, however, often prove substantial.

Bill Hornadge has done a bit of both in his career. Formerly a sub-editor on a Sydney daily, he is one of Australia's more commercially successful self-publishers. Now a professional bookseller, writer and publisher living in Dubbo, central New South Wales, he has self-published since the mid-1940s, specializing in books about stamp collecting as well as general books with an off-beat Australian historical bias and his own vein of popular humour. One of the latter, *The Yellow Peril,* a look at Australian attitudes to Chinese, to the author's surprise became a school textbook for multicultural studies.

Some of Hornadge's books were written to fill a perceived market niche, and these generally sold well; others which were written for fun, he says, generally bombed. *Ern Malley and the Angry Penguin Hoax*, his first self-published book, could not be sold for ninepence a copy in 1945 and almost the whole edition was destroyed. Hornadge believes it was ill-timed, the public being sated with stories about the famous literary hoax. Twenty years later he was mortified to see it listed in antiquarian booksellers' catalogues for $30-$40. The Hornadge *Down Under Calendars* ran for seven years. Starting as an in-house project with a lot of stamp jokes produced for stamp collectors, they appealed to the general market and ran for another six years, with annual sales reaching 20,000 before the author ran out of steam. In the hands of a commercial publisher the series bombed and was dropped.

The Ugly Australian contained 1000 or so anti-Australian quotes. No publisher was interested so the author published 5000 copies. With enthusiastic reviews and radio coverage, it sold out very quickly. Taken up by a commercial house, it sold another 40,000 copies, mostly through newsagents, railway bookstalls and airport terminals before the publisher folded. *How to Publish Your Own Book*, first published in 1983, was written to fill a perceived niche in the market. The first two editions of 2000 each sold out quickly, and the third updated edition of 7000 was published, about 700 copies of these being sold to Doubleday's book club. It still sells steadily.

Stamp books were published because Hornadge owned Seven Seas Stamps, and published *Stamp News*. The core of these publications were 1960s stamp catalogues. Basically lists of stamps and prices, these were unusual in carrying historical information and extensive background notes. His *Australasian Stamp Catalogue* is still published annually by Readers Digest. Print runs have been as high as 80,000. Printed continuously for thirty years, it probably has sold about a million, although Hornadge is not now connected with it. *Stamp Investment Guidelines*, a sixty-four-page booklet, which has sold 40,000 copies, has returned Hornadge more profit than any other writing. 'It is successful because it taps into one of the basic human weaknesses, greed.' *Stamps – a Collector's Guide* started as a giveaway in the 1960s. It was then commissioned as a paperback by SunBooks. The author's suggestions for the cover were ignored, it flopped and 7000 copies were remaindered. Hornadge bought these and self-distributed through the stamp trade without discounting. A revised self-published edition with new cover sold another 5000. A new edition for a commercial press, with colour illustrations and different title, is still in print. 'The market was there, if SunBooks had known how to go about it.'

Since the 1940s Hornadge has published about eighteen of his own books. He says he has made a fair bit of money out of *some* but lost a lot on others, and except for an odd year could never have existed on this income alone. 'It's been more of a hobby than anything else.' His background in journalism helps in self-publishing, especially knowing how to design and prepare a book, and to write press releases and advertisements. On finishing a non-commissioned book, he usually tries to get it commercially published, thus saving distribution hassles. If no publisher is interested, he looks very carefully at the potential market before deciding to self-publish.

Distribution and promotion are the most difficult areas and are different for every book. Some books will sell entirely by mail and others not at all, others by a mixture of mail and wholesale. Pre-selling on subscription or as a premium offer works for one title but not another. Aiming at an Australia-wide distribution, Hornadge finds launches pointless but book reviews important. Radio is very valuable, especially round-Australia 'phone hook-ups.

Hornadge's advice is: 'It's tremendously satisfying to see your name in print, so if you have what you think is a worthwhile manuscript and can't get it professionally published, give it a go, but be realistic enough to understand it might cost you a packet. Decide a retail price after you get all your quotes in, and do your sums properly before signing the printing contract. If you want to make money though, you must be able to sell it at a four or even five times markup.'

A Very Workable Formula Indeed!

While Ron Edwards' black and white art mostly complements his publishing, Melbourne painter Dacre Smyth self-publishes books with full colour reproductions which complement his painting. Since retiring from the Navy in 1978, he has successfully self-published seven books of paintings, prose and poetry. A prolific artist in the realist tradition, he is a methodical, well organized and successful publisher of full colour reproductions, although this is an expensive area usually avoided by self-publishers.

Smyth combines publishing with exhibitions of his own paintings. Indeed, it was only weeks before his first exhibition in 1979 that he decided on a book. The trade was interested, but the usual delay of approximately eighteen months was unacceptable. Any experienced author would have assured him that publishing in the time was impossible. However, unaware of the difficulties, Smyth found another art book, the design of which suited his own work, and a printer to accept the challenge. The job was delivered within six weeks, ahead of time and slightly under quote! The author-artist-publisher has built on this beginner's luck, with a book based on an exhibition every second year.

As well as being attractive, Smyth's books present interesting collections: bridges of the Yarra, lighthouses of Victoria, historic ships of Australia, waterfalls of Victoria, views of Victoria in the steps of Von Guerard and more. His publications are also interesting, useful, eminently sensible, and his poetry, cheerfully recognized as doggerel, is often amusing. The books are works of reference in themselves, the information being systematically presented. For example, in *Historic Ships of Australia* each left-hand page carries relevant technical details and historical information. Endpaper maps show the location of the vessels, a numbered list of contents defines them as paddle steamer, lifeboat, aircraft carrier, pearling lugger, whale chaser and so on. They are also listed again in chronological and alphabetical order. The author has been fortunate enough to find a workable formula, style and format, and sensible enough to stick to it, so his books are distinctive and constitute a recognizable series.

The series has been modestly priced at $14.95 with most titles selling 4000 copies. For example, *Historic Ships of Australia* (1982) cost $14.95, hard cover, full colour jacket, 144 pages, including sixty-seven pages of quality full colour reproductions. Costs, however, are rising, and *Gallipoli Pilgrimage*, dedicated to the memory of his father, General Sir Nevill Smyth VC, and father-in-law, Commander Geoffrey Haggard DSC, will be priced at $29.95. Spin-offs can be profitable. Twenty-three plates of riverboats from *Historic Ships of Australia* became *Old Riverboats of the Murray*, a title which sold well on the river.

With his first book Smyth visited 187 book shops, of which only two refused to stock them. Two thousand copies were sold in six weeks, and another printing ordered. On his rounds he encountered a book distributor to whom he eventually delegated this time-consuming task. His publishing path has been remarkably smooth, although inevitably he has suffered some of the disappointments common in publishing – a distributor collapsed, finally paying about 20 cents in the dollar, and the retirement of his original printer resulted in one book having unsatisfactory colour. Nor did it arrive in time for the launching – always disastrous for sales – and it was remaindered.

Smyth's orderliness is such that he can look in his notebook and announce that in twenty years he has sold 1657 paintings and about 24,000 books. He financed his first book himself, and subsequent publications have been financed out of the proceeds of earlier books and made 'reasonable' profits. He builds up a mailing list in a large alphabetical indexed notebook, ticking off each name as invitations are sent, carries invitations to his launchings in his pocket, does his own catalogues, frames and hangs his own pictures, and with his family runs his own launchings and exhibitions. He sends out review copies, and sometimes gets press or radio exposure, but concedes that he could boost sales with better promotion. But he is happy enough with his results not to want to spend more time and energy on marketing. There is always another exhibition and another book in the pipeline.

Get Every Agreement and Every Variation Thereof in Writing, and File Carefully!

Wendy Lowenstein has worked as a proofreader, journalist and editor and experienced successful commercial publication before self-publishing; she admits that a reputation as a successful author makes selling her self-published work much easier. She was founding editor of the folklore quarterly, *Australian Tradition*, published under the aegis of the Victorian Folk Music Club. Club editors, she says, are usually de facto self-publishers. While Ron Edwards was publishing *Northern Folk*, Lowenstein produced a more ambitious journal in letterpress with two-colour cover, and containing notes, articles, photographs, music, traditional and contemporary folk song, and achieving a modest Australian and international circulation. In the folklore area she also collected children's rhymes in the field. Her collection was self-published in *Shocking, Shocking, Shocking*: the improper play rhymes of Australian children (1974, 50 pages $3.50), now a collector's item. It is now published by Rams Skull as a Folk Lore Occasional Paper.

In 1978-1979 Lowenstein became a pioneer of oral history in Australia, with two commercially published best-sellers, *Weevils in the Flour*, an oral record of the 1930s depression, and *The Immigrants* with Morag Loh (Hyland House). However, finding commercial publication slow and inefficient, financial rewards trivial and author-publisher relationships unfairly loaded, she decided to publish herself. *Under the Hook: Melbourne Waterside Workers Remember Working Lives and Class War* was published by her Melbourne Bookworkers' Press in 1982 (192 pages, many black and white photographs, $20.00). Veteran wharfie Tom Hills, who had smoothed the way on the waterfront, was named joint author as a courtesy.

Early experience had taught Lowenstein that, to at least one printer, the customer was always wrong. 'I've since realized that printers and typesetters habitually accept too much work, give unrealistic delivery dates to get jobs, and serve the big customers first.' Dealing with an established book printer acquaintance was a mistake, because it was hard to make too much fuss about bad quality control. The printer delivered on time, but had not read instructions, and covers were not laminated. Launching, radio and press publicity were already fixed; it was impossible to reject the job. 'I still cringe when I see these dilapidated volumes on friends' bookshelves.' Many covers were also badly smudged and unsaleable. Because the bill was not yet paid, the author was at least able to insist on these covers being replaced. With this experience behind her she now says: 'Never start promotion, or fix launching/publication date, until you've a satisfactory book in hand and have inspected the goods minutely. Large publishers automatically reject sub-standard work. Self-publishers can't afford to be any more tolerant. And the only small customer with any power at all is the one who hasn't paid the bill.'

More than half of the first printing had been sold in advance at a discount to the Australian Society of Labour History, the Waterside Workers' Federation or on subscription. The books was well reviewed and enough bookseller orders came in after a mailed-out notice that no other distribution was needed. Waterside workers and communities were seen as the major primary market, but ship lovers, waterfront folk museums, waterfront employers and the labour movement have all proved fruitful secondary markets, along with industrial relations courses and, recently, secondary schools. Profits from this fairly short-run book continue to compare very favourably with Lowenstein's commercially published work, which has sold many times the number. 'It was labour intensive, an enormous amount of work and worry, a series of small finicky jobs which often had to be done under pressure. But it made me feel independent in dealing with commercial publishers.'

In 1989, after the three-volume *What Happened When in Australia* (with Kathleen Kane) was accepted on very good terms by Angus and Robertson, the book became a casualty of a multinational takeover. A financial settlement did not compensate for five years' work. This has led again to self-publishing new work. Together with a friend, Lowenstein now runs successful seminars on how to publish and sell your own book. Seminar papers have now become the low-tech, A4 volume *Self-Publishing Without Pain* (1989, 100 pages, $18.50 inc. post), commercially photocopied in editions of fifty, coil-bound at home and sold only at seminars and by mail-order. This book complements most existing how-to-do-it books on the subject because it concentrates not only on what should happen but also on what all-too-often goes wrong, suggesting strategies for avoiding disaster. Updates on editing and publicity are now in production, and all will eventually be compiled into a larger work on painless self-publishing.

Lowenstein's advice is: 'Use appropriate technology. Ron Edwards' black and white magazines were more sensible than mine. Mail-order can save massive distribution costs, and low-tech will suffice because you aren't competing in the shops. Small runs don't cost much, you can test the market, correct errors and update text. If I print another book commercially, I'll do it first in parts, and compile them later.'

Better to Go Out of Print Than Have a Garage Full of Books That No One Wants

Ronald Parsons uses very simple technology for his self-published work. A professional writer and editor, he has five books in print with commercial publishers and has self-published more than thirty books or booklets. Parsons, a retired naval officer of Lobethal, South Australia, writes and publishes in the fields of maritime and/or municipal history; he finds that the hardest thing about self-publishing is keeping up with requests for further publications.

Of his self-published work, *Paddle Steamers of Australia and New Zealand* ($6.50, three editions) has sold 3000 copies, *Ketches of South Australia* ($4.00, many editions) has sold about 5000 copies and is still in print, and *Port Misery and the New Port* ($1.95, many editions), also still in print, has sold 6000 copies. Although publishers in Australia, England and the USA saw no hope of a return from his work, his self-published books have all been more profitable than his commercially published work, and only one commercially published title, *Sail in the South*, has equalled the above sales.

Parsons had no prior experience with printing or publishing, never employs anyone for any aspect of publishing, and does not employ a printer. He produced his early books, which contain black and white photographs, cutting the wax stencils himself on a typewriter and using a hand-turned duplicator. He has recently acquired a simple wordprocessor. He considers 500 a major run, and often prints as few as 100, keeping the carbon ribbon printed masters in case demand exceeds expectations. He finds self-publishing enjoyable, not financially rewarding, but a better than break-even affair.

As the president of the Australasian Maritime History Society, he is often called on for specialized information by other writers and scholars. Although some society members make a point of buying everything he writes, and he benefits by references to his books in newsletter articles and research papers, he finds the Association not particularly important in sales.

Selling through bookshops is generally uneconomic, and he distributes his publications personally, mostly by mail and through some selected outlets, occasionally including advertising with other material. Bulk sales are sometimes made to local history societies and various National Trust branches. He also has a catalogue, available on receipt of a stamped, addressed envelope. 'I do sometimes send review copies to nautical interest associations, but the response is muted at best.... I have, from time to time, been interviewed by TV and radio...but I never try for such publicity.' However, he did announce the availability of some original publications such as *Paddle Steamers of Australia and New Zealand* in various Australian, Belgian and British maritime interest newsletters. On the whole, however, he finds his most effective advertising is word of mouth and recommendations of librarians.

His advice to anyone starting a similar venture is: 'Know your material, be clear and concise, thoroughly understand your method of reproduction, don't overprint for a perceived saving whatever the printer says, and be conservative in estimates of possible sales. Try not to produce to a deadline – it always means problems, usually grave errors and dissatisfaction. If unsure, take time, use the equipment available, a duplicator or copier, and produce a trial copy. This will reveal problems, give some idea of costs, and when you see it in print you will probably want to revise and rewrite.'

A New and Needed Product with a Long-term Demand

Murray River Charts is a perfect example of a one-off book that fills a market niche without attracting competitors. In 1973-1974 Maureen and Barry Wright, of Burra, South Australia, made a fourteen-month Murray River voyage in a small boat, from Murray Bridge to Yarrawonga and back. Motoring upstream, they noted houses, locks, windmills, fishing reaches and points of interest. These casual jottings became more urgent when they discovered that the quiet-looking river had numerous navigation hazards, many unmarked. Sometimes they 'sailed on the dew', seeking an elusive deep channel in the otherwise shallow river. When the limited maps ran out at Mildura, many river miles from their destination, Maureen drew the river systematically, the sketches being checked against the maps and redrawn each night. The original river captains used charts which were in effect long strip maps, drawn on cloth and mounted on rollers. From some surviving charts, Wright found reef names, mileages, dangerous snags and station names.

In the style of the old charts, she has drawn and labelled hers by hand, showing cliffs, houses, sheds and huts, launching ramps, Aboriginal campsites, tourist facilities, picnic spots, wineries, stores, windmills, pumps, locks, punts, ferries and waste disposal points, sand bars, old and new sections of the river, lagoons and billabongs, snags, ironstone reefs and tributaries. Snippets of historical or local information, river heights and mileage (distances are given in miles as on the old charts) are typeset. Line drawings of river birds and animals, buildings and riverboats by the author's brother, Neville Kroemer, enhance an eminently useful and most attractive item of Australiana.

River Murray Charts (1975, 2000 copies, $3.95) was originally rejected by two publishers and seriously considered by a third who eventually suggested self-publishing. Credit was available from the printer. The author says that she was lucky because Gillingham, who print a lot of self-published works, provided a great deal of advice, 'almost like a publisher', and the first edition was published in a foolscap format, bound with plastic coil to allow for opening flat while in use, and slotted into a heavy-duty clear plastic bag.

Media publicity and reviews in Adelaide and Melbourne papers enabled the first edition of 2000 to be sold out in less than three weeks, mainly in Adelaide. Subsequently, revision trips up-river offered opportunities for promotion and publicity. People undertaking long river trips were seen as the main market, with tourists as a secondary market. In fact far more copies are bought by people who do not use them as charts – armchair travellers, schools, tourists and river lovers. This allowed the Wrights to use a cheaper stitched (stapled) binding for subsequent editions.

The charts have now been revised and completely redrawn three times, with sales totalling 32,000, and the fourth edition (7000 copies) costs $11.95. Revision is needed every four years, and each update means a six-week trip down-river, trips which have been sponsored by Ampol and Gillingham Printers. Press releases are sent to the river towns when the revision trip is under way, which leads to an increased demand for the current issue. To meet this demand, they carry stocks of the existing edition with them, and arrange to exchange any surplus for the new edition when ready. The old edition is then remaindered and discounted for tourists, while those who need up-to-date charts buy the new edition.

Recent river trips have been expedited by a land party of friends who prepared camping spots and fetched supplies. The Wrights, who keep a boat specially for these trips, realize that the need for constant revision, boat maintenance, promotion costs and time means that it would not be profitable to a commercial publisher. Overall a 'reasonably' profitable project, *Murray River Charts* was started as a hobby by a pair of unfettered wanderers, and the work is still enjoyed by the author. But revision is not now quite so easy. In the past river trips have just meant changing jobs and taking time off in between; now the Wrights are in business and may find the next trip more difficult.

Retail bookshops in the river towns and Adelaide and Melbourne are the main outlets, many having carried stock for fifteen years. Small distributors are used in Melbourne and Sydney, but most are self-distributed. When a new edition appears, the Wrights simply ring around their outlets. In river towns especially the charts sell steadily. The hardest job is watching for breaches of their copyright.

Maureen Wright's advice is: 'Establish friendly relations with your outlets and be reliable – commercial distributors tend to be short on both these qualities.'

Networks Are Essential to Self-Publishers of Local History

Helen Hannah was a school teacher before moving to the Bulga Plateau near Taree, New South Wales during the 1970s. On the Bulga she lived in a communally owned former sawmill, raised three children, wrote and published three local histories, using mainly oral sources: *The Mountain Speaks*, a folk history of the Bulga Plateau (1979); *Together in This Jungle Scrub*, a folk history of the Comboyne Plateau (1981); and *Voices*, a folk history of the Manning Valley (1988). She took a major responsibility for design, layout, production and distribution of her first book.

Until moving to the Bulga, she had no experience with publishing. The Bulga, settled by timber getters and dairy farmers early this century, was poor country, with a living hard to earn. Now dairying had declined and the timber was cut out. The stories of pioneers still living nearby fascinated her, just as the rape of the environment saddened her.

Without material resources other than the supporting mother's pension, very old car and tape recorder, Hannah researched and wrote her first book over several years. With help from a friend with access to typesetting, and a family loan to pay the printer, *The Mountain Speaks* was published. This was a new sort of local history, a revelation for people who had never thought their own lives worthy of note; it transformed their perceptions of themselves. It was relevant to their lives, written in the words of local people, presented in short sentences and paragraphs, immediately accessible. 'I had to think about a broad local market, and fairly unsophisticated readers. And most people want to pick up something and read it easily.'

A pleasantly folksy publication, its limp cover is printed economically in sepia on beige card with a lovely old photograph and attractive type. With seventy-two pages, about fifty black and white photographs, A4 format and a stapled binding, the 30,000-word volume sold for a low $5.00 and was an immediate success. 'You've got to say "What will they pay?" People who aren't used to buying books may think $10.00 is an immense amount to pay for a book. I sold lots more because it was only $5.00. And made more money than on may later, more professional looking and expensive books.'

'Country papers will keep things going for you. I told them early in the piece, "This is what I'm doing. Isn't it wonderful for the area? I want a write-up and picture!" I'd often write it myself, try to be in the paper or radio every few months. I worked at developing a local profile.'

The Mountain Speaks was launched at the local school fete. During the years of interviewing and research an impressive network of friends of the project had developed. Without this support, the author says her book would have been far less successful. Informants had been promised a free copy, and most bought more for friends and family. Local press publicity and favourable reviews in the local press and an ABC interview resulted in a wide interest. The first printing of 1000 was quickly exhausted and a reprint was needed. The book became a favourite Christmas present. At a nearby folk museum the shop manager, interested in good local material, ordered 3000 copies at a time, kept a pile on the counter and promoted it actively, becoming the best commercial outlet. When a reprint was needed, she made a large order and paid in advance to help pay the printer. Local bookshops also took it on consignment, and accepted a lower-than-trade discount.

The book was reprinted twice, returning a very satisfactory profit, and established the author's credentials so that she received an Australia Council grant for the writing of her next book. She also was commissioned to write a history of the New South Wales Forestry Commission. Later she won a North Coast Writing Award which helped with the publication of *Voices*. She has now returned to teaching and moved away from the area. This, she finds, has made it difficult to keep her third book, *Voices*, in the public eye. Being part of the local community makes distribution so much easier.

Hannah prefers the independence of self-publishing. 'I wanted to be in control. To have my books the way I wanted them, the way I thought the readers would relate best to them. I've done what I set out to, but I don't want to do it again. Self-publishing – typing, layout, editing and organizing the material and distribution – is a lot of hard work. I'm going to use my tapes for community radio in the future.'

Her advice is: 'Always have two or three others, people who know something about how words are put together, to advise you. Otherwise you might publish something that's really crummy without realizing it. And have a good launching. An inexpensive party in the local hall worked well for *Together in This Jungle Scrub*. Launchings are really essential for a local history. If possible have several in different parts of the area.'

Conclusion

In the writer's library one shelf, three metres long, contains only self-published works by many authors. In a bewildering variety of size, shape, binding, paper, printing, illustration and subject matter, they range in extent from 400-page tertiary texts to ten-page booklets. New titles are acquired quite selectively, yet the next shelf is filling up fast. In discussion with booksellers, their knowledge of self-published titles seldom overlaps with mine. One wonders just how many books are self-published annually, because despite distribution difficulties, this is clearly a lively part of the industry, and one which appears to be growing as big publishers merge and look for benefits of rationalization and economies of scale. Freedom of the press clearly also belongs to those with access even to a little one!

Note

Titles quoted in this article may be hard to trace, as not all self-publishers yet bother with ISBN numbers or list publications in *Australian Books in Print*. Enquiries may be sent to Bookworkers' Press, PO Box 33, Hawthorn, Vic. 3142, Australia.

Appendix: Publishers Interviewed

Ron Edwards
The Rams Skull Press
PO Box 274
Kuranda, Qld 4872, Australia

Helen Hannah
PO Box 620
Leeton, NSW 2705, Australia

Bill Hornadge
Review Publications
PO Box 1463
Dubbo, NSW 2830, Australia

Wendy Lowenstein
Bookworkers' Press
PO Box 33
Hawksburn, Vic. 3142, Australia

Ronald Parsons
PO Box 89
Lobethal, SA 5241, Australia

H. Dacre Smyth
22 Douglas Street
Toorak, Vic. 3142, Australia

Maureen Wright
1 Young Street
Burra, SA 5417, Australia

Part 3. Selecting and Purchasing Australian Publications

8 Selecting In-print Australian Material: Some General Information and a List of Australian Selection Aids

Jerelynn Brown

This paper presents a range of basic information about collecting current Australian publications. It explores the question, 'What is an Australian book?' in the light of figures on the size of the Australian publishing output. The processes used to select material for the Bennett Australian Blanket Order Service are outlined. Information on the average Australian book price is given. A select list of Australian selection aids for those collecting in-print Australiana is included.

What Is an 'Australian' Book?

The *Australian National Bibliography (ANB)* in its preface sets out general criteria for selection to the *Bibliography*. Further detailed criteria are spelled out in *ANB Documentation*.[1] Generally, the *ANB* includes books and pamphlets published within the current and two preceding years. Specifically included are substantial exhibition catalogues; conferences held in Australia or with substantial Australian emphasis; publications of social or historical significance; first issues of significant serials; printed music as selected; and individually titled monographs in series. Specifically excluded are reprints; 'imprint only' material; novelty and toy books; Acts, Bills and Ordinances; standards; and patents – to list the major categories. These criteria are broad, reflecting the National Library's role as the major collector and bibliographer of Australian publications.

D.W. Thorpe's criteria for inclusion in *Australian Books in Print (ABIP)* define as 'Australian books' those 'books published in Australia including foreign works which have National Library of Australia cataloguing-in-publication data, books written by Australians, and books written about Australia or containing substantial references to Australia.'[2] Thorpe, like Bowker or Whitaker, relies on publishers to submit details of new publications, resulting in a largely 'trade' oriented bibliography. The Thorpe definition reflects Thorpe's role as Australia's major trade bibliographer.

Bennett's Australian Blanket Order definition includes both trade and non-commercial publications, and generally uses the *ANB* definition as a guide. Many of the publications, however, are identified through commercial channels before they are listed in the *ANB*. Like *ANB* and Thorpe, Bennett includes books written by Australians or about Australia, even if not published in Australia. If published in Australia, books are generally classed as 'Australian', except when they have an 'imprint page only'. (Examples of this category are often published by overseas publishers with Australian branches and include books on decorating, cooking and needlework, for example, with no discernible Australian author or content, but with an Australian imprint page.) Categories specifically included in the Bennett definition are the publications of societies, associations, committees, organizations, university departments, families (as in family histories), semi-autonomous government-linked bodies and school texts. Federal, state and local government publications are not usually included, unless they are publications of significance in their own right, or have unique content. These are included, despite their parentage, where they will be of interest to clients. The Bennett definition reflects Bennett's role as Australia's major supplier of blanket orders to libraries.

Blanket Orders for Australian Publications

Most librarians charged with collecting a large proportion of any country's publishing output can avoid some expense on selection aids by using a reputable dealer to supply publications on the basis of a profiled blanket order. This is an assumption which, however, can only be proven by having access to at least the major selection aids, and using these to evaluate the blanket order selections for coverage and currency, if not regularly, at least periodically. Even the best and most conscientious vendor may have problems from time to time, and this could have a minimal to major impact on a given collection. Whatever the cause, including change of personnel, procedure or system, restructuring of services or profile, disputes with individual publishers and so on, the single most important factor for the collector is that he will generally learn of these 'hiccups' only retrospectively. Filling holes which may have occurred, or retrospective collecting, is well known to be both expensive and time-consuming.

At Bennett it is seen as essential to identify and purchase new material as early as possible to ensure currency and coverage. The publishers are therefore the primary source of information. The selection aids listed in this article, at a minimum, are used to check coverage, to verify details, and to identify non-trade publishers such as societies, associations, families, university departments and semi-autonomous government-linked authorities. The selection procedures used are described below:

1 Major trade and non-trade publishers are interviewed systematically by the buyer. The information gleaned from these interviews is used to place orders in advance of publication to fill library blanket order requirements. (A byproduct of this blanket order activity is the gathering of information for the pre-publication Australian New Title 'slip' Service.)

2 Other publishers, normally small and reliable ones, are controlled on a standing order basis. In this case the bibliographic tools are used to check that supply has, in fact, occurred as anticipated.

3 Another important source is the reviewing media, and often journals outside the mainstream are most valuable, as major Australian titles found in mainstream papers and journals are normally advised by the publisher well in advanced of any review. Nonetheless, major daily papers like the *Sydney Morning Herald* and *The Age* are digested methodically, along with the major provincial weeklies and journals such as the *Australian Book Review* to ensure complete coverage.

4 The fourth important source to a supplier is personal contacts, including customers. Obscure publications are often picked up by individuals who are interested to note personal ads in journals, unique monographs seen at markets and publications of local interest. Colleagues in specialized areas of the book trade or study often have priceless knowledge and expertise which they may be willing to share.

5 Of last resort and used primarily for checking are the *Australian Bookseller and Publisher (ABP)*, state library deposit lists and the *ANB*. Many publications of societies and associations are first noted in the *ANB*, because its contents reflect both the legal deposit requirement and the Cataloguing-in-Publication (CIP) roles of the National Library.

As supplier of Australian publications to the National Library of Australia, there is an ongoing race to see how often Bennett can get a new title to the National Library through the blanket order before the legal deposit copy arrives from the publisher. Currently, the Bennett copy arrives before the legal deposit copy about 50 per cent of the time.[3]

The Australian Publishing Output

It may be somewhat amusing, if not bemusing, for readers to note the 'size of the Australian publishing output' or the number of original Australian titles published per year, which is variously stated. A few examples are set out below.

The National Library's CIP figure (1989-90)	4,242[4]
The National Library's legal deposit figure (1990)	8,107[5]
The National Library's *ANB* figure (1990)	13,668[6]
The National Library's Australian Bibliographic Network (ABN) figure (1990)	21,043[7]
The UNESCO figure (1990)	12,235[8]
Thorpe's *Guide to New Australian Books (GNAB)* figure (1990-91)	2,904[9]
Thorpe's *ABP* figure (1990)	2,884[10]
Guldenberg's annual figure in *Books, Who Reads Them?*	4,000[11]
Australian Book Publishers' Association (ABPA) figure (1989)	3,035[12]
Titles allocated on the Bennett Australian Blanket Order (1990-91)	9,990[13]

The parameters for each of the figures are set out below, and the references give greater detail where necessary.

The National Library figures reflect respectively titles for which CIP entries have been made; titles which have been received on legal deposit; the figure for titles published in Australia in the current and two preceding years (which tends to give an 'annual average'); and the number of records for books published in Australia in 1990, as catalogued by ABN members. The UNESCO figure is also calculated by the National Library and reflects one year's *ANB* output, less duplicate entries which occur when a CIP entry is duplicated by the legal deposit entry.

Trade figures include the *GNAB* figure for twelve months which represents those books sent by publishers to D.W. Thorpe for review. As *GNAB* has only been published since October 1990, this twelve-month figure is an extrapolation. The *ABP* figures represent trade or commercial publications reported by publishers. The Guldenberg figure is based on a title count of *ABIP*. The ABPA figure is a compilation of members' figures for original new titles published in 1989. ABPA members are said to represent 80 per cent of the Australian publishing industry.[14] The Bennett blanket order figure counts the actual number of titles treated through the Australian Blanket Order Service in a twelve-month period.[15] It is easy to see from these examples that the 'size of the Australian publishing output' is a different thing to different people. This has implications for bibliographic control, and specifically the need to check a number of selection aids to cover the range of publications described as 'Australian'.

Selection Aids

The Australian publishing output represents only a small percentage (almost certainly less than 5 per cent) of the world's annual English-language publishing output. There is, however, a large and varied range of bibliographic resources available to assist in the selection of current Australian material. Most libraries in overseas institutions hold only a small part of the Australian publishing output. Therefore, overseas selectors may consider the situation in either of the following ways:

1 as the required selection is small, the purchase of only a limited number of selection resources is justified; or
2 as the required selection is small, it is necessary to be as well informed as possible in making those few selections. In this case it follows that the widest possible range of selection resources should be consulted to make the best choices.

Obviously all library suppliers would prefer the second option (not only do they sell more selection aids, but the quality of the orders should be better). In either case there are some selection aids which are central to the selection of general in-print Australian material, and these are listed alphabetically at the end of this section. The list is not comprehensive, nor does it touch on retrospective selection.

A Note on the National Bibliography

When asked (often by librarians collecting only a small amount of Australian material) to suggest an appropriate general selection aid, I prefer to recommend the *ANB* in the monthly hardcopy for its ease of use through its classified arrangement, broad coverage and helpful annotations. The indexes allow easy access to any author or title. The only possible drawback is the lead time, which may yield delays of up to three months.

Now that the National Library of Australia has automated many of its bibliographic functions (to popular acclaim) one must wonder how much longer the *ANB* will continue to be available in the current comfortable and useful format. I advise you to obtain a copy soon in order to appreciate it while the opportunity exists!

Ease of Use/Searching Strategies

Technological change, including the availability of online and CD-ROM formats, has served to heighten expectations, particularly with regard to searching strategies. Change is occurring, but most major Australian selection aids continue to be available manually, and some are still produced manually. This may present the user with difficulties in searching with respect to arrangement, currency and completeness of indexing. There is recognition of these shortcomings from both private and public sector service providers, and there is no doubt that redesign has already been addressed by some. One possible explanation for the seeming lack of speed in responding to technological developments in Australia is the small market size and the relatively high cost of development when the probable return on investment is considered.

The Cost of Australian Publications

Like the size of the publishing output, the average cost of an Australian book is hard to pin down. If one surveys the wide range of material described as 'Australian publications', and compares this with the 'trade' publishing figures provided by Thorpe and the ABPA, it becomes apparent that much Australian material is not 'commercially' published. Non-commercial publishers or those whose primary purpose in publishing is something other than profitability are responsible for a large portion of the Australian publishing output. In sourcing these titles it is necessary for librarians to look at the costs involved in direct purchase, and for the library supplier to create a margin or make a service charge to cover these costs (if they value survival). It is quite normal for non-trade publishers to sell at list price, require prepayment, and charge freight. An important factor related to Australia's small population/large area ratio is the relatively (when compared to the USA, for example) high cost of internal freight and postage. Australia Post offers no book rate within Australia, nor is there a freight carrier which operates similarly to UPS. Particularly in cases of non-commercially published titles, where no margin is made available, freight charges must be passed on to the customer. These aspects of pricing need to be considered when committing funds for non-commercial publications. Some examples of non-commercial publishers already listed include societies, committees, university departments and so on.

However, the average price of Australian books is still substantially lower than average US or UK book prices. With small print runs and relatively high costs of production and distribution which are 'givens' in Australia, this is difficult to understand and may help to explain the liquidity problems common in the Australian book trade for both publishers and booksellers. The production of a high proportion of quality Australian fiction in paperback format serves to underline the difficulties inherent in the small Australian market environment.[16]

It is abundantly clear that US and UK libraries receive excellent value for money when purchasing Australian publications, particularly when exchange rates are as favourable as they are currently. The information below gives some interesting price comparisons.

	Average Price
Australian Average Price - *ABP* (1990)	AU$ 21.62[17]
Australian Blanket Order Average Price - Bennetts (1990)	AU$ 21.30[18]
UK Price - *Bookseller* (1990)	£ 21.12[19]
US Price - *Publishers Weekly* (1990)	US$ 29.84[20]

At May 1991 conversion rates (A$ = £0.4319 and US$ .7525) the variation is even more pronounced:

Average Price Converted to Australian Dollars

	Country of Origin Currency	Australian Dollars
Australian *(ABP)*	AU$ 21.62	21.62
Australian (Bennetts)	AU$21.30	21.30
United Kingdom *(Bookseller)*	£ 21.12	48.90
United States *(Publishers Weekly)*	US$ 29.84	39.65

It is easy to see that the average price of a book published in the US or UK is substantially higher than the average price of a book published in Australia.

Select List of Australian Selection Aids

In the list of selection aids which follows, all formats currently available of each title have been listed. However, many changes are now under consideration and it may be worth checking for the latest information. Reference has been made to networks through which a range of bibliographies are available.

AUSINET, a product of Ferntree Information, is a computerized information retrieval service which provides a range of bibliographic and full text databases in the areas of business, technology and research. Databases currently available and described elsewhere in this list include *ABIP, AEI, APAIS* and *Worklit*. Other databases available and of possible interest include the *Directory of Australian Databases, Australian Business Index* and the *Australasian Industry Reporter*. Further information may be obtained from Ferntree Computer Services, 310 Ferntree Gully Road, Clayton, Victoria, 3168.

AUSTLIT Database. Canberra: Australian Defence Force Academy, 1988- .
AUSTLIT is the major online bibliographic tool for Australian literary studies. It is produced by the department of English and the Library at the Australian Defence Force Academy. Coverage includes creative literature, criticism, biographical

information, reviews, awards, prizes and grants, publishing and distribution of Australian literature and translations by Australians. Seven hundred serials are indexed; ninety of these comprehensively. The first phase of database compilation aims to achieve comprehensiveness from 1970 to present, updating continuously. *AUSTLIT* is available on subscription via AUSTPAC, ILANET, AARNet, and Direct Dial.

Australian Book Review. Carlton, Vic.: National Book Council, 1978- (10 issues per year). ISSN 0155-2864
The *ABR* is Australia's main reviewing journal and is billed by the publisher as 'the only review magazine totally committed to Australian books and writing.'[21] The reviews cover a range of subjects and genres. While the quality of reviews varies, the contribution made by this journal should not be underrated. Reports on events and issues of interest complement the reviews. Full bibliographic details are given for each item reviewed. An effort is made to publish reviews close to publication, and this assists those using *ABR* as a selection aid.*ABR* has an annual index to reviews published only in the previous year in the February/March issue. Hardcopy only.

Australian Books: A Select List of Recent Publications and Standard Works in Print. Canberra: National Library of Australia, 1950- (annual). ISSN 0067-1738
Australian Books is an excellent source of recent mainstream publications. It is arranged by broad subject and its prime aim is to recommend a range of books of general interest. This bibliography is sometimes used by the National Library and other institutions to select material sent to overseas libraries as gifts. Staff preparing this work ascertain that titles are in print prior to publication. Hardcopy only.

Australian Books in Print. Port Melbourne, Vic.: D.W. Thorpe, 1967- . ISSN 0067-172X
ABIP provides information about Australian books and the Australian publishing and bookselling trade. *ABIP* in hardcopy lists each book under author and title, and gives publication details. Other sections list and give details about associations, literary prizes and awards; series of books; and overseas publishers with Australian agents and representatives. In a sense, *ABIP* could be described as a directory to the Australian book trade. A directory of code names with full names and addresses of Australian publishers, representatives and agents is included. *ABIP* is available annually in hardcopy; on

microfiche, updated monthly and online via AUSINET. *A Subject Guide to Australian Books in Print* is published separately. The ISBN for the last published volume (1990) is 0909532702.

Australian Bookseller and Publisher. Port Melbourne, Vic.: D.W. Thorpe: 1921- . ISSN 0004-8763
ABP provides information about Australian books and the Australian publishing and bookselling trade. It lists new and forthcoming books by Australian publishers, and includes an alphabetical listing (by author) of books published in the previous month. A review section is included. In the April and November issues new titles are listed by broad subject area. Articles, announcements and advertisements of interest to Australian booksellers, publishers and librarians are included, as are descriptions of new titles in several categories. *ABP* is available eleven months per year in hardcopy. The subscription includes a copy of the annual, *Australian Book Scene*. Much of the information which appears in *ABP* first appears in Thorpe's *Weekly Book Newsletter*, ISSN 0812 7042. Hardcopy only.

Australian Bureau of Statistics Catalogue of Publications and Products. Canberra: Australian Bureau of Statistics, 1967- (annual). ISSN 1032-805X. Catalogue number 1101.0
The ABS publishes approximately 500 individual statistical titles per year. This catalogue lists all current and forthcoming ABS printed publications and other standard products available from federal or state ABS offices. Each entry comprises a catalogue number, title, publication details, price and a brief description. The catalogue is indexed by subject and by state. Hardcopy only.

Australian Education Index. Hawthorn, Vic.: Australian Council for Educational Research, 1957- . ISSN 0004-9026
AEI is an index to current literature related to Australian education. Books, conference papers, research reports, journal articles, tests, curriculum materials, legislation, newspaper articles and parliamentary debates published in or about Australia are included. The arrangement of *AEI* is three main sections: The Main Entry Section, The Author and Institution Index and The Subject Index. *AEI* is published quarterly with an annual cumulation in hardcopy, is available online via AUSINET and is available on AUSTROM (1978-).

Australian Government Publications. Canberra: National Library of Australia, 1952-1960, 1961- . ISSN 0067-1878
AGP lists material issued by agencies of the Commonwealth of Australia and its Territories, the states of Australia and by local government authorities within those jurisdictions. *AGP* is produced from the National Bibliographic Database and contains records produced by the National Library of Australia for the *Australian National Bibliography* and for its film and video recording acquisitions. *AGP* is cumulated quarterly and produced on microfiche, and is also available online via ABN and OZLINE (1983-1987 only).

Australian Government Publishing Service Catalogue on Microfiche. Canberra: Australian Government Publishing Service, 1976- . ISSN 0811-9201
The *AGPS Catalogue* is a complete listing of publications issued by the Australian Government Publishing Service. Each entry lists full bibliographic details including ISBNs and AGPS catalogue numbers. Prices are included for those titles currently available for purchase from the AGPS. Titles marked 'N.S.' (No Stock) are generally gratis items that are available directly from the government departments concerned. The *AGPS Catalogue* is completely cumulated every two weeks, and is available on a subscription basis fortnightly, monthly or quarterly in microfiche only. It is possible to purchase an annual cumulation separately.

Australian National Bibliographic Database (NBD). Canberra: Australian Bibliographic Network, National Library of Australia, 1981- .
The *NBD* contains over 7 million bibliographic records for monographs, serials, films, videos, maps, pictures, sheet music and other types of non-book material. These records are cataloguing data from national agencies in Australia, US, UK, Canada, New Zealand and Singapore, as well as original cataloguing records contributed by ABN users. Because it is the 'Australian' NBD, it is particularly rich in records for Australian material. The *NBD* may be accessed via online and dial-up connections and is also available from the National Library of Australia on microfiche as the *National Union Catalogue of Monographs*, ISSN 0810-2333 (*NUCOM*), the *National Union Catalogue of Serials*, ISSN 0812-9258 (*NUCOS*) and the *National Union Catalogue of Nonbook Materials*, ISSN 1031-9425 (*NUC:N*).

Australian National Bibliography. Canberra: National Library of Australia, 1961- . ISSN 0004-9916
The *ANB* includes books and pamphlets, new serial titles, government publications except legislation, and printed music. It excludes standards, maps and films. All items listed are published in Australia, have Australian content or are written by Australians (greater detail on *ANB* coverage is available in the introductory segment of this paper, 'What Is an Australian Book?'). *ANB* is arranged in three sections: The Classified Sequence; The Author, Title and Series Index; and the Subject Index. The *ANB* is available in hardcopy as monthly issues with an annual cumulation and is most useful for selection in this format. It is also available on microfiche in three, four-monthly cumulations per year. The content is accessible via online databases as part of the Australian Bibliographic Network (ABN) and via OZLINE.

The Australian New Title Service. Collaroy, NSW: James Bennett Library Services, 1983- .
This service is produced twice monthly by James Bennett Library Services to provide pre-publication information to customers, based on individual subject profiles. Coverage is broad as described above in the section called 'What Is an Australian Book?'. The format is 3 x 5 slips. Entries include a full citation, anticipated price and short annotations.

Australian Periodicals in Print. Port Melbourne, Vic.: D.W. Thorpe, 1981- . ISSN 1030-2474
APIP, previously *Australian Serials in Print*, includes periodicals, magazines, yearbooks, newspapers and proceedings, but not series. Government publications, with the exception of major serials generally available to the public, are excluded. (They are listed in *Australian Government Publications*.) Each serial has three entries: one under publisher, one under title, and one by subject or the key word in the title. *APIP* is available in hardcopy only and frequency varies.

Australian Public Affairs Information Service: A Subject Index to Current Literature. Canberra: National Library of Australia, 1972- . ISSN 0727-8926
APAIS is an indexing service which covers a wide range of current Australian journals, newspapers, articles, conference proceedings and books in the social sciences and humanities. Its level is described as 'scholarly.' Areas of special interest

include cultural, social, political and economic affairs. *APAIS* is available monthly except December in hardcopy, on AUSTROM (1978-) via OZLINE (1978-), or via AUSINET.

Australian Standards: Catalogue of SAA Publications. North Sydney: Standards Association of Australia, 1984- . ISSN 0815-3272
This catalogue is published annually and lists all SAA publications which are available when it goes to print. Information is updated by the SAA's monthly journal, *The Australian Standard* (ISSN 0158-3999). Arrangement is by numerical sequence of the standards. An alphabetical subject index is included. Hardcopy only.

Australian Social Science and Education Databases on CD-ROM (AUSTROM). Melbourne: INFORMIT, RMIT Libraries, Victoria University of Technology, 1990- .
AUSTROM is a CD-ROM compilation of thirteen databases and has been cooperatively produced by INFORMIT, the National Library of Australia and the other database producers. The databases of most interest for selection include *Australian Education Index, Australian Public Affairs Information Service, Australian Criminology Database, EDLINE, Family and Society Abstracts* and *Index to Review of Australian Books*. The information in each database continues to be prepared by the individual database producers. *AUSTROM* is available on either a subscription or single issue basis.

Directory of Australian Associations. 10th ed. Melbourne: Information Australia, 1985- . ISSN 0110-666X
The *DAA* gives information including contact name, address, 'phone, date formed and purpose of more than 6000 associations throughout Australia. It lists both Australian and international organizations present in Australia. Arrangement is alphabetically by name of organization, and a subject index is included. Subscribers receive updates to the *DAA*. Available in hardcopy only and in looseleaf format, this directory is useful for tracing organizations which may publish material of interest.

Guide to New Australian Books. Melbourne: D.W. Thorpe, 1990- . ISSN 1035-5391
GNAB is a new journal which aims to list new Australian publications with full bibliographic details and brief annotations. Annotations are prepared by staff at the Centre for

Australian Studies at Monash University. It is intended for use in the selection of new material by bookshop owners, librarians and members of the public. The entries are classified by general subject (the same seventy subjects used in *ABIP* and *The Subject Guide to Australian Books in Print)*. Arrangement is by title, and each title is indexed by author, illustrator, photographer and subject. Selection of titles for inclusion depends primarily upon a review copy being sent by the publisher. Strategies are under consideration by the publisher to make coverage more deliberate. Hardcopy only.

OZLINE

OZLINE is a subsection of the National Library of Australia, established in 1987; it is responsible for providing access to a network of databases in the humanities and social sciences. Those of major interest for selection include *APAIS, ANB, AGP, Multicultural Australia Information System* or *MAIS*, and *The Australian Family and Society Abstracts (FAMILY)*. OZLINE is available through AUSTPAC and AARNet. Further information may be obtained from the OZLINE subsection, National Library of Australian, Canberra, ACT 2600.

Publishers

A list of publishers and their addresses can be found in *ABIP* or at the back of each bound annual volume of the *ANB*. Most publishers produce catalogues or lists and are delighted to send these to libraries interested in collecting their publications. Send individual requests to publishers of interest.

Worklit. Canberra: Department of Employment, Education and Training, 1987- .

Worklit is a bibliographic database incorporating details of monographs and journal articles relating to industrial relations, employment, staff training, wages, personnel management and technological change. The database is compiled from the combined resources of several government departments and is updated monthly. *Worklit* is available online through AUSINET.

The information presented here indicates that the Australian book trade is alive, well and producing new publications so quickly that it is difficult to count the output accurately. It is clear that appropriate, professionally produced general selection aids exist, giving a reasonable view of the current publishing output and sufficient information for ordering specific titles as required.

Notes

1 'Selection Policy,' *ANB Documentation*, 4 (January 1990): 1.

2 D.W. Thorpe, now the bibliographic segment of Butterworths (Australia), is the publisher of *Australian Bookseller and Publisher, Australian Books in Print, Guide to New Australian Books* and *Australian Periodicals in Print*. Information about the scope of *ABIP* was provided by John Nieuwenhuizen, publishing manager, in May 1991.

3 Information from Australian Selection Services staff, National Library of Australia, April 1991.

4 Figure provided by Pam Dunlop, Cataloguing Section, National Library of Australia, April 1991.

5 Figure provided by Rosemary Turner, Australian Selection Services, National Library of Australia, April 1991.

6 Figure provided by Pam Dunlop, Cataloguing Section, National Library of Australia, April 1991.

7 Figure provided by Briony Wilcox, ABN Office, National Library of Australia, May 1991.

8 Figure provided by Pam Dunlop, Cataloguing Section, National Library of Australia, April 1991.

9 Figure obtained by counting entries in the *Guide to New Australian Books*, 1, 1-4, October 1990-May 1991. An issue average was then calculated and multiplied by six to arrive at an annual figure.

10 Figure obtained by counting 1990 publications listed in 'New Australian Books' column of *Australian Bookseller and Publisher*, 69, 999 (November 1989)-70, 1011 (December 1990).

11 Hans Guldenberg, *Books: Who Reads Them? A Study of Borrowing and Buying in Australia*. Sydney: Australia Council, 1990, p. 201. Figure is an annual estimate based on a count of titles in *Australian Books in Print*.

12 Figure provided by Susan Blackwell, Executive Director, Australian Book Publishers' Association, Sydney, May 1991.

13 Figure provided by Portia Barnes, Chief Buyer, James Bennett Library Services, April 1991.

14 Information provided by Rebecca Kaiser, Deputy Director, Australian Book Publishers' Association, Sydney, May 1991.

15 Figure provided by Portia Barnes, Chief Buyer, James Bennett Library Services, May 1991.

16 In 1989 only thirty Australian fiction titles were published in hardcover; 857 were published in paperback. Information provided by Susan Blackwell, Executive Director, Australian Book Publishers' Association, Sydney, May 1991.

17 Figure obtained by calculating the average price of all 1990 publications in the 'New Australian Books' column of *Australian Bookseller and Publisher*, 69, 999 (November 1989)-70, 1011 (December 1990).

18 Figure provided from Bennett database.

19 'Output Up, Prices Slow,' *The Bookseller*, 4444 (22 February 1991): 509.

20 Chandler B. Grannis, 'Title Output Down, Prices Stable,' *Publisher's Weekly*, 238, 12 (8 March 1991): 36-39.

21 *Australian Book Review*, 128 (March-April 1991): 43.

9 Resources for Collecting Australiana

John Arnold

Australia is one of the few countries which was discovered after the invention of printing and whose history of English-speaking settlement occurs almost entirely in the age of machine printing. Its annual publishing output is relatively small, and it has been possible for a few select libraries to collect this output comprehensively, many others selectively. Although there are some weaknesses in the bibliographic record of its output, coverage of relatively recent material is excellent. Through the various publications and databases of the National Library of Australia, librarians can find out what is being published. Using these and the various trade publications, they can find out about new and forthcoming titles and the necessary details for ordering. A network of library suppliers is available to assist with this, as are retail chains and owner operated bookshops. An active trade is available to assist with the acquisition of retrospective material. This paper surveys the bibliographic record of the country's publishing output from the viewpoint of book purchasers, be they bookshop proprietors, librarians or general readers. Emphasis is also given to retrospective and out-of-print material. It concentrates on resources for collecting separately published monographs, with some attention given to newspapers and serials, and to reformatted texts. The acquisition of non-book materials is not dealt with here.

Around 6000 books are published in Australia each year.[1] These range from deluxe limited editions to standard hardback monographs, textbooks, cookbooks and other 'how-tos', paperback novels, through to self-published family histories or literary efforts. In addition there are the 11,000 or so publications produced by various government departments and statutory authorities and published under the auspices of the Australian Government Publishing Service.[2] Finally, there are the thousands of magazines, periodicals and newsletters produced either for mass consumption or, through the universities, special interest groups, sporting clubs and church congregations, for specific audiences.[3] There are also around 700 newspapers published daily, weekly or fortnightly in Australia.[4] Only one library – the National Library of Australia[5] – attempts to collect all of the country's output;

others try for state or regional comprehensiveness.[6] However, no one institution can expect to acquire or record *everything*. Australia is fortunate in having through its national bibliographic database various subject bibliographies and several trade publications, the necessary record of its publications to answer almost all the questions about what has been published, who published it and from where it is obtainable.

This paper surveys the bibliographic record of the country's publishing output from the viewpoint of book purchasers, be they bookshop proprietors wanting to know what to stock, casual buyers wanting books as Christmas presents, public librarians wanting to know what is available and possibly suitable for their borrowers, through to research librarians with responsibility for establishing and/or maintaining a reference and research collection of Australiana. Emphasis is also given to retrospective and out-of-print material. Such items are obtainable. Their acquisition involves an understanding of the antiquarian and secondhand book trade combined with patience and diligence in searching. The paper concentrates on resources for collecting separately published monographs, with some attention given to newspapers and serials, and to reformatted texts. The acquisition of non-book material such as manuscripts, pictures, oral history and other audiovisual material, despite their obvious importance for both research and recreational use, is not dealt with.

The progress towards national bibliographic control in Australia can be divided roughly into five periods: pre-1936, 1936-1950, 1951-1970, 1971-1982 and 1983 to the present. The time divisions are naturally arbitrary but serve some purpose. Interestingly enough, they tend to reflect both public and private initiatives during the particular periods. Before 1936 there was virtually no national bibliographic record of the country's publishing output, either past or present. Helpful aids were the three-part *Australasian Bibliography* (1893), published by the Public Library of New South Wales,[7] the *Catalogue of the York Gate Library* (1882 and 1886), compiled by Australia's first notable bibliographer, Edward Petherick,[8] and the *Australian Catalogue* (1911), compiled by A.B. Foxcroft, then on the staff of the Public Library of Victoria.[9] There were also the unpublished catalogues of the major libraries, particularly those of the Mitchell Library, Commonwealth Parliamentary/National Library and the Public Library of Victoria. However, there was only one copy of each of these.

Information for the book trade was through the *Australian Stationer and Fancy Goods Journal*,[10] and its off-shoot, *All about Books*, published by D.W. Thorpe.[11] Both were geared to books emanating from England, although attention was given to local publications. If one knew the author or title of a book by an Australian author published in England, then the publication details could be found in the *English Catalogue of Books* and the various British trade publications such as *The Bookseller*.[12]

This was hardly bibliographic control. The first steps towards this came in 1937 with the publication of the *Annual Catalogue of Australian Publications* by the Commonwealth National Library.[13] Although not comprehensive, it provided an author listing of 658 titles published during the previous year and was the forerunner of the *Australian National Bibliography (ANB)*. At the time of the first issue of the *Annual Catalogue*, E. Morris Miller, Librarian and Vice-Chancellor of the University of Tasmania, and the book collector and judge, John (later Sir John) Ferguson, were putting the finishing touches to their own outstanding works of individual and dedicated scholarship.[14] 1940 saw the publication of Morris Miller's two-volume bibliography of Australian literature,[15] and in 1941 the first volume of Ferguson's *Bibliography of Australia* was published by Angus and Robertson.[16] In this Ferguson attempted to list every printed item ever issued relating to Australia between 1784 and 1830. A further six volumes were to follow, the last published posthumously in 1969. Although the scale was modified as the project progressed, his bibliography of Australian publications to 1900 contains over 19,000 entries and is still the standard reference for details on nineteenth-century Australiana.

It is now considered that by 1951 the *Annual Catalogue of Publications* provided an adequate bibliographic record of Australian publications.[17] Issue number 16 contained details on 2322 books published during that year. The volume covering 1952 also included a cumulation of the new monthly listing of government publications.[18] This listed government initiated publications arranged by issuing body within each state. *The Australian Stationery and Fancy Goods Journal* was now *Ideas*, and in 1956 its publisher, D.W. Thorpe, issued the first *Australian Books in Print*.[19] This was to become the standard reference to Australian books for the book trade. The first issue was fifty-two pages in length; the twenty-eighth edition of 1990 totals almost 1000 pages. 1956 also saw the publication of the revised edition of Morris Miller's *Australian Literature*.[20]

The third period of progress towards national bibliographic control ends roughly in the late 1960s, following the publication of the catalogue of the Mitchell Library and the final volume of Ferguson's bibliography.[21] Librarians, researchers and collectors now had a very good record of what was published before 1900, what books about or relating to Australia published before 1968 were held by a particular library which aimed to collect comprehensively in the field, what books were being published each year, and what titles were available for purchase regardless of their year of publication. There were also separate guides to government publications and a union list of newspaper holdings.[22]

In October 1969 the National Library of Australia assumed responsibility for the allocation of International Standard Book Numbers (ISBNs) in Australia, and in 1972 the *Australian National Bibliography* was published for the first time in a classified sequence.[23] This allowed for a subject as well as the traditional author/title approach. In 1974 the first *National Union Catalogue of Monographs (NUCOM)* was released on microfilm.[24] This was a copy of an alphabetical card index held in the National Library of the holdings of Australian books in major libraries. During this period the National Library also issued the second and substantially revised *Serials in Australian Libraries: Social Sciences and Humanities (SALSSH)*, which replaced an interim list published in 1963.[25] A revised edition of *Scientific Serials in Australian Libraries* also appeared during this period.[26] *SALSSH* was complemented by Lurline Stuart's detailed bibliographical guide to literary and semi-literary periodicals published in Australia in the nineteenth century and Alfred Pong's *Checklist of Nineteenth Century Australian Periodicals*.[27] Contemporary periodicals and their availability were listed in Thorpe's *Australian Serials in Print,* which replaced the National Library's defunct *Current Australian Serials*, published from 1964 to 1975.[28]

The final period in the progress towards national bibliographic control is associated with the development of computer technology and begins in 1983 with the establishment by the National Library of the Australian Bibliographic Network.[29] This was a cooperative national project, the first step towards a national online catalogue. Bibliographic records are added to the database primarily by the National Library but also by participating libraries which include all the state libraries and the major research libraries. As an online catalogue it is also available for consultation in all the participating libraries.

In 1986 the National Library produced addenda to the early Ferguson volumes and, as part of its contribution to the Bicentenary celebrations of European settlement in Australia, published *Australian National Bibliography, 1901-1950*.[30] This attempts to bridge what was known as the 'Ferguson gap', namely the period from the cut-off date for Ferguson (1900) and the period (1951 onwards) when the coverage in *ANB* is considered to be adequate. Although obviously not complete,

ANB, 1901-1950 lists over 49,000 items, all of which can also be read online via the Australian Bibliographic Network.

These sophisticated developments were matched, although to a much lesser extent, in the publications designed to service the book trade. D.W. Thorpe still dominates the field here. *Australian Books in Print* is now available in microfiche as well as in book form. It also has a companion volume in *Australian Books in Print by Subject*, which lists available Australian books under seventy-seven subject headings.[31] Thorpe also publishes a *Weekly Book Newsletter* and a regularly updated *Book Trade Fax Directory*. The firm is also investigating making these services available online via a CD-ROM disk through its AusBib database.

Librarians and booksellers now have through the various databases and publications emanating from both public and private sectors detailed bibliographical information on what is being published and what is available for acquisition. To date, the public sector (through the National Library) has concentrated on the bibliographical record of Australian publications, while the private sector (almost entirely through D.W. Thorpe) has concentrated on providing information on the distribution and availability of those publications. These sources are supported by a mass of publishers' catalogues, advertising and promotional material. The use of fliers in targeted journals is now also an accepted form of advertising by publishers.

There is still work to be done before full bibliographical control of the country's publishing output is obtained. There are considerable gaps in the record of retrospective material, especially creative literature;[32] a new edition of *Newspapers in Australian Libraries* is long overdue; and a bibliography of twentieth-century periodicals to complement the Stuart and Pong checklists would be a welcome addition to any reference collection.

Having established what is available and who has published a particular title, how does the acquisitions librarian or individual purchase a desired item? The former has two options, the latter only one. The acquisitions librarian can order the required item from an established bookshop with a reputation for mail order business. School libraries often work in this manner, using an active local bookseller. Libraries also regularly buy direct from small publishers who sell via leaflet mail rather than through a distributor or the retail trade. This is becoming increasingly more common with desktop preparation and publication.

Public and larger libraries are more often likely to use a library supplier to acquire their stock rather than buy directly from the trade. In Australia these library suppliers were established in the 1930s to supply books to the many commercial circulating or subscription libraries that flourished from 1920 to 1970.[33] They now deal with public, state and university libraries. The biggest in Australia is James Bennett Library Services in New South Wales.[34] Founded in 1958 by its namesake, the firm was responsible for pioneering the blanket Australiana order system now used by almost all major state and university libraries throughout the country. Other established suppliers include the Victorian family firm of B.H. Walshe and Sons founded in 1938, Hills and DA Books and Journals.[35] Some suppliers specialize, such as the booksellers Linehan and Shrimpton in Melbourne who handle children's books and educational texts.

The library suppliers operate on smaller margins than the retail trade. Although their overheads in relation to stock and equipment may be high, no shop front is required, and their market is more predictable. Libraries will be sent slips with appropriate bibliographic details as a basis for ordering, others may use a blanket order system to buy everything via a supplier in certain fields or areas within a specified price range. The advantages to libraries in using a supplier are in the economies of scale. The supplier can also follow up problem orders and generally act as a link between the publisher and the library market.

The individual book buyer has no such 'support' group. Popular titles are sure to be available at the local branch of a chain like Angus and Robertson/Bookworld, retail stores with a book section such as Myer Melbourne, and possibly on sale at newsagents or even in all-purpose stores such as K-Marts. For specialist titles and those published by small publishers, individual book buyers must rely on their own knowledge and the goodwill and expertise of their local bookseller.

The acquisition of retrospective material is particularly important in collecting Australian books. Given patience and a little work, most (if not all) out-of-print titles can be purchased. Australia has a flourishing antiquarian and secondhand book trade. A recent directory listed over 190 such businesses, all of which deal with retrospective material.[36] The difference between the two aspects of the trade is not always clear. An antiquarian bookseller is one who deals in out-of-print, valuable and sought after books, often specializing in particular subjects or areas, and has usually been in the trade for a number of years. A secondhand dealer will have as many in-print titles as out-of-print ones in stock, and a large proportion of these will be paperbacks sold at less than their original published price. They also rely more on passing trade and are less likely to issue catalogues.

Both categories of dealers are listed together in the business sections of telephone directories, and a 'phone call to a local dealer should establish the scarcity of a particular title and its approximate cost. Librarians and collectors who regularly buy secondhand books will soon gain a knowledge of the local trade and make dealers aware of their wants. They may also receive catalogues. These are usually sent free and range from simple lists of books with prices to sophisticated scholarly descriptions of rare items in a particular subject area. Those of Serendipity Booksellers in Perth, Burge-Lopez and Craft in Sydney are examples of the former; those of Peter Arnold and Kenneth Hince in Melbourne and James Dally in Adelaide are examples of the latter variety. All can be used to advantage. Most dealers are happy to search for particular titles or at least to record customers' requests for scarce titles. When they see or acquire a wanted title, they then offer it to the particular customer. This may take time, but most books turn up eventually. There is usually no cost for the search service nor any obligation to buy a quoted title; any astute librarian will have desiderata listed with several booksellers.

Scarce and valuable items are often sold at auction. Sotheby's in Melbourne, Lawson's in Sydney and Kenneth Hince (Book Auctions) in Melbourne hold regular sales of Australian books. At these sales caveat emptor applies, and potential buyers should consider using a dealer to bid on their behalf. For a charge, usually 10 per cent of the purchase price, the buyer gains access to the professional knowledge of the dealer, who will examine material and recommend on its approximate realization figure. Also, by acting as your agent, they are out of the market themselves for the title in question. Almost all secondhand dealers will bid for people at auctions. It would be advisable, however, to use one of the members of the Australia and New Zealand Association of Antiquarian Booksellers. This association was formed in 1977 'to promote the standing, welfare and growth of the local antiquarian booktrade.' It now has over thirty members.[37]

Whether using a dealer at auction or buying scarce and valuable material from them, librarians and collectors should familiarize themselves with the terminology of the trade, some of which they will have picked up, or at least noticed, in the various booksellers' catalogues. John Carter's *ABC for Book Collectors* is an informative and entertaining read as well as a useful ready reference.[38] Those requiring detailed information on early Australian imprints can do no better than consult Jonathan Wantrup's learned *Australian Rare Books, 1788-1900*.[39] Besides various descriptive chapters, including one on 'Anatomy for Bookcollectors', Wantrup gives the full bibliographical details on 265 desirable items of Australiana. Desirable they may be, but many are so scarce as to be virtually unobtainable, and the rest will be above most libraries' and collectors' budgets. A guide to the value of some of the books described by Wantrup can be found in the biennial *Australian Book Auction Records*.[40] This gives the details of individual titles sold for over $50 at major book auctions held over the previous two years. Although somewhat out-of-date, Brian Howes' two-volume *Guide to Fine and Rare Australasian Books* provides a guide to books offered for sale from 1982 to 1987 by dealers through their catalogues.[41]

Because of their scarcity and value, collectors and institutions may have to be satisfied with facsimile or reprints of rare Australiana. The Libraries Board of South Australia in the 1960s and early 1970s published over 200 facsimiles of early Australian titles, mainly accounts of voyages and land exploration and descriptions of early settlements. These are now sought after themselves by some collectors. A checklist of these facsimiles is about to be published,[42] and their desirability as collectables is covered in *Spalding's Collecting Australian Books*.[43]

Many other Australian publishers have issued series of facsimiles or edited reprints. There are a few booksellers such as the Library of Australian History, which specializes in this type of material.[44] In addition, several major libraries have microfilmed or microfiched scarce and valuable newspapers and genealogical sources such as directories and electoral rolls. The State Library of Victoria has, for example, an extensive filming programme and currently offers over 480 Victorian and Australian newspapers on microfilm for sale, plus numerous sets of genealogical-related microfiche.[45] The reissuing of scarce literary texts in recent years has resulted in the 'discovery' of certain authors and the reassessment of others, and provided texts for teaching and research purposes. A useful listing of these reprints can be found in *ANCLIP: Australian Nineteenth Century Literature in Print*.[46]

There are several guides to the best Australian books or the most suitable for establishing or developing an Australian collection. The first is the Australian volume in the Clio World Bibliographical Series.[47] Compiled by Indulis Kepars of the National Library of Australia, it lists 964 books about Australia in some forty-two subject areas. Kepars also gives a brief description of the contents of each title. The books listed in *Australia* may be in- or out-of-print. This is the same for the more ambitious volume, *Australia: A Guide to Sources*.[48] One of the reference volumes in the bicentennial series, Australians: An Historical

Library, this lists over 4000 titles in approximately sixty subject areas grouped under the broad areas of general reference works and statistics, environment, Aborigines, general history, European discovery and colonization, politics, the economy, society and culture. Each citation includes a brief assessment of the book and its virtues, and the various subject listings are preceded by an essay which attempts to give an overview of the literature on the subject in question.

The above are complemented by the National Library's *Australian Books: A Select List*.[49] The issue for 1989 lists approximately 1400 books in print in some thirty-one subject areas. However, no assessment or description of the individual titles listed is given. The proposed *Australia: A Readers Guide*, being prepared by the National Centre for Australian Studies (NCAS) at Monash University, will attempt to evaluate an estimated 2500 titles, both in- and out-of-print, in a subject guide to the basic and important books about Australia. When finished in 1992, the guide, as well as being a valuable reference for students and those undertaking or interested in Australian studies, will also serve as a selection tool for libraries, especially those attached to institutions overseas offering Australian studies, in developing their collections. In addition, it will suggest relevant gaps in the literature about Australia and, it is hoped, encourage publishers to commission books in these areas and to reissue basic titles that are currently unavailable.

The various reviewing media in Australia can be used by librarians and book buyers in general to assist their own evaluation of new books. The weekend issues of the main dailies all carry book reviews, and specialist journals devote a section to reviewing. There is also the *Australian Book Review*.[50] Published monthly by the National Book Council, it attempts to cover a wide range of new Australian books. Since the Libraries Board of South Australia ceased publishing its quarterly book review index in 1981,[51] there has been no accessible or systematic guide to reviews of Australian books, and the lack of such an index is seen as a deficiency in Australian studies research.

The National Centre for Australian Studies decided to run a pilot project covering all reviews of Australian books that appeared in sixty-eight newspapers and journals over the period December 1989-January 1990. The printed index provides access by authors, titles, editors and reviewers.[52] The Centre is seeking support funding to continue the index, but, despite favourable comments and the inclusion of the pilot in the AUSTROM CD-ROM package produced by INFORMIT, financial assistance or other institutional commitment has not been forthcoming.[53]

In the more specialized but problematic area of fiction selection there are several guides to reviews. Helen Daniel's *Good Reading Guide* is a guide to recent Australian fiction arranged alphabetically by author with extracts from reviews of their various novels.[54] Over 650 works by 290 authors are referred to, and it is a useful reference for libraries wanting to know what contemporary Australian fiction they should purchase. The journal *Australian Literary Studies* includes book reviews in its annual bibliography of Australian literature,[55] and they are also indexed in the AUSTLIT database, compiled by the Library and the English Department at the Australian Defence Force Academy in Canberra.[56] This is available online in most major research libraries and is being considered for inclusion in the AUSTROM CD package referred to above. The above generally deal with recent Australian fiction. The *Allen and Unwin Good Reading Guide*, compiled by Robin Lucas, gives a brief summary of over 500 novels by some 150 Australian and New Zealand authors both past and present.[57] The arrangement is alphabetical by author with interspersed subject guides to novels in seventeen categories. Those dealing with more than one subject are cross referenced, and there are also author and title indexes.

Another useful publication for acquisitions librarians is *Guide to New Australian Books (GNAB)*, a joint initiative of the National Centre for Australian Studies and D.W. Thorpe.[58] *GNAB* is an annotated bimonthly bibliographic and descriptive guide to books about Australia or books by Australians, published both locally and overseas. The annotations are written by NCAS staff from an examination of the books themselves and are intended to be a guide to the contents of the book, its special features, potential audience and whether it is a new title, a revised edition or simply a reissue. The arrangement is alphabetical by title with author, illustrator and photographer indexes, and an overall subject index based on the subject descriptors given for each title. The text of *GNAB* is stored online, and the possibility of producing a yearly cumulation and/or special subject or author indexes is being investigated.

Australia is one of the few countries which was discovered after the invention of printing and whose history of English-speaking settlement occurs almost entirely in the machine age. Its publishing output is relatively small – its annual tally representing only about 6-8 per cent of the 100,000 titles published annually in all English-speaking countries[59] – and it has been possible for a few select libraries to collect this output comprehensively, many others selectively. Although there are some weaknesses in the bibliographic record of its output, coverage of relatively recent material is excellent. Through the various publications and databases of the National Library of Australia, librarians can find out what is being published. Using these and the various trade publications, they can find out about new and forthcoming titles and the necessary details for ordering. A network of library suppliers is available to assist with this, as are retail chains and owner operated bookshops. Various bibliographies, ranging from the all-embracing or individual subject or author listings, are available to provide information about gaps and retrospective material. An active trade is available to assist with the acquisition of retrospective material. In short, the necessary resources for collecting Australiana are available. The necessary finance is, however, a different matter.

Notes

1 Hans Guldberg in *Books: Who Reads Them? A Study of Borrowing and Buying in Australia.* Sydney: Australia Council, 1990, p. 201, gives an estimate of around 4000 based on a count of titles in *Australian Books in Print* (see Note 19). However, given the amount of desktop, small interest group, local history and genealogical publishing, the total Australian output would be around the 7000 mark.

2 For details, see *Australian Government Publications.* Canberra: Australian Government Publishing Service, quarterly microfiche. The estimate of 11,000 is based on the 1987 annual volume, the last one to be so published. See note 18 for full publishing details.

3 *Australian Periodicals in Print, 1990.* 8th ed. Melbourne: D.W. Thorpe, 1990 lists some 8740 different titles.

4 Figure extracted from Margaret Gee's *Media Guide. 35th edition, November 1990-March 1991.* Melbourne: Information Australia, 1990. The guide provides relevant details including personnel, advertising and subscription rates for newspapers, magazines, newsletters and the electronic media and is issued three times a year. It is also available on disk.

5 See National Library of Australia, *Collection Development Policy.* Canberra: National Library of Australia, 1990. Ch. 5, 'The Australian Collections'.

6 See, for example, *State Library of Victoria Selection Policy.* Melbourne: State Library of Victoria, 1986, Ch. 3, 'Victorian Imprints'; and State Library of New South Wales, *Collection Development Policy.* Sydney: State Library of New South Wales, 1990, pp. 12, 202-203.

7 Free Public Library, Sydney, *Australasian Bibliography... Part I. Catalogue of Books in the Free Public Library, Sydney. Relating to, or Published in Australasia... Part II. Books on the*

Colonies... Part III. Classified Subject and Title Catalogue of Books.... Sydney: Government Printer, 1893.

8 E.A. Petherick, *Catalogue of the York Gate Library Formed by Mr. S. William Silver. An Index to the Literature of Geography, Maritime and Inland Discovery, Commerce and Colonisation.* 2nd ed. London: John Murray, 1886. First published in 1882. The collection now forms part of the library of the Royal Geographic Society of South Australia housed in the State Library of South Australia. On Edward August Petherick (1847-1917), see *Australian Dictionary of Biography,* Vol. 5, pp. 438-439.

9 A.B. Foxcroft, *The Australian Catalogue: A Reference Index to the Books and Periodicals Published and Still Current in the Commonwealth of Australia.* Melbourne: Whitcombe and Tombs, 1911.

10 First published in 1921; the name was changed shortly afterwards to *The Booksellers, Stationers and Fancy Goods Journal,* later to *Ideas,* and later still to its current title, *The Australian Bookseller and Publisher.*

11 Published from 1928 to 1938, it simply reprinted articles that appeared in the parent journal. D.W. Thorpe is the book trade publications company, now the bibliographic/reference division of Butterworths Australia. It was founded by Dan Thorpe (1889-1976). See Joyce Nicholson, 'Dan Thorpe,' in *The Golden Age of Australian Bookselling: Fifty Years in the Trade.* Sydney: Abbey Press, 1981, pp. 209-220.

12 *The English Catalogue of Books.* Sanderstead, Surrey: The Publishers' Circular Ltd, 1801-1968; title varies; *The Bookseller.* London: Whitaker, 1858- ; title varies.

13 *Annual Catalogue of Australian Publications.* Nos 1-25. Canberra: Commonwealth National Library, 1937-1961.

14 On Edmund Morris Miller (1881-1964), see *Australian Dictionary of Biography,* Vol. 10, pp. 507-509; on Sir John Ferguson (1881-1969), see *An Exhibition in Honour of Sir John Ferguson...August 1965.* Canberra: National Library of Australia, 1965.

15 E. Morris Miller, *Australian Literature from Its Beginnings to 1935: A Descriptive and Bibliographical Survey...with Subsidiary Entries to 1938.* 2 vols. Melbourne: Melbourne University Press, 1940. Facsimile edition, Sydney: Sydney University Press, 1973.

16 John Alexander Ferguson, *Bibliography of Australia.* 7 vols. Sydney: Angus and Robertson, 1941-1969. Facsimile edition, Canberra: National Library of Australia, 1975.

17 1951: '...the beginning of accurate and comprehensive coverage...'. W.M. Horton, introduction to *Australian National Bibliography, 1901-1950*, Vol. 1 (see note 30).

18 *Australian Government Publications*, 1952- ; frequency varies: monthly 1952-1960 with annual cumulation in *Annual Catalogue of Publications*; separate annual publication from 1961 to 1987; from 1988 quarterly microfiche, with each issue being a full cumulation of all titles published since 1986 which have been added to the National Bibliographic Database maintained by the National Library of Australia.

19 *Australian Books in Print*. Melbourne: D.W. Thorpe, 1956- ; title varies.

20 E. Morris Miller and Frederick T. Macartney, *Australian Literature: A Bibliography to 1938... Extended to 1950*. Sydney: Angus and Robertson, 1956.

21 Mitchell Library, Public Library of New South Wales, *Dictionary Catalog of Printed Books*. 28 vols. Boston, Mass.: G.K. Hall, 1968; Ferguson's final volume was published in 1969; see note 16.

22 First published by the National Library in 1959-1960 as *Union List of Newspapers in Australian Libraries*, revised in 1967 with a third edition as *Newspapers in Australian Libraries: A Union List. Part 2. Australian Newspapers*, published in 1975.

23 Successor from 1961 to the *Annual Catalogue of Publications*.

24 Supplements covering holdings reported between 1975-1980 and 1981-1984 were also issued before *NUCOM* was replaced by the Australian Bibliographic Network (ABN); see note 29.

25 *Serials in Australian Libraries: Social Sciences and Humanities, a Union List*. 2nd ed. Canberra: National Library of Australia, 1974.

26 *Scientific Serials in Australian Libraries: A Union List*. 2nd ed. Melbourne: CSIRO, 1964-1974. The first edition was issued in 1959.

27 Lurline Stuart, *Nineteenth Century Australian Periodicals*. Sydney: Hale and Iremonger, 1979; Alfred Pong, *Checklist of Nineteenth Century Australian Periodicals*. Bundoora, Vic.: Borchardt Library, La Trobe University, 1985.

28 *Australian Serials in Print* (now *Australian Periodicals in Print*). Melbourne: D.W. Thorpe, 1981- .

29 For details, see *Guide to the National Union Catalogue of Australia*. Canberra: National Library of Australia, 1985 and *The Australian Bibliographic Network*. Canberra: National Library of Australia, 1985.

30 John Alexander Ferguson, *Bibliography of Australia. Addenda, 1784-1850* (Volumes 1-4). Canberra: National Library of

Australia, 1986; *Australian National Bibliography, 1901-1950*. 4 vols. Canberra: National Library of Australia, 1988.

31 *Australian Books in Print by Subject*. Melbourne: D.W. Thorpe, 1987- ; title varies.

32 A major initiative here is the Bibliography of Australian Literature Project (BALP), coordinated by the National Centre for Australian Studies at Monash University, which is aiming to list all Australian creative literature published in monograph form from 1788 to the end of 1990.

33 At their peak in the early 1940s there were over 500 of these circulating libraries in Sydney and around 400 in Melbourne. See John Arnold, 'Choose Your Author as You Would Choose a Friend: Circulating Libraries in Melbourne, 1930-1960,' *La Trobe Library Journal* 10, 40 (Spring 1987): 77-96.

34 See Alan Bundy, ed., *James Bennett: Supplier to the Nation's Libraries*. Adelaide: Auslib Press, 1988.

35 On B.H. Walshe and Sons, see 'Brothers,' *Good Weekend* (Melbourne *Age* supplement), 30 October 1986, pp. 6-7; on other suppliers, see, for example, their advertisements in *InCite: Newsletter of the Australian Library and Information Association*, 26 November 1990, p. 9, 10 December 1990, p. 15 and 11 March 1990, p. 10. Other suppliers also advertise regularly in this newsletter.

36 Brian Howes, *Antiquarian and Secondhand Book Dealers in Australia: A Directory*. 3rd ed. Angaston, SA: Magpie Books, 1990.

37 Information on the association supplied by Peter Arnold Antiquarian Booksellers, Melbourne.

38 John Carter, *ABC for Book Collectors*. 6th ed. updated by Nicholas Barker. London: Granada, 1980.

39 Jonathan Wantrup, *Australian Rare Books, 1788-1900*. Sydney: Hordern House, 1987.

40 Jill Burdon, ed., *Australian Book Auction Records*. N.S., 1983-1985- .

41 Brian Howes, *Guide to Fine and Rare Australasian Books*. 2 vols. Wagga Wagga, NSW: Brian Howes, 1986 and Angaston, SA: Magpie Books, 1991.

42 Barry Peade, *A Checklist of Facsimile Editions of the Libraries Board of South Australia*. Edited with an introduction by Valmai Hankel. Adelaide: Libraries Board of South Australia, 1991.

43 D.A. Spalding, *Collecting Australian Books: Notes for Beginners*. 2nd ed. Mawson, ACT: D.A. Spalding, 1982.

44 Library of Australian History, 17 Mitchell Street, North Sydney 2060.

45 Details from an in-house 'Newspapers on Microfilm' list dated January 1991 which is currently being reformatted for distribution by the Council of the State Library of Victoria. The genealogical material is available directly from the library (328 Swanston Street, Melbourne 3000) or through specialized booksellers such as Gould Books, PO Box 126, Gumeracha, SA 5233, or Macbeath Genealogical Books, PO Box 136, Hampton, Vic. 3188.

46 Victor Crittenden, ed., *ANCLIP: Australian Nineteenth Century Literature in Print*. Canberra: Mulini Press, 1989- .

47 I. Kepars, *Australia*. World Bibliographical Series, Vol. 46. Oxford: Clio Press, 1984.

48 D.H. Borchardt and Victor Crittenden, eds, *Australians: A Guide to Sources*. Sydney: Fairfax, Syme and Weldon Associates, 1987.

49 *Australian Books: A Select List of Recent Publications and Standard Works in Print*. (Supersedes *Select List of Representative Works Dealing with Australia, 1933-48*.) Canberra: National Library of Australia, 1949- .

50 *Australian Book Review*. N.S. Melbourne: National Book Council, 1978- .

51 *Index to Australian Book Reviews, 1965-1981*. Adelaide: Libraries Board of South Australia.

52 Elizabeth Morrison, ed., *Index to Reviews of Australian Books (IRAB): Pilot Index (December 1989-February 1990) and Project Report*. Clayton, Vic.: National Centre for Research and Development in Australian Studies, 1990.

53 A cooperative venture among several Australian database producers; for a description, see the pamphlet, *AUSTROM: Australian Social Science and Education Information on CD-ROM*. Melbourne: INFORMIT, RMIT Libraries, 1990.

54 Helen Daniel, ed., *The Good Reading Guide: 100 Critics Review Contemporary Australian Fiction*. Melbourne: McPhee Gribble Publishers, 1989.

55 *Australian Literary Studies*. St Lucia, Qld: Department of English, University of Queensland (publisher varies), 1963- ; published twice a year, with the May issue carrying the 'Annual Bibliography of Studies in Australian Literature'.

56 See Michael Denholm, 'Searching and Researching the Australian Literary Scene: The Why and How of AUSTLIT,' *Reference Australia* 6 (October 1990): 1-10.

57 Robin Lucas, ed., *Allen and Unwin Good Reading Guide*. Sydney: Allen and Unwin, 1990.

58 *Guide to New Australian Books,* 1, 1- . Melbourne: D.W. Thorpe in association with the National Centre for Australian Studies, October 1990- .

59 Figure quoted by Guldberg, *op. cit.,* p. 201.

10 Australian Book Supply and Australiana: A Battle against Closed Markets?

Carol Mills

Australian readers and libraries are a part of the greater English-speaking world. It is in this context, the consumption by Australian readers of foreign books, that acquisition difficulties for book buyers have arisen, not from seeking Australian-published titles for Australian consumption, which is largely a closed system. A range of market forces may render English-language foreign titles or editions unavailable from Australian book shops when they are in print in other countries. These same market forces give rise to book prices which are higher in Australia than their original price abroad would seem to warrant. Varying combinations of these forces have been a continuing factor in Australian bookselling history back into colonial times (before 1901). This paper presents an overview of the present situation, its origins, and factors for change which have failed to redirect the essential situation in over forty years.

> And in all of this time there has never been any doubt that the Australian reader, the Australian publisher, the Australian bookseller, get the crummy end of the deal. We have been viewed down the wrong end of the telescope as an enthusiastic, dimwitted, gullible mob. As a fat-cat market of surprising size considering our population. As a lovely colonial jewel in the imperial publishing crown.[1]

The speaker, Max Harris, has been a campaigner on Australian book trade issues for over forty years. Writer, bookseller, publisher and literary figure, what he was saying in 1973 remains essentially the same today because the major attitudes remain the same, however circumstances may have changed. Even the starchiest British publisher would have to admit that the Empire has been gone for the odd decade or so. Australians no longer have imperial allegiances of the moral sort when it comes to trade; nor any desire to commence others. We do have the disadvantage of having a relatively small population, and various foreign business houses purveying a range of commodities have tried to tell us what market is best for *us* (read *them*).

Our booksellers' attempts to purchase what we request, when we want it, at the right price, in a situation of equality with fellow English-speakers in other countries frequently have been thwarted, with arguments which of late have related to the protection of copyright. The Australian bookseller, librarian and reader do not seek freedom to purchase truly pirate editions, but simply to be free to purchase legally published editions available to other book buyers in the English-speaking world when they want them. This is not possible on the home market at present. We are offered the edition for which one publisher has secured the Australian rights (often as a part of a package together with other rights to other areas which do not sit well with the Australian book market) by virtue of provisions of the Federal Copyright Act which were drafted to combat literary piracy. Furthermore, we are offered it at a time chosen by the publisher's local representative, which may be months or occasionally years after reading about it in the reviewing media.

We have a situation in Australia where foreign books are made available to booksellers by one of several means, depending upon their publisher's presence in Australia. The publisher may have no representation in Australia, leaving the bookseller free to import; second, the publisher may engage an agent or subsidiary to carry a limited stock in Australia on an 'open' market basis, still leaving the bookseller to go his own way in his choice of a supplier; or, third, and in terms of sales in the majority of cases, the publisher's agent or subsidiary may operate a 'closed' market warehouse from which the Australian bookseller is required to order his stock, even if the publisher must then import it for him. This last arrangement at its most efficient is closely controlled. Direct attempts to go past it to the principal will result in the return of the orders. This is the situation which the Australian book trade knows as the closed market system. At this point the foreign bookseller or jobber becomes a significant factor in the acquisitions process.

The essential infrastructure which permits the operation of the closed market system in Australia has not always been as it is at present. Going back to late colonial times it was a de facto closed market brought about by astute stocking by local booksellers, the larger of whom had agencies for major UK publishers. Time was on the bookseller's side in holding his market if his stock was good – as it frequently was. Before the advent of airmail, to read a notice or review in Australia, order the book in the UK and wait for it to arrive took over nine months. Good Australian booksellers relied upon efforts on their behalf by publishers in London with whom they had working relationships, by professional buyers acting under instructions, or, in a few notable cases, upon buyers employed in London by large Australian booksellers to seek new stock and get it on to the boat in the shortest possible time from publication. Only very wealthy private book purchasers or the occasional library had agents of their own in London. As the 'colonial' price at this time was frequently close to or identical with the original price, the difficulty which we now experience of inequitable pricing was not at issue, meaning that the small book buyer was well served by the local book trade. Indeed, the value of Australian currency remained identical with that of the UK until the 1930s. One of these buyers was E.A. Petherick, London buyer for George Robertson, Melbourne bookseller. A book collector and bibliographer, Petherick while in London built the collection which bears his name and is now in the National Library of Australia.

The present inability of the bookseller to do his own importing is governed by provisions in the Federal Copyright Act, one of whose real functions was to support international copyright agreements to which Australia is signatory. These provisions were invoked by publishers after the 1974 US Attorney-General's Anti-Trust Suit against twenty-one US publishers over the way in which British and US publishers were operating in agreed mutually exclusive publishing territories. These territories were known in the trade as 'traditional markets', and evolved as the Australian market grew and publishers' Australian sales became significant. Canada, another example, had no say in the matter of becoming a part of the US traditional market; New Zealand and Australia became a part of Britain's. To sell the Australian rights on their own was and is rare, and is largely restricted to domestic editions of international-selling Australian authors.

The 'big two' left each other's markets alone, and, by agreement, publishers contracted authors for their traditional segment of the market, frequently offering the balance of the rights to a transatlantic publisher with whom a regular working relationship existed. This came to an end after the Anti-Trust Suit, whose consent decree was hailed by many in Australia as the end of an era. Tempers were high in Australia, and it was in the climate of the approaching consent decree that Max Harris made his radio broadcast which was quoted from above. Things did not change. Instead foreign publishers enlisted the import provisions of the Copyright Act to maintain a near-identical situation. Publishers now structured contracts so that authors were advised of how their rights would be apportioned. The import clauses of the Copyright Act were invoked to obstruct the importation of alternative editions for resale. Closed markets were back within the year! All but the most saleable authors continue to be required to allocate copyright regionally as a part of their contract.

Libraries, like private individuals, may import for themselves, and do. Because they do not import for resale they are exempt. This is quite important, as under a closed market situation prices in Australia for foreign books are frequently inflated beyond the real costs of importing, handling and storage for the Australian market, and the books may not be available when wanted. Apart from big-selling titles such as best-sellers, where prices may be pegged at a level closer to a direct conversion of the original published price, it is not unusual for the price of an imported book via the local warehouse to retail at a significant margin above a direct currency conversion of the original retail price.

In this situation, libraries which are in a position to import do so, regardless of what has been, until recently, a consequent long order lead time; which in turn creates larger order banks than are the experience of the northern hemisphere acquisitions librarian. Recent changes, the introduction of online ordering direct to suppliers abroad, coupled with air-freight consignment of books by suppliers into Australian, including rapid Customs clearance by the library supplier for the library, have brought about a marked improvement. These two factors together mean that order lead time can now be as little as three weeks – a happy contrast to the fourteen-plus weeks which previously prevailed for all orders, and which still applies to orders which cannot be sent to large dealers geared to their Australian customers.

Because of the need for astute management of acquisitions in a variety of foreign currencies, coupled with the management skills associated with controlling large order banks, the level of skill of Australian acquisitions librarians is excellent. These larger order banks have been a factor, incidentally, of which it has been difficult to persuade foreign computer companies; they have little experience of it, their own research says otherwise, and within limits advising a potential client to purchase a larger computer in order to be able to carry an acquisitions file may make or break a sale. This goes some way to explaining the relatively slow adoption of automated acquisitions in Australia; efficient manual files and the uneven experience of some libraries which have introduced acquisitions systems with response times across the system as a whole when acquisitions order banks grow have had a disincentive effect.

In recent years the previously somewhat uninterested US publishers, with their larger domestic market and their less pressing concern with book exports, have become restive at the traditional market situation. Those of the UK, for whom exports are closer to being a matter of economic survival, have tried to protect their markets. The US publishing industry began to generate an increasing number of unique titles which were of interest to Australian readers, but which would not be sold in Australia if the transatlantic publisher was indifferent to publishing them because of relatively small sales potential in his area. Some US books never make it into print in the UK, even if the rights to do so have been sold, making some US books hard to get from Australian booksellers.

When the US rights are not sold off, books published in North America alone constitute a different situation. These are not governed by traditional market territories, giving rise to a desire as US publishers have become more export-minded that the markets for these books be expanded. These titles constituted the vanguard of the move of US publishers into the Australian market in direct competition with the publishers of the UK for titles for which they both hold rights.

Finally, there is a third group: books in English originating from a number of major European publishers, insignificant in market size, but significant in their scholarship and in the increases in price which are demanded for them in Australia in relation to their original prices. Local warehouses have recently attempted to control the distribution of these by entering into agreements with their publishers which are enforced by invoking various provisions of the Federal Trade Practices Act – in some cases with more success against libraries and private buyers who try to 'buy around' abroad than has been the case with the utilization of the Copyright Act for similar purposes. It is expected that this last practice will come under the attention of the Trade Practices Commission shortly. This practice is spreading, and is now employed by a number of UK and US, as well as European, publishers.

In June 1989 the Federal Attorney-General announced that an enquiry would be held by the Prices Surveillance Authority into the price of books in Australia. One of the principal functions of this enquiry would be to examine the ramifications of the so-called import clauses of the Copyright Act, in order to make recommendations to the Federal Government regarding the adequacy of that legislation.

This was by no means the first government enquiry into elements of the book trade. The Australian book trade has been plagued with enquiries which have had no positive outcome, as foreign publishers rebuilt the infrastructure after each enquiry regardless of the recommendations made. At a level limited by circumstances, the best friends of the truly Australian publishing industry have been disasters. In the 1914-1918 war, and again in 1939-1945, small, but relatively strong, independent, Australian publishing grew, even in the face of manpower and paper shortages, fostered by shipping priorities to Australia which limited the import of books. During the Great Depression import restrictions associated with currency controls performed the same service. Active publishing of Australian titles took place, and even foreign titles were published here for the local market.

Almost as if this strength had been recognized, in 1945-1946, as one of the earliest government efforts directed towards post-war reconstruction, the Federal Tariff Board conducted an enquiry into the Australian publishing industry. A follow-up to their enquiry of 1930, this was the first of the major enquiries which has shaped today's Australian book market. The issue was the obverse of that of today: the fear of a flood of cheap British books following the loss of the controls kept in place by war, and the damage which this would do to any attempt to develop an Australian publishing industry. Among its conclusions was the statement: 'High-grade Australian work can and does find a ready market, not only in Australia but also in other parts of the world.'[2] This was an idealistic and uninformed opinion, as Australian publishing at the time was by no means strong enough to sustain its viability, or even keep its authors at home in the face of the larger foreign publishers' activities.

During the 1950s the Statement of Terms, a document drawn up between the Australian Book Publishers' Association, the Publishers' Association (UK) and the Australian Booksellers' Association came into use. By the 1960s most foreign publishers operating in Australia had 'closed the market', thus centring book orders on their warehouses. The Statement was a direct lineal descendant of the British Net Book Agreement, established by Frederic Macmillan in 1890, which provided for sanctions for booksellers who did not adhere to its terms.

The statement had the effect of controlling the price at which a bookseller could purchase, and hence of governing the retail price. The Statement of Terms' hold was not universal once library suppliers began to emerge in Australia in the 1950s, as the structure of their business was such that they were able to ignore it. It died in 1972 when the Federal Trade Practices Tribunal disallowed it from exemption under the then Restrictive Trade Practices Act. At this stage a non-enforceable recommended retail price ('rrp') came into being. This still operates. The retail price set by the Australian warehouser is the basis on which the price to the bookseller is calculated, not the original trade price in the country of origin. For financial reasons it is rare to find Australian booksellers who are able to undercut this.

In 1978 the Secretary of the Industries Assistance Commission (successor to the old Tariff Board) announced yet another enquiry into the Publishing Industry. Its report was published in 1979. As an agent for change it was a non-event, doing little more than provide a benchmark by reporting on the situation; a situation which remains in essence largely as we know it today.

In 1986 the Federal Copyright Law Review Committee announced an enquiry into the import clauses of the Copyright Act (1968). Its report made a number of recommendations, none of which has been implemented, although it provided the dubious reassurance that the situation still remained unchanged. Under the import clauses it is perfectly legal for a book to be imported, provided that it is not for resale. This means that libraries are exempt under the Act, and may do what they please. However satisfactory this is, it is not wholly so. To import a large proportion of library stock from abroad lengthens the line of supply, creating its own problems.

Libraries commenced to order abroad as a part of their routine procedures in the late 1950s for three major reasons: better budgets, more assured availability abroad and price. The larger book-buying budgets which libraries began to receive about that time gave them the ability to arrange their operations on a larger scale which made this economic. It was also in the late 1950s that professional Australian library suppliers began to emerge, some of whom employed foreign-based 'jobbers' to 'buy around' on their behalf, and who entered into special pricing arrangements with local publishers' warehouses which were designed by publishers to keep the market onshore.

The benefits of special pricing arrangements were and are inconsistent. Many publishers claim to carry a near-representative stock in the warehouses of their Australian subsidiaries or agents, but this is not always the case, particularly with less popular titles, and levels of stock of a less-commercial title are likely to be unreliable for meeting the demands of immediate supply. The publisher's having to import the book places an additional intermediary into the ordering chain, causing further delay. There is the problem, too, of local release dates. The fact that a book has been publisher abroad does not mean that it is necessarily available at the same time in Australia. There is also the problem that because an author signs a contract which assigns the 'rights' to publish other editions does not mean that these will be published, thus potentially excluding the book from the Australian retail trade.

To import has its attractions. The 'rrp', according to the Prices Surveillance Authority, can be 30 per cent or more above the price in the country of origin, converted using current bank exchange rates. As many or most libraries are directly or indirectly publicly funded, most would prefer to order locally, given the costing structure to do so, but budgets are finite, and to do so is to buy fewer books.

Some booksellers have on occasion sought to purchase stock 'illegally' from abroad, usually for reasons of non-availability in Australia. A classic case in the 1970s was the action of a bookseller who wanted to sell *Jonathon Livingston, Seagull.* Although the British rights had been sold, there was for a time no British edition available, and hence no edition which could be sold in Australia legally. This was exacerbated when the book was published in the UK by delays in publishing it in Australia. The stated penalty for such action is seizure of stock and litigation by the aggrieved party. This did occur. The situation for booksellers in such cases has not been fully defined because very few copyright complaints have been taken to the courts as test cases; most booksellers are unable to afford the financial risks which litigation may entail, or the risks to their livelihood of a possible publisher blacklisting.

Booksellers have been further discouraged from attempts to contest the situation in the past few years since prices of more popular titles where sales are likely to be higher may be offered to them at something closer to the original trade price. This may suit the main street retailer, but as it is a practice which is linked to a relatively brief marketing campaign, supply at any given time beyond that is not reliable. For management reasons it is not economic to divert portions of the library acquisitions workflow to utilize such prices.

The conclusions of the Prices Surveillance Authority (PSA) are still subject to discussion and legislation by Parliament, and hence have not had any particular effect. In brief, they are as follows: 'The importation provisions of the *Copyright Act 1968* have been used by publishers to exercise international price discrimination, which has resulted in excessively high prices for books in Australia.'[3] The PSA's *Interim Report* states that: 'As an overwhelming net importer of books, Australia suffers a net loss from the operation of these [import] provisions.'[4]

Delays in publication of foreign titles in Australia are to be discouraged, with a legal definition of a 'reasonable time' within which these books must be published in Australia, or be supplied on back orders, being recommended. A Bill to amend the Copyright Act of 1968 has since been drafted for the consideration of the Federal Parliament. The revised s.44A(1) of the Act reads: 'The copyright in a work first published in a foreign country...is not infringed by a person who, without the licence of the owner of the copyright, imports a noninfringing book into Australia....' The sole classes of infringing books which it is proposed to retain are pirate editions and books by Australian authors for which there is a separate Australian copyright.

Since the authority's reports were released, public debate has been energetic. The interim report recommended allowing the Australian book market to become totally open, with market forces determining future sources of supply. Not surprisingly, the Australian Book Publishers' Association, many of whose influential members are foreign publishers' subsidiaries, was extremely vocal. Present arrangements provide publishers, at the least, with a market control which assists in the conduct of their business. This outcry was particularly vocal from the representatives of British publishers, although for the first time American publishers, goaded no doubt by their by now significant Australian sales, were more active than heretofore.

The more surprising activity came from a fully Australian organization, the Australian Society of Authors (ASA). Under Australian law there is no requirement to publish, print, or register copyright locally in order to secure copyright. Spearheaded by a number of well-known Society members with international sales such as Peter Carey and Thomas Keneally, the ASA launched a vociferous, successful, high-profile campaign against the recommendations of the draft report. Their fear was of foreign remainders of their works competing locally with full-price Australian editions, denying them royalties. Their campaign was successful, as has been stated. They have successfully impeded future imports on a freer basis of the greater portion of the books which library readers require.

The authors launched a wholesale campaign against the report, and the public at large, not being fully informed, was in sympathy. For a while it appeared as if the wider problem of the prices of books which Australians want to read was in jeopardy. Their principal opponent was a large Sydney bookseller, while the publishers used the controversy which they caused to promote their case. It is thanks largely to the authors' response that the draft report was modified from a position of total freedom to the situation outlined above.

In any case, by modifying its report, it seems that the Authority has opened the loophole of the next generation. Revisions to the appropriate clauses of the Copyright Act have been drafted for legislative consideration. The draft legislation provides guidelines as to 'reasonable time', but not on the size of edition which is required to secure for the publisher a continuing hold on the Australian market.

Consequently, one can see potential for token gestures designed to hold the Australian market open to the publisher.

As is the case with publications in and about other countries, much Australiana is locally published, and as such is largely outside world publishing market forces. In world terms Australian publishers are small, and their potential markets abroad are not usually significant. For the foreign librarian, obtaining any but commercially published Australian titles is a problem of its own, both as regards their identification and finding a suitable supplier. The principal field in which world market forces operate on Australiana is literature or fiction, and to a lesser extent in fields such as anthropology. The rare title which transcends this, such as Robert Hughes' *The Fatal Shore,* is the exception rather than the rule, as Australia publishes between 10,000 and 15,000 titles each year, most with sales of under 1000 copies.

With the rise of interest in Australian studies in universities and colleges around the world, getting those Australian titles which are not commercially published has its own problems for their libraries. There is no absolute means by which a library can choose an Australian supplier to meet its acquisitions requirements. Like its publishing world, the Australian world of bookselling in the area of new titles is small. It has been in a state of change in recent years, thanks to changes of ownership, mergers, etc. Skilful library suppliers and booksellers exist, but it is probably most appropriate that a library wishing to go into this area contact a colleague in Australia and seek current advice at the time of wishing to make orders.

Notes

1 Max Harris, Australian Broadcasting Commission 'Guest of Honour' script, 28 January 1973.

2 *Tariff Board's Report on Publishing Industry, 7th November, 1946*. Canberra: Government Printer, 1947, p. 43.

3 Prices Surveillance Authority, *Inquiry into Book Prices: Final Report.* Report No. 25. Canberra: Prices Surveillance Authority, 1989, p. 39.

4 Prices Surveillance Authority, *Inquiry into Book Prices: Interim Report.* Report No. 24. Canberra: Prices Surveillance Authority, 1989, p. 70.

Part 4. Australiana Collections: Experiences from Three Countries

11 The Acquisition of Australiana in the National Library of Australia

Richard Stone

The National Library of Australia has developed a major collection of Australian printed and microform materials. Means of acquisitions have included legal deposit, formed collections and other deposit arrangements for government publications. In the context of a Distributed National Collection the Library is redefining its Australiana collection development policies. This involves scrutiny of all publishing genres and the concept of collecting comprehensively. There is close consultation with the state libraries, which are also redefining their aims and achievable goals.

'Of the World, and of All Time'

The Australiana collections of the National Library of Australia have existed and developed for eighty-nine years. They have evolved as the institution itself has evolved through the twentieth century. Along with the Federal Parliament, the Library will be celebrating its centenary in 2001. There are no other major national collecting institutions in Canberra, which will be celebrating a similar anniversary.

For the first sixty years of its existence, the fortunes and development of the National Library were inextricably bound with the fortunes and development of the Federal Parliament and the federal capital. One of the first moves of the first Prime Minister, Sir Edmund Barton, was to establish a Library Committee which considered the information services necessary for the operation of the new Federal Parliament. It also took on a visionary role: 'The Library Committee is keeping before it the ideal of building up...a great Public Library on the lines of the world-famed Library of Congress at Washington; such a library, indeed, as shall be worthy of the Australian Nation; the home of the literature, not of a State, or of a period but of the world, and of all time.' This statement, full of the heightened idealism of the time, provides what can be seen in today's management environment as the first mission statement for a national library in Australia.

Ninety Years On

As the end of the century approaches, the National Library has been conducting a soul-searching exercise on its role and purpose. This long process, the first for the institution on such a scale, resulted in the publication of a strategic plan for 1900-1995.[1] This document includes a mission statement reflecting the changed nature of the Library's role and its collections.

In the intervening years the commitment to the collecting of Australiana has remained a constant factor in spite of changing fortunes and the vagaries of history. The collecting of Australiana has encompassed many materials: printed, microforms, original manuscripts, pictorial works, such as photographs, drawings, oil paintings, lithographs and posters, oral history tapes, music scores, maps, sound recordings and films. All have been collected for their relevance to Australia and the Australian experience. Within the confines of this paper the discussion of collecting Australiana in the National Library will be limited to printed and microform materials.

'A Comprehensive Collection'

With the establishment of the National Library of Australia as a separate entity in 1960 the collecting of Australiana received unequivocal affirmation: '...to maintain and develop a national collection of library material, including a comprehensive collection of library material relating to Australia and the Australian people....'[2] It is this policy statement which has been at the heart of developing the Australiana collections of the National Library in the last thirty years. It is, in fact, one which has caused considerable debate both within the Library and in the Australian library community as a whole. Most debate has centred on the definition and redefinition of what is meant by 'comprehensive'. For many years the statement was taken at face value and accepted as the achievable standard. However, in recent years structured collection development terminology has been increasingly applied until the recent adoption of RLG Conspectus by the National Library. Serious questioning is taking place which raises doubts as to whether the Library's Australiana collection is truly comprehensive in all aspects of Australian publishing, and whether, in fact, it ever can be.

Parallel with these considerations, the concept of a Distributed National Collection has emerged as a dominant focus in recent years. It was one which was accorded close scrutiny at the Australian Libraries Summit in 1988. One of the Summit's many resolutions was to foster the publication of collection development policies for major collecting institutions such as the National Library and state libraries.[3] The National Library had already undertaken a trail-blazing effort with the publication of its own *Selection Policy* in 1982.[4] It is significant that by the end of 1990 all state libraries except one had published collection development policies, and the National Library had issued a new document replacing the 1982 *Selection Policy*.[5]

The final effects of the publication of these policies and the ensuing debate and consultation have yet to be seen. It is reasonable to predict, however, that the degree of cooperation between the state libraries and National Library in collecting printed and non-print Australiana will increase further. All institutions have had to face trends of declining resources. Realistic assessments of what is achievable in terms of claiming deposit material and storage of material are being made by all libraries. In addition, the geographic spread of a large continent places practical limits on the possible collecting reach of any one library.

Building a Collection of Australiana

All these factors are impinging on the collection of Australiana by the National Library. It is a process which is building on the historical evolution of the National Library's collecting of Australiana. That evolution possesses many threads and strands. Is it an historical accident or the result of inspired planning that two of the major means of national collection development occurred within twelve months of each other? In 1911 the Library acquired the Petherick collection. In 1912 the Copyright Act with its provisions for the legal deposit of publications was passed by Parliament. The national library collection, still very much subsumed within the young Parliamentary Library, was provided with two substantial bricks upon which to build.

As another sign of early maturity, the library published its first catalogue in 1912.[6] It is a substantial volume of 974 pages describing a carefully chosen collection serving the information needs of the parliamentarians as well as laying the foundations of a strong Australiana collection.

Formed Collections and Retrospective Acquisitions

A major means of developing collection strength is by the acquisition of formed collections. In one move, or a series of moves, a library can acquire large bodies of material which, if well selected and conscientiously collected, can significantly enrich and advance a collection. Such a means has been utilized well by the National Library.

The first such acquisition came as early as 1911 with the transfer of the collection assembled by Edward Augustus Petherick. A bookseller, book collector and bibliographer, Petherick had been adding to his collection relating to Australia, New Zealand and the Pacific for thirty years before it was finally acquired by the fledgling national library in 1911. In this case the man himself came with the collection. Petherick worked on the bibliography of his collection of 10,000 volumes and 6500 pamphlets, maps, manuscripts and pictures. This valuable bibliography remains unpublished. His collection, however, became the core of the Library's Australiana resources.

The acquisition of the Petherick collection gave the Australiana collection a national profile which it otherwise would not have achieved quite so rapidly. It was a profile which had to be built from the ground up with careful selection of retrospective material which charted the history of the young nation and the factors which had gone into its creation. With a fortuitous succession of head librarians who were visionary collectors and the cooperation of a parallel series of book collectors who combined scholarship and doggedness in seeking the rare and valuable, a unique partnership evolved which ensured the enrichment of the Australiana collection.

Two names stand out in the book collector field: those of Sir John Ferguson and Rex de C. Nan Kivell. Between them, these two men contributed nearly 40,000 printed and manuscript items, including most of the rarest and earliest Australian imprints, to the National Library's collection. In the case of Nan Kivell a rich collection of pictorial materials is a dominant focus of the collection. What made Sir John Ferguson's contribution so significant was not only the gathering together of a great collection, but also the bibliographical scholarship he undertook. It resulted in the publication of the Ferguson bibliography. This monumental undertaking to record the bibliography of Australia up to 1900 began in 1941 with the final seventh volume being published in 1969.[7] It is the standard bibliography of nineteenth-century Australiana. It is also a union list recording other holdings of the national imprint of the nineteenth century.

The Ferguson bibliography is a record of the National Library's retrospective Australiana holdings for imprints of the nineteenth century and the last sixteen years of the eighteenth century. Alas, not everything in the Ferguson bibliography is held by the National Library. It is one of the aims of the Library's retrospective acquisitions programme for Australiana to fill in gaps in its holdings of Ferguson material when possible. Even more desirable is the ability to be able to add a nineteenth-century item which is 'not in Ferguson'. The additions to the collection and the bibliography continue a great tradition of Australiana collecting.

Both the Ferguson and Nan Kivell collections were acquired by the Library in the post-Second World War period. There are smaller, specialist collections of Australiana acquired before then and subsequently. One of the largest in its field is the unique collection on ornithology formed by Gregory Mathews, author of the classic work, *Birds of Australia.* The Library has published a catalogue of this collection.[8] A brief list of other collections indicates the scope of the assiduous collectors and astute librarians, who identified the potential of these collections and secured them for the Library: collections such as Holmes (Australian federation), Cumpston (public health), Crome and Ellison (aviation), Riley (trade unionism), Kenafick (left-wing politics), Ellis (political movements), McLaren (local history), J.C. Williamson (theatre), Pearce (literature). Further details of these and other Australiana collections can be found in the indispensable *Guide to the Collections* by C.A. Burmester.[9]

In addition to acquiring formed collections, the Library has long pursued an active programme to acquire retrospective Australiana through the antiquarian book trade, both in Australia and overseas, either at auction or through individual selections from catalogues. As far as retrospective Australiana is concerned, the Library has a one-copy acquisition policy in general. The danger of unnecessary duplication does not permit the acquisition of formed collections to such a degree in these days. The ability to select desired items from a rich collection is a luxury that does not occur with great frequency. A recent case, however, was in the field of juvenile literature with the O'Neill collection. The Library was able to select material not held and thus add considerably to its resources in this genre of material.[10]

Legal Deposit

Legal deposit provisions first appeared in the Australian Copyright Act in 1912. Under the current legislation one copy of all Australian publications is to be made available free of charge.[11] Until the establishment of the National Library in 1960, all items deposited were housed in the collection of the Commonwealth Parliamentary Library, but housed in a separate 'N' (National) stack. At the time of separation of the two libraries this N stack was transferred to the National Library. It forms the core of the twentieth-century Australian printed collections of the Library. The Library receives an average of between 7000 and 8000 monographs on legal deposit per year.

The successful operation of a legal deposit system depends on the degree to which the receiving library can actively follow up and claim those publications not deposited. This role is one which has not been consistently pursued by the Library. Up to the end of the Second World War the pressures of servicing the needs of federal parliamentarians and of limited financial resources spread over a total acquisitions programme meant that the library took a passive role in relation to legal deposit. Major commercial publishers appear to have been consistent depositors. However, the small presses outside the mainstream of publishing, and genres of popular publishing such as women's magazines, comics, trade catalogues, etc. appear to have escaped the deposit net. There was a suggestion also that such materials were not deemed suitable for a national collection, which was perceived to be of a scholarly rather than popular nature. The publication of the *Australian National Bibliography 1901-1950* has given focus to the Australian national imprint of the first half of the twentieth century.[12] The National Library is actively acquiring items not held in its collection for this period as part of the overall retrospective acquisitions programme.

Since the 1950s the Library has taken a more active role in educating the Australian publishing community at all levels. Particular emphasis has been given in recent years to keeping up with the small presses, the private presses, local sources, etc. For example, an area such as family history publishing continues to be a highly productive growth genre of Australian publishing and needs constant monitoring to capture the output.

Many devices are used in an attempt to ensure that the Library is aware of the range of Australian publishing output. This is in spite of the relative isolation of Canberra from the centres of mainstream publishing in the state capital cities, as well as the geographic spread of all sorts of publishing activity across the continent. Judicious scanning of selected journals and newspapers in 'difficult' fields yields many an obscure citation to claim. The Library maintains a blanket order plan with a library supplier for the supply of one copy of currently published Australian monographs, copies which become the second or lending copy to ensure the preservation of the deposit copy. Items are received in this manner which the Library has not received on deposit. They too are used as alerting mechanisms in an annual claiming cycle.

Expanding Legal Deposit

The provisions of the legal deposit clauses have remained basically unchanged since 1912. The terms of the provisions, in particular the definition of 'published', are out-of-date. They do not reflect the advent of electronic publishing, computer technology and the proliferation of non-print material in general. The Library is embarking on the slow process of examining these non-print materials in relation to legal deposit. Considerations of supporting these materials with appropriate technology and preservation, as well as copyright problems, are being addressed. The Library is a member of the Working Group on Legal Deposit and Electronic Publishing established by the Conference of Directors of National Libraries. It is also an active member of a similar Australian committee working under the auspices of the Australian Libraries and Information Council to examine the same question.

It is of considerable note that the state libraries in Australia are all undergoing the same process. Indeed, they are one step further along the path as each state has enacted legislation in recent years to extend the definition of materials that must be deposited under the state legal deposit provisions. This legislation has usually been in the form of a Libraries Act. This is in marked contrast to the deposit provisions being subsumed in another piece of legislation such as a Copyright Act. The degree to which each state library is tackling the problem of coping with non-print materials varies considerably. Similarly, the exact rate of acquisition of non-print materials is difficult to gauge. Indeed, the size of the 'publishing' field of these materials is a relatively unknown factor at this stage.

Towards the Rationalization of Legal Deposit

Australian libraries have been scrutinizing legal deposit for some time. In 1980 a meeting was held in Canberra involving all the depository libraries around Australia. It ambitiously tried to cover the acquisition of 'special' materials in Australiana, such as manuscripts, pictorial works, etc., as well as printed materials and legal deposit. Much useful information was exchanged in that meeting, but concrete results in terms of cooperation and rationalization were not very numerous.

One result was an agreement between the National Library and the state libraries to rationalize the collecting and preservation of minor serials. It was agreed that the National Library would not necessarily retain and preserve sets of local and parochial serials of a minor informational nature. Examples are numerous but typical of the genre are social club newsletters and bulletins, in-house staff bulletins, serials from amateur hobby groups, etc. When the National Library receives copies as part of legal deposit and a decision is made not to collect, the title and publisher are notified to the relevant state library. The publisher is also notified of the decision.

State libraries have, until recently, undertaken the responsibility to collect and preserve these minor serials. This scheme has operated successfully over the last ten years. However, pressures and priorities have changed, forcing at least two state libraries to rethink their policies on this aspect of the Australian serial output. Diminishing financial and staff resources have forced difficult choices between maintaining acquisition and control activities for the state output and meeting growing user demands. All state libraries have experienced growth in the number of users. In the case of three of them this has been influenced by the completion of new buildings and improved facilities. Difficult decisions have included the library's ability to acquire and retain the state output. At the level of the minor serial this has meant that at least two state libraries have decided not to retain all titles and to rely on local collecting institutions as the preservers of the local serial imprint.

Minor serials featured at the 1980 meeting on legal deposit. They will no doubt be present again in 1992 at a major forum to involve the state libraries and the National Library. Discussions will focus on the sharing of bibliographic information in controlling the national imprint, as well as questions of cooperative collection development. After ten years of collecting Australiana and talking of rationalization there is a need for a definition of responsibilities and the application of cooperative acquisitions.

Publishing Genres

To enable more constructive cooperation, it is necessary to identify genres of publishing and define each of their places in the national imprint. Australia's publishing output remains a complex, multi-level entity, reflecting the cultural, economic, intellectual, political and social diversity of the nation. It includes the mainstream commercial output as well as the non-commercial sector, which in itself includes a multitude of levels and genres. The non-commercial product often presents the most problems in acquisitions for the depository library. Lack of knowledge of legal deposit is common in this field. Print runs can be small, meaning that later claims may not be able to be fulfilled. On the other hand, another genre such as ephemera pours into a library and the difficulty lies in coping with it physically.

The volume of output from some publishing sectors, such as campus literature from tertiary educational institutions and the travel and tourist industries, to take two large-scale examples, makes the task of even approaching a reasonably comprehensive coverage difficult for a single collection institution which is remote from the sources. In another field, the output of the specialist, limited edition presses, and the growth in the production of 'artists' books' with original works of art present special acquisition problems. The growth in an entirely different sector, that of consultants and their printed reports (including environmental impact statements), poses many difficult questions – is it a public document? is it a government publication? is it in fact published?

These and many other questions are being addressed daily by Australiana acquisitions librarians around the country. They have been addressed at the institutional level and to some degree incorporated into collection development policies. They were addressed by the National Library in 1990 and 1991 as part of a detailed re-examination of the Australiana section of the *Collection Development Policy*. This covered all levels and genres of Australian publishing. Without this rigorous self-examination, the refinement of a collecting policy for internal use, as well as the dissemination of one which positively contributes to the further development of cooperative collection development in Australiana, is not truly feasible.

A Further Distributed National Collection?

State libraries have already anticipated some of the trends and developments which might be expected to emerge for discussion. One of these is a wider recognition of a tripartite level of collecting responsibility, which is slowly replacing the accepted two-level concept. The 'new' player in this game is the local institution. This may or may not be library-based. However, the emergence of a local focus and responsibility is the result of many influences, some outside the library world and its acquisition problems.

The dramatic growth in the family history and genealogy movement is but one manifestation of a general move to popular (or populist?) history. The Bicentennial in 1988 encouraged a widespread awareness of history at the personal and community level. Projects such as the Australian Bicentennial Authority's Historic Record Search, conducted in 1988, and the Last Film Search by the National Film and Sound Archive are other potent success stories in raising people's awareness of historical preservation. The dramatic growth in Australian studies as a tertiary course of study in the last twenty years and the sheer variety in courses available are further indications of the popularization of Australian history.

These general influences have combined with the library-based factors already mentioned above to throw the spotlight onto local collecting institutions. Increasingly, they are going to be relied on to collect and preserve the local printed imprint. This may include the output of the local government authority, as well as the serials and monographs and ephemera emanating from all the community groups, institutions and organizations in the town, city, shire or suburb.

Government Publications

Australia has three levels of government: federal, state and local. Each of these produces printed, published material of potential concern to a collecting institution such as the National Library. Of the three, the Library collects federal and state government publications. Local government publications are collected by the relevant state libraries and by local collecting institutions. Neither federal nor state publications are liable to be deposited in the National Library under the legal deposit provisions of the Federal Copyright Act. In contrast, state publications have recently been included in the newly enacted legal deposit provision for each state and, as such, as liable for deposit in state libraries.

The National Library has had to evolve a multi-level system to acquire federal and state government publications. In the federal sphere it receives a 'deposit' set of all publications issued by the Australian Government Publishing Service (AGPS). This includes parliamentary, legislative and departmental publications. However, a significant amount of government publishing does not pass through AGPS and, as such, deposit must be negotiated with individual departments, authorities, including their branches and regional offices. In the state sphere the position (in some cases the existence) of a centralized government printing office has declined. The National Library is obliged to negotiate with each department, authority, etc. to acquire publications. In recent years the intake by the Library of monographs published by both federal and state governments has climbed steadily towards 3000 titles per year.

The acquisition methods employed for government publications necessitate a constant monitoring and a large clerical workload to ensure that acquisitions continue. Despite a long history of acquiring publications of the various governments, the very nature of governments and bureaucracies being subject to change means that nothing can be taken for granted in the way of supply. The National Library will be making greater efforts to ensure that it does in fact collect the output of the Federal Government as comprehensively as possible. Priority will be given to them over and above any attempt to collect state government publications comprehensively. With the operation of the legal deposit provisions for state government publications in state libraries, these institutions will be able to ensure comprehensive state government collections.

The National Library has never seriously attempted to collect local government authority publications on a comprehensive basis. The current intake of financial statements, annual reports, etc. from shire, city, municipal or county government bodies reflects a small number of geographically disparate entities represented in the Library's collection. All state libraries have a policy to collect this material. Most of them appear to be successful, although coverage is not always comprehensive. At the local level mention has already been made of a growing movement for locally based institutions to assume responsibility for preserving the local output, including local government publications.

Newspapers in Microform

In 1969 the National Library entered into an arrangement with the State Library of New South Wales and the commercial microfilming agency W.F. Pascoe Pty Ltd to commence a project to microfilm the current issues of 150 regional newspapers in New South Wales. At the time such a project was a major initiative in the preservation of Australian newspapers. Until then a small amount of retrospective filming had been undertaken and some of the capital city dailies were in the process of being microfilmed. Twenty years later the NSW regional newspapers project is still active. It is now, however, just one part of a much larger mosaic involving the preservation of Australia's newspaper heritage.

As the NSW regional programme has continued for current newspapers, the Library has also been actively engaged in a retrospective programme. This has involved cooperative arrangements with two or three other bodies: (1) a local authority, such as an historical society, public library, or a local government authority; (2) a state library; (3) a microfilming agency. The local authority has usually been the initiator in locating and identifying a set of a newspaper to be preserved, which on occasion has been the sole surviving set. On other occasions a set has been completed from a variety of sources. The financial arrangements have been split, with contributions from each participant for the filming and creation of a master negative and then the supply of a positive copy. The geographical emphasis of this retrospective programme has been in New South Wales and to a lesser extent in Victoria. It has usually involved country or rural newspapers rather than those from urban or suburban sources. It has resulted in the preservation of long runs of newspapers as well as runs of short-lived papers. Priority has been given to the preservation of nineteenth-century newspapers. Often these cooperative projects can stretch on for years as the financial resources of the participants fluctuate. However, the end result has been the preservation of a large number of newspapers.

Most of the newspapers filmed and acquired in this way have not been previously held by the National Library. With the commencement of the development of its collecting in the first years of the twentieth century, the Library had missed out on collecting the Australian newsprint of the nineteenth century. In subsequent acquisitions, such as the formed collections of Ferguson, some rare early newspapers were acquired. However, the bulk of the collection development for retrospective newspapers has been in microform.

Current Developments in Newspaper Microfilming

The environment for preservation of historical materials and the pattern of newspaper microform publishing have changed in the twenty years since the regional NSW programme began. It has accelerated, particularly in recent years, having been given a boost by the heritage euphoria engendered by the celebration of Australia's Bicentennial. State libraries are focusing on their own collections and progressively having them filmed. For example, in 1988 the State Library of New South Wales received a Bicentennial grant to film New South Wales newspapers from its own collections. A list of over eighty titles was completed. As a result of this considerable achievement, the State Library has continued to focus on the preservation of its own newspaper collection. It has diverted a large part of its binding vote funds to a greatly expanded microfilming programme devoted to newspapers. All state libraries now have active microfilming programmes for the preservation of newspapers of their state.

In addition, microfilming agencies have expanded both in number and in the scope of their activities. An interesting case study crossing both worlds is the Regional Library Service in Warrnambool in south-western Victoria. What began as a small agency filming a few local records and newspapers has expanded to become a major filming agency processing newspapers and archival records from around the state of Victoria. Its list includes over 160 titles, over one-third of which has been acquired by the National Library. As a result of these developments, the newspapers available have grown dramatically, allowing a collecting institution such as the National Library to add extensively to its holdings. The Library has an active policy of acquiring Australian newspapers in microform which are available on the commercial market. In the financial year 1989/1990 a supplemented budget of $192,000 was spent on such newspaper acquisitions.

The role of the National Library in initiating preservation of newspapers by microfilming can be expected to expand as the Preservation Services Section of the Library becomes more actively involved in a national preservation programme. Enlarged, and provided with unequalled technical facilities in 1986, the unit has developed an ongoing programme of assessing the Library's own collections and arranging microfilming of materials where the need for preservation has been identified. The unit does not have its own microfilming facilities but uses commercial agencies. Newspapers have not yet assumed a high profile in the programme, but they can be expected to.

In the meantime the Library will continue to develop a collection of Australian newspapers, either in hard copy or in microfilm, to represent the social and political history of the nation. It still enters into a small number of appropriate cooperative projects, as well as expanding its role in initiating preservation. With the dramatic expansion of the availability of newspapers in microform it will continue to acquire new titles for the collection.

There is a very real user demand for a wider range of newspapers in the National Library. In particular, this emanates from the family history and genealogical research group. Nineteenth-century newspapers are a fount of information in the form of court reports, social events, obituaries, local government reports, advertising, etc., all of which are eagerly demanded by the family history researcher. The geographic mobility of Australia's population and the newness of Canberra as a population centre mean that most of these researchers in the National Library are seeking newspapers from around the country.

Other Microform Collections

A development paralleling that of newspapers is the increased availability of archival records in microform. This is a recent phenomenon that builds strongly on the model set by newspapers in microform. Births, deaths, marriages, convict indents, passenger lists, land grants, official correspondence, shipping lists, prison records – the list is growing every year as authorities in all Australian states gradually commit vast amounts of official records to microform and make them available for purchase. The National Library acquires all these sets. They serve a voracious genealogy user group. They also provide an opportunity to enrich the Australiana collections with unique records which would otherwise be available only at their source, inevitably remote from Canberra and the National Library.

The Organizational Environment

The change in emphasis given the acquisition of Australiana by the Library can be charted over the years. The limited resources and small staff numbers militated against any large degree of concentration before the Second World War. However, separate sections dealing with special materials (maps, music, pictorial manuscripts, oral history) all evolved in the post-1950 period). A selection unit for all printed materials, whether Australian or overseas imprints, was a standard feature from the 1960s. This umbrella unit included two divisions: Overseas and Australian Selection. The Australian Selection Unit included the operation of legal deposit.

In 1984 Australian Selection became a separate unit, devoted to the acquisition of all Australian printed and microform material. The Library had formalized a fact which had existed for some time by giving a suitable profile to the acquisition of Australiana. This is the unit which exists today with a staff of thirteen. It includes most processing and accessioning activities, as well as legal deposit, the deposit of state and federal government publications, the selection and acquisition of all retrospective materials, and monitoring and acquiring microform materials. The unit is part of the Australian Collections and Services programme which has been in existence for two years, following a restructuring of the Library in line with programme management principles adopted across the Australian Public Service.

In this way the acquisition of Australiana in all its aspects, the bibliographical control of the national imprint, and the use of those collections are administratively concentrated together. Discussions have been taking place for some time within the Library which may result in another reorganization or a refinement of the patterns described above. However, the focus on collecting Australiana in all its aspects will remain.

Acquisitions in all areas can be closely linked: printed materials can be included in manuscript collections, just as annotated books may rightly take their place in the manuscript collection. A published book of views of Townsville circa 1920 is a pictorial record as well as a book. Sheet music is a published item and liable to legal deposit, just as maps are, with both of them having their own special storage and reference facilities in the Library. The great collections such as the Nan Kivell or the Ferguson cross many library material boundaries which must be taken into consideration when searching retrospective offers of rare material. It is this creative interaction in the acquisition of Australiana which has enriched the Library collections over the years.

The Future

A process of change is gathering momentum. It is a culmination of historical trends as well as being hastened by new technology and information sharing. The future for collecting and preserving the national imprint on a national scale lies in increased networking among major collecting institutions in Australia. A rationalization of aims and the realization of achievable goals are developments already well underway in the state libraries and the National Library. Further refinement of policies and the creative monitoring of current publishing trends are both being actively pursued. Contact and discussion by staff at all key levels of operation in the libraries concerned are vital as far as the tyranny of distance in Australia allows.

One hundred years ago the Australian nation did not exist as a political entity. A national library did not exist. Today the National Library of Australia houses a major collection of Australiana. A Distributed National Collection is in the process of further evolution, one which is shared by libraries around Australia. It is a process which is a challenge for all librarians involved in the collecting of Australiana.

Notes

1 *Shaping Our Future: Preserving Our Past. National Library of Australia Strategic Plan 1990-1995*. Canberra: National Library of Australia, 1990.

2 National Library Act, 1960-1973, s. 6.

3 Australian Libraries Summit (1988, Canberra, ACT), *Resolutions*. Canberra: National Library of Australia, 1988. See Resolutions AA1-AA10.

4 National Library of Australia, *National Library of Australia Selection Policy*. Canberra: National Library of Australia, 1981.

5 The state library policies which have appeared to date are: Library Board of Queensland, *Collection Development Policies*. Brisbane: Library Board of Queensland, 1989; Mortlock Library of South Australiana, *The Mortlock Library of South Australiana Interim Collection Development Policy, May 1989*. Adelaide: Mortlock Library of South Australiana, 1989; South Australia. Department of Local Government, Libraries Division, Public Libraries Branch, *Collections Management Policy 1990*, ed. by L.K. Harris. Adelaide: Libraries Board of South Australia, 1990; Library and Information Service of Western Australia, *Past Imperfect, Future Imperative: Collection Development at the Library and Information Service of Western Australia. Volume 1:*

The Alexander Library Building Collections, 1990. Perth: Library and Information Service of Western Australia, 1990; State Library of New South Wales, *Collection Development Policy*, eds-in-chief: Janine Schmidt and Alan Ventress. Sydney: State Library of New South Wales, 1990.

6 Commonwealth Parliament Library, *Catalogue of the Books, Pamphlets, Pictures, and Maps in the Library of the Parliament, to September, 1911*. Melbourne: Government Printer, 1912.

7 John Alexander Ferguson, *Bibliography of Australia*. Sydney: Angus and Robertson, 1941-1969 (Vol. 1 1784-1830, Vol. 2 1831-1838, Vol. 3 1839-1845, Vol. 4 1846-1850, Vol. 5 1851-1900 A-G, Vol. 5 1851-1890 H-P, Vol. 7 1851-1900 Q-Z; addenda to Vols 1-4 published by the National Library of Canberra, 1986).

8 Gregory Macalister Mathews, *The Birds of Australia, with Handcoloured Plates*. 14 vols in 12. London: Witherby, 1910-1927; *Checklist to the Mathews Ornithological Collection*. Canberra: National Library of Australia, 1966.

9 *National Library of Australia: Guide to the Collections*. 4 vols. Comp. by C.A. Burmester. Canberra: National Library of Australia, 1971-1982.

10 Terence O'Neill, *Australian Children's Books to 1980: A Select Bibliography of the Collection Held in the National Library of Australia*. Comp. by Terence and Frances O'Neill. Canberra: National Library of Australia, 1989.

11 Copyright Act 1968, s. 201.

12 *Australian National Bibliography, 1901-1950*. 4 vols. Canberra: National Library of Australia, 1988.

12 Australiana in the British Library

James D. Egles and Graham P. Cornish

The collections of the British Library in the field of Australiana are extensive and date back to the late eighteenth century. The rich and varied collections of printed books and journals are described in some depth, emphasizing the breadth and rarity of the holdings. Current collection practices are less extensive but still fairly comprehensive. Apart from the main printed books collection, the British Library has extensive collections of Australian government and other official publications, as well as maps and music. The manuscript collection is also valuable; and the newspaper library in North London has long runs of Australian newspapers, including the very first one published in 1803. The National South Archive (part of the British Library) has extensive Australian recordings, both imported from Australia direct and recordings by Australian artists produced in the UK. There are also extensive Aboriginal materials in the Archive. Collections are not limited to the historical and cultural areas, and both the Science Reference and Information Services and the Document Supply Centre (at Boston Spa in Yorkshire) collect all worthwhile scientific and technical literature from Australia. The basic functions and services of thr British Library are also outlined during the course of describing the various collections.

The British Library, the national library of the United Kingdom, was established on 1 July 1973 under the British Library Act 1972. It brought together the library departments of the British Museum, the National Central Library, the National Lending Library for Science and Technology, and in subsequent years the British National Bibliography Ltd, the Office for Scientific and Technical Information, the Library Association Library, the India Office Library and Records and the National Sound Archive. The Library's services are based on collections which include over 18 million volumes (books, manuscripts, maps, newspapers, serials, music) , 8 million stamps, 1 million disks and 55,000 hours of tape recordings currently housed in more than twenty buildings in London and one complex in Yorkshire. From 1991 to 1996 the bulk of the London collections will be brought to a single site at St Pancras, the new British Library whose first phase opens in 1993.

The Library's principal research collection of Australiana is the responsibility of Humanities and Social Sciences, formerly the Reference Division. Since the Division's holdings are so large (approximately 12 million volumes) and so wide-ranging in subject matter, period and country of origin, it is impossible to quantify Australian material, but the library undoubtedly contains the major collection of Australiana in the United Kingdom. An attempt will be made, however, to review the major phases of the Library's collection development: first, concentrating on printed material with mention of some important holdings, particularly earlier works; and then more briefly surveying the specialized collections, excluding the Science Reference and Information Service and the Document Supply Centre which will be dealt with separately.

The Bloomsbury Collection: Early Years

The Library has its origins in the foundation collections of the British Museum which was established in 1753. The acquisition of the great semi-private collections which were characteristic of the bibliographical scholarship of the eighteenth century dominated the development of the Library until the reforms under the 'Prince of Librarians', the great Antonio Panizzi in the 1840s. They include the libraries of statesmen and kings such as the Harleys, George II (The Old Royal Library), George III (The King's Library) and Grenville; and the libraries of scholars and scientists, most importantly Sir Hans Sloane and Sir Joseph Banks. Ten years after Banks equipped and accompanied Captain Cook's voyage of exploration in the *Endeavour* he was elected President of the Royal Society. He was also an active and influential Trustee of the British Museum. His library, and those of the other early collections, are crucial for the study of the voyages of commercial and scientific exploration of the Pacific from Tasman to Cook and Banks himself.

The richness of the Library's holdings in this field is apparent from checking the bibliography to the first volume of Manning Clark's *History of Australia.* All the British, French and Dutch accounts of voyages listed there are in the Library's collections. Among them may be found, for example, Banks' own copy of *The Voyage of Governor Phillip to Botany Bay* (1789), bound in kangaroo skin; and one of four copies in the Library of Bougainville's *Voyage autour du Monde* (1771), originally belonging to George Burney, which has on its first map Captain Cook's autograph tracing of the course of his own voyage from 1765 to 1771.

The Library is also well endowed with works dating from the early days of the colony founded at Botany Bay by Arthur Phillip in 1788. Rare items from this period include: Watkin Tench's *A Narrative of the Expedition to Botany Bay* (1789); the anonymous *An Authentic and Interesting Narrative of the Late Expedition to Botany Bay* (1789); the three editions of Judge Advocate David Collins' *An Account of the English Colony in New South Wales* (1789, 1802, 1804); Reverend Richard Johnson's tract, *An Address to the Inhabitants of the Colonies* (1794); the important *Journals* of Surgeon-General John White (1790) and Governor John Hunter (1793); various works attributed to the notorious convict, George Barrington; the convict artist Thomas Watling's *Letters from an Exile at Botany Bay* (1794) (one of three known copies); both issues of the sailor George Thompson's *Slavery and Famine, Punishments for Sedition* (1792, 1794); and Ensign George Bond's description of the convict system and the attendant economic corruption, *A Brief Account of the Colony of Port Jackson* (1803).

Between 1788 and 1806 New South Wales had been ruled by First Fleet Governors Phillip, Hunter and King. The turbulent years that followed under William Bligh and Lachlan Macquarie saw the evolution of New South Wales from an uncertain penal colony to an emerging nation. Bligh's life was plagued by mutiny, and the Rum Rebellion against him in Sydney is fully documented in the *Proceedings of a General Court-Martial...for the Trial of Lieut Col. Geo Johnston* (1811). In the same year D.D. Mann, a supporter of the rebellion and a convict, published his *The Present Picture of New South Wales* (1811), which was the last of the personal journals describing life in the colony. Both of these very scarce works are in the Library's collections.

The following decade is known as the 'golden age of Macquarie' and saw rapid development in the colony, although Governor Macquarie was attacked in the colony and in England and eventually destroyed for his patronage of ex-convicts – the emancipists. Important works in the Library of books devoted to the Macquarie years include some of the finest Australian books ever published. To mention only a few, there is convict Joseph Lycett's celebrated plate book, *Views in Australia* (1824); the untitled and equally rare *Views in New South Wales*, published by Absalom West (1813-1814); the first book of poetry published in Australia, Judge Barron Field's *First Fruits of Australian Poetry* (1819); and the first published work by a native Australian, William Wentworth's *Statistical Historical and Political Description of the Colony of New South Wales* (1819). The Library also has a copy of a very rare work, important for the study of Macquarie, which was published in 1826, two years after his death. This is the pamphlet, *An Answer to Certain Calumnies in the Late Governor Macquarie's Pamphlet, and the Third Edition of Mr Wentworth's Account of Australia*. This attack on Macquarie was written by Samuel Marsden, known as the 'Flogging Parson', who had been recommended to the New South Wales chaplaincy by William Wilberforce, but whose colonial career is generally regarded as a disgrace to his calling.

Equally notorious was Michael Howe, who across the Bass Strait in Van Diemen's Land (Tasmania) terrorized the pioneer settlers. Howe was the subject of the first non-official book or pamphlet published in Tasmania, Thomas Wells's *Michael Howe, the Last and Worst of the Bushrangers of Van Diemen's Land*, published in 1818, the year of his death. Bound together with the Library's copy of *Michael Howe* is another important early Tasmanian work, Pindar Juvenal's *The Van Diemen's Land Warriors* (1827), the first book of verse published locally.

Actual promotion of Australia as a land for emigration may be said to have begun with Wentworth's book mentioned above. The first emigrant's guide and the first description of Van Diemen's Land is the work of the disreputable Lieutenant Charles Jeffreys, *Van Diemen's Land* (1820). Jeffreys had stolen the papers of George William Evans, Surveyor General of Van Diemen's Land, and for his own work used Evans' manuscript of a book he was to have published. Evans managed to retrieve his manuscript and two years later published his superior version, *A Geographical, Historical and Topographical Description of Van Diemen's Land*. Both of these works are in the Library.

Few emigrants could be expected to be aware of the immensity of the continent that awaited them. Throughout the nineteenth century there were voyages of discovery around the coast and epic journals of exploration inland. Numerous accounts of these travels were published, and the Library's holdings are too strong for more than a cursory glance. Notable volumes in the collection include the following on coastal exploration: Matthew Flinders' *Observations on the Coast of Van Diemen's Land* (1801); Flinders' monumental *A Voyage to Terra Australis...Prosecuted in the Years 1801, 1802 and 1803*, published in 1814; James Grant's *The Narrative of a Voyage of Discovery* (1803), which has the longest title page of any Australian book and which describes Grant's journey through the Bass Strait; Philip Parker King's *Narrative of a Survey of the Intertropical and Western Coasts of Australia* (1846), an account of a journey in the *HMS Beagle*, in which

Darwin had sailed, and which completed the discovery of the Australian coast. Works on inland exploration before 1850 include: John Oxley's foundation work, *Journals of Two Expeditions into the Interior of New South Wales* (1820); Charles Sturt's *Two Expeditions into the Interior of Southern Australia* (1833) and his *Narrative of an Exploration into Central Australia* (1847); the major works of Thomas Mitchell, Surveyor General of New South Wales; the *Journals* of George Grey in the north-west, Edward John Eyre in central Australia, and that of the expedition into 3000 miles of unknown territory in 1844-1845 undertaken by the romantic figure Ludwig Leichhardt, who was to disappear without trace three years later; and, finally, William Carron's *Narrative of an Expedition Undertaken Under the Direction of the Late Mr Assistant Surveyor E.B. Kennedy* (1849), which tells of Kennedy's tragic journey to Cape York where he was killed by hostile natives despite the devotion and courage of his Aboriginal guide, Jacky Jacky.

After Panizzi

The decade of these heroic and tragic explorations in the Australian interior, the 1840s, saw the beginning, many miles away, of a new phase in the development of the British Museum Library's collections. If one travels (metaphorically) from Cape York to Bloomsbury, one can briefly examine the period that began with the reforms that Panizzi made in the Library's acquisitions policy.

The second half of the nineteenth century was the classic phase of institutional collecting which consisted chiefly of the three methods of acquisition still central to the collection development of national research libraries, namely: (1) effective enforcement of legal deposit legislation; (2) use of a government-funded annual purchase grant for foreign material; and (3) exchange agreements between governments and their national libraries for the collecting of official publications.

Novels and historical and descriptive monographs written in or about Australia or by Australians were frequently published in Britain (and thus acquired by legal deposit at the British Museum), as such genres were favourites of the Victorian reading public. The first Australian novel in book form, Henry Savery's *Quintus Servinton*, had, however, been published in Hobart in 1830-1831. The Library acquired this by purchase in 1839 and has continued to purchase desiderata to the present day.

Novelists from the colonial period whose works are in the Library's collections as a result of legal deposit include such writers important for

Australian studies as Catherine Spence, Caroline Leakey (author of *The Broad Arrow*, 1859, a forerunner of Marcus Clarke), Henry Kingsley, Rolf Boldrewood, Mrs Campbell Praed and Ethel Turner. Similarly received by legal deposit were the descriptive and historical works of writers such as Alexander Harris *(Settlers and Convicts)*, John Dunmore Lang, George William Rusden and Edward Curr, son of the Edward Curr whose scarce *An Account of the Colony of Van Diemen's Land* (1824), the first emigrant's guide written by a real resident, had been acquired by the Library in pre-Panizzi days. Finally, to show the effect of legal deposit, it is notable that of the 160 or so contemporary (largely nineteenth-century) books listed in the bibliography of *The Other Side of the Frontier*, Henry Reynolds's recent study of Aborigines, over ninety were published in Britain.

Some books published in Australia, principally those published by George Robertson in Melbourne, were distributed in the UK and thus received by legal deposit. There were, for example, the *Poems* of Henry Kendall and the Robertson first edition of Marcus Clarke's *For the Term of His Natural Life* (its original appearance was in the *Australian Journal* from March 1870 to June 1872, also held by the Library). Also in Melbourne, the bookseller and publisher F.F. Bailliere acted as an agent for the Library. Australian purchases, included newspapers listed by Reynolds (thirty-six are in the Newspaper Library) and such works as *The Eureka Stockade* (1855) by Carboni Raffaello, very scarce even when acquired in 1864. Bailliere also obtained for the Library a copy of the first book printed in Australia, the 1802 *New South Wales General Standing Orders* of which only three copies are known to Ferguson in his *Bibliography of Australia.*

Bailliere was the publisher of John McDouall Stuart's *Explorations across the Continent of Australia* (1863), an account of his crossing of Australia from south to north. The following year an edition of his six expedition journals, *Explorations in Australia*, was published in London, thus enabling the Library to obtain the major volumes devoted to his career. Stuart's crossing of the continent took place in competition with the costly (£60,000 and seven lives lost) Burke and Wills expedition sponsored by the Royal Society of Victoria. This disastrous and geographically insignificant expedition has long been enshrined in Australian folklore, inspiring writers and artists such as Adam Lindsay Gordon, Henry Kendall, Sir John Longstaff and Sidney Nolan. A considerable number of contemporary works relating to Burke and Wills, and of the expeditions sent in search of them, were published, and the Library possesses a good selection of these.

By the 1860s the eastern half of Australia had been well explored, but much of the west and the interior desert remained unknown. The 'last of the Australian explorers', Ernest Giles, added greatly to the knowledge of this part of the continent by crossing from South Australia to Perth in 1875. His *Australia Twice Traversed*, published in London in 1889, is one of the most handsomely produced Australian books, enlivened by Giles' perceptive and literary writing. Finally, to conclude this brief description of the Library's holdings of exploration literature, mention must be made of the work of another fine writer, David W. Carnegie. Carnegie was born in London in 1871, the younger son of the Earl of Southesk, and travelled to Western Australia in 1892 to work on the Coolgardie goldfields. Financed by successful prospecting, his expedition of 1896-1897 covered 3000 miles of the unexplored deserts of the interior. Returning to England, he published in 1898 *Spinifex and Sand*, the enthralling account of his five years in Western Australia, which is unequalled in the entire literature of Australian inland exploration. Sadly, his short life ended two years later. Having been appointed Assistant Resident in Northern Nigeria, he was killed there in November 1900 by a poisoned arrow.

Before leaving the nineteenth century a few more examples of superbly produced and very rare topographical plate books published during Australia's first century that were chiefly acquired from Bailliere are: Augustus Earle's *Views in New South Wales, and Van Diemen's Land*, published in 1830, the year before his voyage as artist on Darwin's *Beagle*; Joseph Fowles' 1848-1849 quarto volume, *Sydney in 1848*, which is the most comprehensive topographical account of early Sydney street architecture; George French Angas' greatest work, *South Australia Illustrated* (1847); S.T. Gill's *Victoria Illustrated* (1857) and his *Diggers and Diggings of Victoria as They Are in 1855*, classic views of Victoria and the goldfields; W.C. Piguenit's *Salmon Ponds and Vicinity New Norfolk Tasmania* (1867), the first and only topographical plate book by a native-born Australian artist published during the first century of settlement; and, finally, the finest work of urban topography produced in nineteenth-century Australia, Charles Troedel's *Melbourne Album* (1863).

The Twentieth Century

The number of books published in the twentieth century is, of course, far greater than the 20,000 books and pamphlets of Australian interest that were published between 1789 and 1900. But the turn of the century saw a comparative decline in books acquired for the Library from Australia – unlike Canada, from where the Library received everything published between 1895 and 1924. Unfortunately, the newer 'nationalist' publishers like the Sydney *Bulletin* did not, like their nineteenth-century predecessors, deposit either directly, or through an agent, in London. Thus the Library did not receive by deposit, or purchase at or near time of publication, the two classic texts that followed *For the Term of His Natural Life*: Henry Lawson's *While the Billy Boils* and Joseph Furphy's *Such Is Life*. The Lawson title was not to be purchased until 1957, nor the Furphy until as recently as 1983.

However, the sense of a European audience continued, and continues to be important to many leading Australian novelists and writers of scholarly texts who seek to be published by British firms which are subject to UK deposit. Novelists such as Miles Franklin, Henry Handel Richardson, William Gossey Hay, Eleanor Dark, Martin Boyd, and even the more self-consciously 'Australian' Vance Palmer and Katharine Susannah Prichard all had their major fiction published in London or Edinburgh. In this period also local publishers, particularly the new university presses and Angus and Robertson, began to participate in the transnational English-language book distribution which involved London offices or agencies and British legal deposit. A check of the Library's holdings of twenty-five major novelists and poets (from Boldrewood to Wright) listed in Miller and Macartney's *Australian Literature* (1956) reveals that the Library holds 285 out of 375 titles, with most gaps being of early or limited Australian editions and so not liable to deposit.

The fourth and present phase of collection development began in the years of cultural expansion following the Second World War. As funding increased and staffing levels improved, the Library in the 1950s began to reinstate the encyclopedic acquisition strategy that had been prevalent in the nineteenth century. Consequently, gaps such as the Furphy and Lawson already mentioned were filled; the exchange of official publications with Australia expanded considerably; the growth of Anglo-Australian publishing ensured that many important works were deposited; the printing of much Australian material in Hong Kong (where deposit by the printer in the British Library is part of their Copyright Act) also led to legal deposit in the British Library; and selection of current material to be purchased was systematized.

As an indication of the level of acquisition since 1900 of Australian material, we have examined items received since that date that were used in the British Library's modest Australian Bicentennial exhibition, *Prison or Paradise?*. Three of the thirty-four pre-1900 books were acquired after 1950: Charles Harpur's *Poems* (1883); Henry Lawson's first book, *Short Stories in Prose and Verse*, published by his mother

Louisa Lawson in 1894; and C.J. Dennis's copy of Steele Rudd's *On Our Selection!* (1899) were purchased from Australian booksellers in the 1960s or 1970s.

Of the books published after 1890 six were published in the UK: R.F. Irvine, *Bubbles, His Book* (1900), an Art Nouveau influenced children's book not published in Australia until 1927; Miles Franklin's classic *My Brilliant Career* (Edinburgh, 1901); Louise Mack, *Teens: A Story of Girl Life in Australia* (1903, but originally published in Australia in 1897); Ernest Favenc's only book of verse, *Voices of the Desert* (1905); Frank Fox, *Australia* (1910), with illustrations by Percy Spence; and Mary Grant Bruce's delightful children's story, *Timothy in Bushland* (1912). Of the other books in the exhibition (which did not include works published after 1939) the following with Australian publishers were received by legal deposit: *Australian Echoes* (1902), a book of poems by John Mathew, author of the study of Aboriginal life, *Eaglehawk and Crow*; the soldier-poet Leon Gellert's *Songs of a Campaign* (1918), with illustrations by Norman Lindsay; and a children's book written in his 70s by the chief folk-poet of Australia, 'Banjo' Paterson, *The Animals Noah Forgot* (1933), also illustrated by Norman Lindsay. At the behest of the authors, who wished to see their books in the British Museum Library, two books were donated to the Library through the publishers: Norman Lindsay's own *The Magic Pudding* (1930) and Dorothy Wall's *Blinky Bill, the Quaint Little Australian* (1933), two more classic works of Australian children's literature, a genre well represented in the Library. Christopher Brennan's *Poems* (1913) was purchased from Angus and Robertson via the Australian Book Company in London in 1932.

The remaining books in the exhibition were all purchased from Australian booksellers in the 1960s or 1970s: Louis Lavater's collection of verse, *Blue Days and Grey Days* (1915); C.J. Dennis' *Backblock Ballads and Later Verses* (1918); a copy of the limited edition *The Fairyland of Ida Rentoul Outhwaite* (1926), with its beautifully drawn bush fairies; an American private printing of the 'Philosopher of Love' Havelock Ellis' experiences in Australia, *Kanga Creek: An Australian Idyll* (1938); and a limited edition of Henry Lawson's *The Romance of the Swag* (1939), illustrated and signed by Lionel Lindsay.

The efficacy of the Library's collecting policy in recent decades is demonstrated by comparing the holdings to titles listed in standard bibliographies. Two have been selectively examined for this article. Fred Lock and Alan Lawson's *Australian Literature: A Reference Guide* (1977) includes reference material much of which will be available in any major research library, as well as works devoted to individual authors. In this latter section 105 sources are described, of which the Library has all but twenty, and of this twenty more than one-half are checklists issued in typescript by the Fryer Memorial Library in Queensland. Of the twenty periodicals listed in the bibliography, all the major titles are in the Library, although five less substantial titles have not been collected. I. Kepars' *Australia* (1984), Volume 46 in the World Bibliographical Series, has been checked in the following categories: the country and its people, discovery and exploration, history, politics, Aborigines, art, literature and language. Of 272 titles, 170 are in the Library. This figure of 60 per cent is lower than one would anticipate, partly due to the decline in funding in recent years. However, when resources become available, these and other important gaps in the collection will be filled whenever possible.

Although many people's primary image of the Library is of the Reading Room (to be vacated in 1996) and the humanities collection of printed books, there are other collections and reading rooms which contain material of interest to researchers studying Australia. These will now be examined briefly.

Official Publications

Official publications are generally received by international exchange, although a few are purchased and some are donated. The earliest Australian exchange commenced in 1883 with Tasmania. This was soon followed by exchanges with Queensland (1885), Victoria (1886) and New South Wales (1894). In the present century agreements were set up with the Commonwealth Government (1904), Western Australia (1908), South Australia (1935) and, more recently, the Northern Territory (1982). The central government exchange is now with the National Library, whereas in most states it is with the State or Parliamentary Library, except in Western Australia where it is with the Library and Information Service, and the Northern Territory with the Northern Territory Library Service. A comprehensive set of federal government publications is received, while the material sent by the states varies from a few Northern Territory to a large selection of Western Australian official and semi-official publications. As pressures of space and conservation priorities increase, the British Library will inevitably become more selective in its retention policy of this low-use material. However, priority is given to categories such as official gazettes, parliamentary proceedings and debates, treaties, law and secondary legislation, official yearbooks, statistics, official histories, major reports and enquiries, law reports and journal and departmental annual reports. The collection is extensive but difficult to quantify, because of limited bibliographic control. An indication of the extent can be suggested by the 2250 official serials received in 1985, of which 800 were federal and 600 from Western Australia. There is also a comprehensive collection of British official publications which contains a substantial amount of material on Australia, especially for the colonial period.

Maps

The British Library's collection of maps, both manuscript and printed, is undoubtedly one of the most important in the world. Even by 1800 the British Museum held a remarkable range of cartographic records illustrating the discovery of Australia. The foundation collections included maps, charts and atlases documenting the discovery of New Holland (Australia) by Tasman and others from the seventeenth and early eighteenth century and also maps and charts of the Dieppe School which indicate possible Portuguese discovery of Australia in the 1520s or 1530s. In the early nineteenth century Joseph Banks was influential in the Museum's acquisition of the manuscripts of Captain Cook, Archibald Menzies and others, and his own bequest to the Museum included many atlases, maps and early engraved charts of the Pacific region, including those of Matthew Flinders. Major acquisitions since Banks include King George III's Topographical Collection and the King's Maritime Collection; and the Map Library acquired much of its British Empire cartographic material by colonial deposit, thus making its holdings of Australian maps up to the First World War nearly complete.

Later maps and atlases by James Arrowsmith, James Wyld and the Surveyors General of the colonies include many plans of settlement in Australia. Ballarat, for instance, has nearly forty entries (to 1964) in the *General Catalogue*. Charts of internal exploration include, for example, the track of the expedition from Coopers Creek to Carpentaria by Burke and Wills. The Map Library currently obtains topographic series produced by federal authorities and large-scale mapping by state authorities. It also acquires the national thematic atlas, geological series, the atlas of Australian soils, and gazetteers, and is a depository for charts published by the Australian Hydrographic Service.

Music

The Music Library maintains the Library's collection of printed music. The collection consists of nearly one and a half million music scores and is one of the most comprehensive in the world, covering all countries and all periods from the sixteenth century to the present day. British music is received by legal deposit, and antiquarian items to fill gaps are purchased. Foreign music is acquired by purchase and donation. It is impossible to estimate the extent of the Australian collections as the catalogue is based on composer or main title. However, a brief examination of the catalogue indicates a representative selection of Australian music beginning with *Botany Bay* and *Broadsides Botany Bay* (1789). More serious music begins with itinerant or immigrant composers such as Vincent Wallace (more than 1000 titles) or Isaac Nathan (about fifty), who organized chamber or virtuoso concerts for the free settlers as they begun to arrive in Australian in the 1830s. Later nineteenth-century composers include Charles E. Horsley (about sixty titles), who went to Australia in 1866 and in 1870 set Henry Kendall's *Euterpe* for the opening of Melbourne Town Hall.

In the period around the founding of the Commonwealth of Australia, 1901, there was a spate of patriotic compositions including songs by Joseph Gillot (*Australia's Cherished Dream: Songs of the Southern Seas*) and Charles Thomson (*Australia, I Love Thee: A Trip to Manly)*. At this time an increasing awareness of serious music also became evident, including the earliest string quartets written in Australia. Composers from this period represented in the Library include Leon Caron, Alfred Hill, Ernest Truman and Ernest Hutcheson; Hill, active in Australia from 1897 as a conductor, composer and teacher, was a vigorous champion of Australia's latent musical nationalism. In the 1920s and 1930s there was a new search for a national identity in Australian music, most notably by Percy Grainger (more than 400 titles in the catalogue).

The inter-war years also produced a generation of composers influenced by contemporary European music, including Margaret Sutherland, Peggy Glanville-Hicks, Arthur Benjamin and Malcolm Williamson, who are well represented in the Library because much of their careers have been spent outside Australia, usually in Britain. After the Second World War Australia's music began to absorb more advanced twentieth-century compositional techniques and to show the influence of jazz, pop and East Asian music. Composers of this and the following generation represented include Don Banks, Peter Sculthorpe, Richard Meale, Barry Conyngham, Ross Edwards and Don Boyd.

The catalogue of national and folk music contains a number of Australian items. There are collections of Aboriginal songs, songs with words by Henry Lawson, bush songs, children's songs, and Isaac Nathan's *The Southern Euphrosyne and Australian Miscellany* (1848). As a final note on Australian music, the Library holds fifteen versions of *Waltzing Matilda.*

Manuscripts

Both manuscript music and maps are held in the Department of Manuscripts. The entire collection of the Department's holdings (up to 1968) of Australian material has been described in Phyllis Mander-Jones, *Manuscripts in the British Isles Relating to Australia, New Zealand and the Pacific* (1972). The entry for the Department covers seventy pages. It contains a number of separately named collections of which Sloane, Egerton, Hargrave, Harley, Stowe and the Old Royal Library include material of Australian interest. From the Old Royal Library John Rotz's *Boke of Idography* (1542) shows a coastline in the latitude of Australia; Sloane includes accounts of Dampier's voyages and John Welbe's scheme for the discovery of Terra Australia incognita; the Harleian manuscripts contain sixteenth- and seventeenth-century charts of Australia; and Egerton includes Cook's *Resolution* journal and his secret instructions for the voyage, as well as other material relating to his second and third voyages. Apart from the Bathurst Papers, which are on permanent loan and contain letters relating to Australia in the 1820s, including one from William Wilberforce concerning the lack of clergymen in Van Diemen's Land, the remainder of the manuscripts of Australian interest are 'Additional', i.e. later acquisitions. These have been acquired after the foundation collections, generally by gift, bequest or purchase. They greatly outnumber the named collections, accounting for sixty-seven pages in Mander-Jones, and are an invaluable source for the study of Australia, in particular for the colonial period. They are strong in subjects such as transportation, emigration, political and social history, and exploration. For the last, the material on Cook, including many remarkable drawings made on the voyages, is especially noteworthy.

Relevant acquisitions not in the Mander-Jones compilation but obtained by the Department since 1968 include: 610 volumes of the Dropmore (Grenville) Papers, the papers of William Lord Grenville, Prime Minister 1806-1807, which contain important material from 1789-1791 concerning the transportation of convicts to New South Wales; the Carnarvon Papers of the 4th Earl of Carnarvon, Colonial Secretary 1866-1867 and 1874-1878, important for Australian history shortly before Federation; and the Wrench Diaries of Sir Evelyn Wrench, founder of the Royal Overseas League and the English Speaking Union, which contain observations on Australia for the years preceding the First World War. Finally, a recently acquired literary manuscript should be mentioned: Peter Porter's *Sydney Cove, 1788*.

Philately

The National Philatelic Collections, now maintained by the British Library, originate in the stamp collection first formed in the British Museum in 1864 by John Gray, Keeper of Natural History, and William Vaux, Keeper of Coins and Medals. Dr Gray was a collector from 1840, the year when stamps were first issued. In 1891 the Museum acquired, by bequest, the collection of stamps and postal stationery of Thomas K. Tapling, MP, making it the largest public collection of early and classic issues of the world from 1840 to 1887 to be found in any public institution, and probably the only major one formed during the nineteenth century which is still intact. The early issues of the Australian states are extensively covered and include the major rarity of the 1854 4d issue of Western Australia with the frame inverted. Tapling's stamp collection contains approximately 100,000 items, and in addition there are several thousand examples of postal stationery. In the philatelic library there are approximately thirty other identifiable collections and archives. The Universal Postal Union Collection, dating from about 1920, is the major reference collection. Its authentic status makes it invaluable for comparison with forgeries. Other collections are generally highly specialized or confined to a particular country. For example, the Fitzgerald Air Mail Collection, given to the Museum in 1947, contains stamps, letters and other material of pioneer and early flights throughout the world. The first postal flight in Australia was on 16 July 1914 from Melbourne to Sydney by the French aviator, Maurice Guillaux, who carried souvenir cards on the flight. On 26 February 1920 Ross Smith arrived in Australia from England, and a special stamp was designed for this first England-Australia flight and printed at the Commonwealth Stamp Printing Office. These stamps were fixed by the Australian postal authorities and cancelled on envelopes containing letters that were carried on the Ross Smith flight and then forwarded to the addresses through the normal mails.

The Library also holds a major collection of philatelic literature covering every aspect of the subject. These holdings were greatly augmented by the Philatelic Library of the 26th Earl of Crawford, bequeathed in 1913. The Crawford Library, comprising some 4500 volumes, is probably the most complete collection of philatelic literature in the world for the period 1861 to 1913.

India Office Library and Records

The India Office Library and Records has been administered by the British Library since 1982. It contains nearly 400,000 books in

European and Asian languages, as well as substantial holdings of serials, newspapers, records, official publications, manuscripts, maps, prints and drawings, and a small collection of oil paintings, sculpture and antique furniture. The original Library was established in 1801 by the East India Company to house its collection of oriental books and manuscripts. It was transferred to the newly created India Office in 1858 and subsequently to its successors, the Commonwealth Office and the Foreign and Commonwealth Office. The Library forms a major international specialist collection of South Asian material, especially for the period of British rule. In the nineteenth century its acquisitions ranged wider than the subcontinent and many works were acquired relating to the rest of Asia and the Pacific. One of the subjects in the Library's *Catalogue* (1888) and *Supplement* (1895) is 'Australasia and the Pacific Islands'. There are many books on discovery and exploration, and general descriptive and historical works. The earliest work of Australian interest is William Eden, *The History of New Holland* (1787). There are items relating to possible Indian immigration to Australia, works on ethnology, and several superb plate books, including J.S. Gould, *The Birds of Australia* (1848) and his *The Mammals of Australia* (1858), held as a result of the East India Company's patronage of publishing. Modern acquisitions on Australia are confined to works dealing with cultural, political or economic links with South Asia and with the position of Indians in Australia.

The India Office Records also contains material relating to Australia, most notably emigration from India to Australia, whether of Britons leaving service or of Indian indentured labour from the 1830s until the Immigration Act of 1901. The Marine Records include ships' logs of voyages to Australia and demonstrate the East India Company's involvement with the transportation of convicts. The records of the Company's General Correspondence show that, in the other direction, Australia supplied the Company with horses for its armies, a source for the Indian Army which continued into this century.

BLISS

The British Library Information Sciences Service (BLISS), formerly the Library Association Library, was established in 1934, although its collections date back to 1900. The Service, under British Library control since 1974, holds some 90,000 monographs and 52,000 serial volumes in the field of librarianship. Coverage aims to be world-wide and comprehensive, particularly of English-language serials, which includes a strong Commonwealth representation. Material on Australia ranges from general directories and surveys of libraries and librarianship to detailed studies of special topics like collection development and networking. The Service acquires reports and documents issued by such institutions as the Library Association of Australia, the Australian Advisory Council on Bibliographic Services, the National Library and various library schools. A number of more specialized titles are available on microfiche. Approximately fifty current periodicals are taken from Australia, including such titles as *Australasian College Libraries, Archives and Manuscripts, Cataloguing Australia* and *Education for Librarianship*. All theses accepted for the FLA are in stock, as well as higher degree dissertations in the field of librarianship submitted to UK universities. Some theses, mainly on microfiche, have been obtained from Australian library schools.

National Sound Archive

The National Sound Archive (NSA), formerly the British Institute of Recorded Sound (BIRS), was founded in 1948 and has been administered by the British Library since 1983. The holdings of the Archive comprise nearly 1 million discs, over 55,000 hours of tape recordings, 8500 books and over 3000 videograms. About 90 per cent of the output of the British recording industry is acquired through voluntary deposit. The Archive has an active recording programme of its own, chiefly in the fields of drama, literature, traditional music and oral history. BBC Sound Archive and Transcription discs are supplied to the National Sound Archive, and selected programmes are recorded off the air. There is a representative collection of Australian music composed in the Western tradition. Holdings tend to be of items available in Britain but do include the entire Festival label series and a selection of discs issued by Australian EMI and Australian RCA.

The International Music Collection is a specialist archive within the NSA and consists of recordings and commercially published discs. All of the discs produced by the Australian Institute of Aboriginal Studies have been acquired, and privately recorded collections include: forty-three privately pressed discs edited by Professor A.P. Elkin of music recorded between 1950 and 1956 in Australia and New Guinea; and recordings made by John Hutchinson in Western Australia in 1960-1961. The Sound Archive's oldest ethnographic recordings are in a set of 283 wax cylinders which were made during the course of four anthropological expeditions, in Australia and the Torres Strait Islands, between 1898 and 1912. The cylinders found their way to England, where they were acquired by Sir James Frazer, author of *The Golden Bough*. After the First World War the collection was taken over by the Cambridge Institute of Psychology, where for thirty-odd years they languished in the obscurity of a boiler room. In the 1950s Professor Zangwill of the Department of Psychology at Cambridge arranged for the entire collection to be transferred to the BIRS. The cylinders represent some of the earliest sound records made of Aboriginal music and language. In recent years the NSA has transferred the recordings to tape.

Australians living in England such as Peter Porter, Germaine Greer and Clive James are represented in the section of the NSA devoted to recordings of drama and literature. Readings by Michael Wilding and Chris Wallace-Crabbe, among others, have been recorded at seminars at the Commonwealth Institute and other venues. There are BBC recordings of authors such as Patrick White. The Archive also holds a rare recording of the *Oz* trial of the 1960s with Richard Neville.

The British Library of Wildlife Sounds, founded in 1969, is possibly the most comprehensive wildlife sound library in the world. Most of the commercially published Australian wildlife material is in its collection, together with tape recordings made by professionals and amateurs. The latter includes a copy of the 'Preliminary Field Guide to the Bird Sounds of Australia', prepared in 1974 by Norman Robinson, and comprising some 400 recordings of 300 different species, as well as recordings contributed by individuals and a few recordings of mammals.

Newspapers

The final port of call in this survey of the principal holdings of Australiana in the British Library in London is the Newspaper Library at Colindale. Here are housed the national collections of newspapers, comprising some 600,000 volumes and parcels of newspapers and nearly 250,000 reels of microfilm. The Australian collections are extensive (more than 400 titles), but runs are sometimes imperfect. During the nineteenth century titles were often received via the Colonial Office, and from 1887 to 1976 by donation from the Royal Commonwealth Society. The library holds the first newspaper to be published in Australia, the *Sydney Gazette* of 5 March 1803. There are titles from mining settlements, newspapers produced for or by ethnic groups, and titles not properly newspapers at all such as *Australian Sketcher with Pen and Pencil*, published in Melbourne from 1873 to 1889. The Newspaper Library's policy is to transfer its foreign collection to 35mm microfilm both for preservation and as a means of saving space. The microfilming of Australian material was completed in 1983. Gaps in retrospective holdings are filled when possible by microfilm. The fifteen current Australian titles are all received on microfilm. The Newspaper Library's 1987-1988 catalogue of *Microfilms of Newspapers and Journals for Sale* includes 241 entries for Australia. As well as major newspapers such as *The Age*, *The Australasian*, the *Port Phillip Herald* (later *The Herald*), and the *West Australian*, the catalogue includes more obscure titles like the *Australasian Brewer's Journal*, the *Australian Spiritualist*, *The Cockatoo and North Queensland Figaro*, and the *Kangaroo out of His Element*.

Science, Technology and Industry Collections

The Science, Technology and Industry collections of the British Library are divided between two major sites: Holborn (in Central London) and Boston Spa in West Yorkshire, some 200 miles north of London. The collections here are of a very different nature when compared with those in the Humanities and Social Sciences Division (commonly called 'Bloomsbury').

The Science Reference and Information Service (SRIS) began life as the Patent Office Library and was subsequently renamed the National Reference Library of Science and Invention (NRLSI) in the 1960s. Its brief was, and is, to collect published materials from all over the world in the fields of science, technology and increasingly business. Originally intended to serve the needs of the patent researchers, the collection has at its core material relating to the physical and chemical sciences, engineering, building and other technological subjects. With the creation of the NRLSI the scope was expanded to include the life sciences. When the British Library was created in 1973, the NRLSI became the Science Reference Library, and the collection now houses most of the British Library's scientific collections in London. Originally a reference service, the Science Reference Library has developed its role to be much more of an information provider to those working in science, industry, commerce, business and patent searching. To reflect this, the name was changed several years ago to Science Reference and Information Service (SRIS). SRIS offers conventional reference facilities (with far fewer restrictions than the Bloomsbury complex) and also online searching, SDI services, business information and assistance with translating. Currently the collections at SRIS number over 29 million patents, including a complete collection of those issued in Australia, 220,000 monographs and subscriptions to about 31,000 serials. It is difficult to isolate Australian materials because of the way stock is arranged and processed, but the collection includes all major Australian technical and scientific journals, as well as a considerable number of trade and industrial publications which would most often be described as 'grey' literature.

The other part of the Science, Technology and Industry division is the Document Supply Centre at Boston Spa (DSC). The Centre, whose primary function is to provide a loan and photocopy service to libraries both in the United Kingdom and overseas, began life at the Lending Library Unit (LLU) in 1958 to collect Russian scientific literature and translations made from it. In 1961 it became the National Lending Library for Science and Technology (NLLST – often referred to simply as NLL) and its brief was to collect literature in science and technology from all over the world regardless of language and specialization. The brief was extended in the early 1960s to medicine and biological sciences and in 1969-1970 to the social sciences. When the British Library was formed in 1973, the National Central Library (an independently funded library dealing mostly with humanities and social sciences and based in London) was moved to Boston Spa and merged with the NLL to form the British Library Lending Division (BLLD) and scope was extended to cover all fields of knowledge. In 1985 the name was changed to Document Supply Centre to reflect the shifting emphasis from lending to copying.

The collections at BLDSC are extensive, consisting of over 2.8 million monographs, 211,000 serial titles, 3.3 million technical reports and considerable quantities of official publications, theses and translations. The acquisitions policy of the Centre has been narrowed somewhat over the years, to cope with dwindling financial resources, but basically the aim is to collect all English-language materials likely to be requested through inter-library loan. There is no subject limitation, but some kinds of material are excluded, notably fiction, school and children's books and popular magazines and purely recreational material. Currently the Centre is adding about 800 Australian monographs to its collections annually and subscribes to 800 Australian journals ranging from the *Medical Journal of Australia* and *Chemical Engineering in Australia* in the sciences to *Journal of Christian Education* and *Sydney Studies in English* in the humanities. The Centre also has backruns of nearly 6000 journals from Australia no longer being published. The material is quite heavily used by the Centre's 13,000 customers. Not surprisingly, most heavily used titles have been in the medical, engineering and social sciences.

The Centre also has extensive collections of technical report literature from Australia, including virtually complete collections of reports from such organizations as the Australian Road Research Laboratory and the Australian Atomic Energy Commission. University theses from Australia are not normally collected, but the Centre has extensive holdings of Australian government publications, as well as those from the states and territories. The collection of government publications from Western Australia is particularly strong.

The Future

All the collections of the British Library currently scattered in twenty-one sites around London, apart from the Newspaper Library at Colindale and the National Sound Archive at Kensington, will be brought together under one roof at St Pancras. The move, the largest in library history, begins in 1991 and continues until 1996. It will bring together over 11 million volumes onto a single site, where more than 300 linear kilometres of shelving will accommodate them in a purpose-built, environmentally friendly building. The new library will offer enhanced services and improve possibilities for multi-disciplinary research. Already the British Library contains one of the world's leading research collections and its Australian holdings are unequalled in the United Kingdom, Europe, and possibly elsewhere outside Australia. At St Pancras, one of the greatest cultural achievements of the twentieth century, according to Richard Luce, former Minister for the Arts, a larger part of these collections will be concentrated on one site. New technology will make storage and retrieval more efficient. For more than 200 years the Library has welcomed the learned and the curious to its reading rooms, providing for its users a 'gateway to the world of recorded knowledge' *(Gateway to Knowledge,* British Library Strategic Plan, 1989). Learned researchers and the curious students of Australiana will continue to be welcome, both at Bloomsbury now and at the new British Library in St Pancras from 1993.

In view of the current developments in the British Library there is considerable rationalization of collections, and material which is rarely required from document supply but regularly used for reference purposes will be centred in Bloomsbury and vice versa. In addition there will be rationalization between DSC and SRIS to achieve maximum use of literature with minimum inconvenience to customers, whether visitors or remote users.

13 Collecting Australian Literature: An Australian Perspective

G.A. Stafford

An Australian perspective is provided in this examination of the development at Flinders University of South Australia of a creative Australian literature collection. Decisions which were crucial to the nature and scope of the collection are discussed; the methods of acquiring material, the main sources of supply and problems of acquisition are treated; and an evaluative description of the collection is provided, with its main strengths and weaknesses being identified. Finally, future prospects for the collection are considered.

During the early years of settlement, literature in Australia, like that in most colonies, was a development and extension of the colonizing country, Britain. The first writers were continuing a style and manner they had learned from their land of birth. The first products of creative writing were written by people from overseas. Barron Field's *First Fruits of Australian Poetry* is generally regarded as the first book of verse published in Australia, published in Sydney in 1819.[1] The first novel published in book form was *Quintus Servinton* by Henry Savery, published in Hobart in 1830.[2] Later in the nineteenth century Australian-born persons began writing, and we find in the poetry of Charles Tompson and Charles Harpur the start of an indigenous Australian literature.

Throughout the latter half of the nineteenth century many Australian writers had their work published both in Australia and overseas. Their writings reflected the growth and development of the Australian colonies and the people living in them. If it is true that creative writing reflects the essence of a nation's culture, then in its 200 years of existence since European settlement Australia has developed a culture and literature of its own. It has produced some outstanding writers who have achieved considerable fame through their output and literary merit. Australian authors such as Patrick White and Morris West have gained a world-wide reputation, yet less than forty years ago academics were having to defend the teaching of Australian literature at our universities. At that time courses in English included works by Scottish, Irish and

American writers, but works by Australian authors were not considered worthy of inclusion. In 1954 A.D. Hope, a professor of English and a well known poet, wrote:

> the study of English is of prime importance. And if we have to choose what shall go into such a course, we are right to choose the best we can get. It would I think be hard to argue that Australian literature has anything comparable to offer. It is not a matter of arguing whether Goldsmith is inferior to Henry Handel Richardson, or Lovelace to Shaw Neilson. It is the more general argument that the great English writers cannot without loss be replaced by even the best of our Australian writers and that if we are to study great writers we ought to study them in their natural context of the lesser writers of their periods. To find a place for Australian literature within the present English courses is a disservice to both.[3]

Four years later Vincent Buckley, also a professor and poet, wrote: 'Certainly, over the past twenty or thirty years, the large assumption has come increasingly to be made that since there is a body of writing that is recognizably Australian and not something else, there is also, or there ought to be, a subject called Australian Literature which our universities have the duty to study and teach.'[4] Happily the situation today has followed Buckley's exhortation and Australian writers are studied as part of the courses on literature at our universities.

From its establishment in 1966, the Flinders University of South Australia has included Australian literature in the courses taught. Naturally the Library had to build up a collection to support this teaching programme, but it also had to acquire material to assist the research carried out by academic staff and higher degree students. It was agreed that the Library should acquire the creative literary works of Australian writers both past and present. It was, therefore, necessary to start acquiring works that were being published currently as well as those already published, many of which were long out of print. It was decided that fiction, poetry and drama would be collected, together with works of criticism, literary history and biography. At a later stage children's literature was also collected.

Using Morris Miller's *Australian Literature: A Bibliography to 1939* and Frederick Macartney's work that extended the bibliography to 1950, a list of the major authors and their works was drawn up and, where possible, purchased. Books by minor authors were not neglected.[5] It was agreed that the collection should represent as many authors as possible, so, regardless of the literary merit of a book, the works of many minor authors were acquired. Thus a collection was formed that contained an example of the work of most Australian writers. This has proved useful for comparative purposes.

One of the first decisions that has to be made when establishing a collection of Australian literature is to define who is to be regarded as an Australian writer. Is it to be all those who were born in Australia? Is it to include those who were born in Australia but then left to live overseas? How are writers who were born overseas but emigrated to Australia and developed their literary reputation here to be regarded? It was decided that no hard and fast rules would be laid down, and we have regarded as Australian those authors who have generally been claimed as Australian. Thus we do not treat Mrs Humphrey Ward as an Australian although she was born in Hobart, Tasmania, because she went to England as a young person and established her career as a writer there. Henry Handel Richardson, however, although she too went to England, continued to write novels with an Australian background and is considered an Australian. Arthur Upfield and Adam Lindsay Gordon were both born overseas but came to Australia as young men and are regarded as Australians. In cases of doubt we consult established bibliographies like Morris Miller's *Australian Literature* to assist our decision.

Many Australian writers have been attracted to move overseas, chiefly to Britain. Apart from the experience gained and the greater opportunities to be found overseas, there was the distinct advantage of being closer to a number of large publishing houses, and the development of Australian publishing has had a direct effect on Australian writing. As long as publishing houses in Australia remained small, authors were unable to have their work widely distributed. Andrew Fabinyi, the publishing manager of F.W. Cheshire, noted in 1954 that in recent years one witnessed 'the tendency of Australian writers to publish their books abroad'.[6] This tendency has continued not only among contemporary authors but also with the reprints of earlier writers of the nineteenth century. We find their works being published in Britain and the United States of America. The short stories of Louis Becke, who lived from 1855 to 1915, are available in editions from Ayer and Co. of New Hampshire,[7] and the novels of Rosa Praed (1851-1935) can be purchased as reprints issued by Pandora Press and Virago Press, both in London.[8] This does not mean that Australian publishers are not also reissuing the classics of Australian literature, but it does show that overseas firms are prepared to reprint and market titles that local publishers will not.

Until 1901 Australia consisted of six separate colonies each with its own governor and parliament. This contributed to several writers acquiring a local reputation within their own colony, either because they only wrote about their immediate region or because they used small local publishers. This practice occurred mainly with minor writers, particularly poets, and continued after the colonies became states. Poets like Dryblower Murphy and Essex Evans gained their reputations within their respective states, Western Australia and Queensland. In common with minor writers in most parts of the world, the size of the editions of their works was small. It is, therefore, often quite difficult to obtain copies of their publications; yet, if one is aiming to have a reasonably comprehensive collection, one must acquire copies of the work of as many authors as possible from all parts of the country.

In establishing a collection of Australian literature at Flinders University we were faced with the challenge of acquiring publications from the whole of the country, many of which would have been unavailable for many years. Currently published material also had to be bought at a time when Australian literature was only just being recognized as worthy of academic study. Fortunately, at that time in the mid-1960s funding was more generous and book prices were lower. Now, after twenty-five years, our collection consists of around 6000 volumes. It may not be the largest collection in Australia, but as it started from nothing, it is quite a respectable achievement.

Ever since the Library was established, book order requests from teaching staff have been the basis of selection of material for the collection. The number of such requests was given an added stimulus with the establishment of the Centre for Research in the New Literatures in English (CRNLE) in 1977. The increase of interest in Commonwealth literature coming from Australasia, Africa, India, the Caribbean and Southeast Asia led to the study of these literatures as part of the courses offered. The Centre was established to foster this study and to develop research of a comparative and cross-cultural nature. Australian literature was included within the scope of interest of CRNLE, and the research staff have continued to place requests for items of Australian literature. They are particularly assiduous in checking booksellers' catalogues. The Library staff augments these requests by ordering works that may have been overlooked. This has helped in the development of a balanced collection without too great an emphasis being placed on one author to the neglect of another. It has also meant that orders are placed regularly for works as they are published.

The main sources of supply for currently published Australian titles are local and interstate booksellers who have little difficulty in providing copies of the books. However, in the case of works by minor writers that are produced at lesser known presses in editions of a small number, we usually order direct from the publisher or author. This particularly applies to some poetry titles where a local poet may have a small edition of their work issued. This type of publication often has a limited distribution and is sometimes difficult to acquire. It is also not unknown for smaller publishers to fail to provide proper invoices for purchase of the item. This in turn will cause difficulties in ensuring that correct payment is made. If the author's work is published overseas, then we will order direct from a large bookseller either in Britain or the US. In doing this we are guaranteed supply of the item and purchase it at the current exchange rate for the overseas price. We did consider placing a blanket order with an overseas bookseller for Australian literature, but a serious problem would be caused with those titles that are published both in Australia and abroad, because, wherever possible, we prefer to have the Australian edition. It was thought that too much checking would be involved to prevent duplication, so blanket orders were never placed.

Earlier printed material is acquired through various channels: the secondhand market, book auctions, donations and serendipity. Secondhand booksellers' catalogues are a valuable source for obtaining works that are out of print. Time has to be spent in reading these lists and marking them for checking against our catalogue to find out if they are already in stock. Because Australiana has been collected by many private book collectors for a number of years, a high price often has to be paid for these books; however, if they are needed for the collection, a value judgment has to be made as to whether the need is worth the cost.

Attendance at book auctions is a useful way of acquiring works, as the catalogue may be checked beforehand and an estimate made of the price that you are prepared to pay. If staff and time are available, then library staff can attend the auction; otherwise an agent is used and this will, of course, add to the cost of the book. However, by regularly watching the prices that books fetch at auctions the librarian soon gains a good working knowledge of the book market in the subject area of interest. It is often enlightening to see the prices at which books are bought. For example, in June 1990 a first edition of Patrick White's *Happy Valley*, published by Harrap in 1939, was sold at auction for A$580.[9] In many libraries the first editions of books by Australian writers are on open access shelving where they are likely to be a prey to vandalism or theft.

The catalogues of publishers who reissue or reprint books by Australian authors provide a good source for obtaining the works of early writers. *Australian Books in Print* will, of course, list all the books that are in print in Australia, but, as mentioned already, a number of overseas publishers are reprinting the works of early Australian authors. This is especially the case with women writers; here there has been a growing interest in works that have been neglected for too long. To help in finding out what has been published in this category of material, both in Australia and overseas, a new bibliography appeared in 1989: *ANCLIP: Australian Nineteenth Century Literature in Print*.[10] It is edited by Victor Crittenden, formerly librarian of what is now the University of Canberra and also a noted bibliographer. Although it is only a slim publication, it contains valuable information concerning the availability of nineteenth-century literature. The price of each item is given and publishers' addresses are available, so that, if a local bookseller is not prepared to obtain a required item, one can order direct from overseas. This publication is very useful in providing an alternative ordering source to the secondhand bookseller. The prices listed in *ANCLIP* are generally far lower than those on the secondhand market. Recently, *Rodman the Boatsteerer and Other Stories* by Louis Becke (1855-1913) appeared in one catalogue for $95, while in *ANCLIP* a reprint published in the US was available for $19.[11] The former was a first edition, but for most libraries building up a collection the reprint would be more suitable.

Gifts and donations can prove to be an excellent avenue through which to build up a collection. Many people acquire and collect books and then at some time in their life may wish to dispose of some or all of their collection. If the general public is made aware that a collection is being built up, donors may make contact and offer their books to the library. Although donations mean savings on purchase costs, other expenses are involved. The gifts may have to be collected, they will have to be sorted and checked against the library's holdings. The donor may wish to receive a tax concession for the gift, in which case there is the expense of having the books valued by a recognized valuer. However, one must always bear in mind that the main purpose is to build up the collection, and if the range of titles has been increased by the acceptance of a gift, then the collection has benefitted.

Serendipity is an enjoyable way to build up a collection. It represents the fun of the unexpected, and there are no guides on applying this approach. It is based on personal knowledge of the literature and the fascination for fossicking. These days there are so many outlets where one can see books being offered for sale. Apart from secondhand dealers, there are jumble sales, white elephant stalls, garage sales,

Rotary fairs, Red Cross shops, Community Aid Abroad shops and trash and treasure outlets. Public libraries have also made use of sales as a means of disposing of books that are no longer read, and as a way of raising funds. These sales are a valuable hunting ground for any librarian building up a literature collection. One never knows when an out-of-the-way piece of Australian writing may turn up. Recently a copy of *Growing towards the Light*, a novel by Mrs Henry Doudy, was bought from a stall for twenty cents.[12] This is not a great work of literature but it was the second edition of the novel and was published in Adelaide by the Woman's Christian Temperance Union of South Australia in 1928. Apart from filling a place in our Australian literature collection, this work has value as a document of social history.

All the above methods of acquisition have been used to build up the collection at Flinders University. It must, however, be understood that no separate funding has been allocated for Australian literature, so this collection has been developed at the same time as the rest of the Library's collection, which covers all subjects taught at the University. This means that at those times when there have been cuts in the allocation of funds to the Library fewer books have been purchased. This has caused an uneven flow of books, so that in one year we would have bought more books on Australian literature than in another. Cuts in funding are experienced by all libraries, but when you are as far away as we are from our book suppliers in Britain and the USA, it is likely that books will go out of print before we have the money to order them. In practice we find that requests from academic staff for purchases take up most of available funds, and library staff have very little money to spend on augmenting the teaching staff's selection. The reduction in the financing of Australian universities has also led to staff cutbacks, and as staff are either not replaced or there is a delay in their replacement, so there are fewer people available to take part in book selection and collection building. In this respect, if the Library has not ordered a book when it is first published, there is always the hope that it may be obtained later as a donation, or be bought secondhand.

Australia's isolation means that we are at least twelve weeks away from overseas suppliers using surface mail. Air mail postage for the delivery of books is too expensive, except for a few cases of extreme urgency. Surface air lift is now an alternative used by many of the main suppliers and this cuts time down to five weeks. Nevertheless, whenever any title is going to be used in teaching a course, it must be ordered well in advance of the start of the course. This is not a problem if the work is published in Australia, but if it has to come from overseas, it may not arrive in time for the commencement of teaching.

Distance from booksellers can also cause difficulties with costs and prices. It is common now for currencies to fluctuate. In 1986 the Australian dollar declined in value against overseas currencies. The 1990 crisis in the Middle East at first caused it to rise in value and then to decline. These movements in the Australian dollar greatly affect the number of books that one may or may not be able to buy from overseas. A sudden fall in the value of the dollar can mean that a large part of the book vote is used up.

In its formative years the Library was fortunate in receiving presentations of books from former institute libraries as they closed down. Flinders University was being established during the 1960s when there were still institute libraries throughout South Australia. These libraries, some of which were established in the last century, were supported by borrowers' subscriptions and a government subsidy. During the 1970s the development of local subsidized public libraries caused a number of the old institute libraries to close down, and their books were disposed of. These books generally consisted of older works on a variety of subjects. Among them were older Australian novels and volumes of poetry, some of which were published in the nineteenth century. Their acquisition was a valuable addition to the Library's collection of Australian literature.

In building up the collection of Australian literature the staff selecting books must have a good knowledge of the names of Australian writers. Because, as already mentioned, so many Australians have their books published outside Australia, it is easy to miss an author relevant to our collection when glancing through publishers' lists. In common with several writers who have their books published outside the country in which they live, the titles of their books may change from one country to another. Arthur Upfield, a writer of detective stories set for the most part in the Australian bush, had his book, *Mr Jelly's Business*, published in Australia and England under that title, but in America it was entitled *Murder Down Under*. Similarly, *Wings above the Diamantina* was published as *Winged Mystery* in England.[13] No doubt these changes of title were made for sound commercial reasons, but one can easily spend money by buying two copies of the same book without realizing it.

In making an evaluative description of the collection that we have brought together it is apparent that the fiction and poetry sections are far stronger than the drama. This has not been done deliberately; it is the way the collection has evolved in satisfying the demands made on it, and the outcome of the selection of works of literature for the collection. Australian dramatists, like the novelists, had to go overseas if they wished to achieve major success. Currently, the majority of Australian drama is published by Currency Press, but earlier Australian plays, if not published overseas, were not issued in large editions. As mentioned above, we have received some very useful additions as donations. The majority of these, however, have been either novels or poetry. Drama as leisure reading is perhaps not as popular with the reading public and has not been present in many gifts. It is a working collection acquired for use, so the majority of the books are on open access shelves, where they are available for borrowing by the staff and students of the University. The works of the major Australian writers are represented in the collection, in some cases in several editions. This applies to authors such as Marcus Clarke, Miles Franklin, Henry Handel Richardson, Henry Lawson and Patrick White, who are studied regularly in the courses taught. A large part of the collection, however, consists of the publications of minor writers, some of whom were very prolific. Guy Boothby, for example, was born in Adelaide, South Australia, in 1867 and wrote the librettos of two operas while a young man. In 1894 he left for London, where he wrote almost fifty novels before his death in 1905. We have a number of these novels but not the early librettos. There are authors like Boothby in the collection who became popular novelists but whose reputation has not endured. Many of them went to Britain to achieve success and, it would appear, to have their work published by Ward Lock. The number of books by Australian authors issued by this publishing house is remarkable.

Although works by minor Australian writers have no great financial value, they have their place in the history of Australian literature, and copies of some of these titles are now quite rare. It is likely, therefore, that for security reasons some of the more rare items will have to be taken from the open shelves and placed in our store.

In arrangement of the books on open shelves the practice has been followed of bringing together in one alphabetical sequence by title all the works of an author, regardless of form. This has meant that when a person has written both novels and poetry, a decision has to be made whether to regard him or her as a novelist or poet. It looks a little strange to find Henry Lawson's poetry shelved in the sequence of fiction alongside his short stories. At one time a chronological arrangement instead of an alphabetical arrangement by title was discussed but was not adopted. As part of the open shelf arrangement, the works of biography and criticism of an author follow the author's literary works. In this way students can easily find the book they want and criticisms of it.

One collection that has not been placed on the open shelves is that relating to Australian children's literature. This collection was acquired from an Adelaide bookseller when the Library was being established and before the first intake of students had arrived. It consists of the works of the major children's writers in Australia. There is a complete set of Ethel Turner's books as well as those of her sister Lilian and her daughter Jean Curlewis. Most of the authors wrote during the inter-war period, and the writers Constance Mackness, Lillian Pyke and Mary Grant Bruce are well represented. All the books are in very good condition, some are first editions and many still retain their original dustjackets. As they have been kept in a closed collection, they have not suffered from a great deal of handling by readers. From 1970 to 1984 a course was taught on children's literature, but for this books were purchased and placed on open access for borrowing. Duplicate copies of titles already held in the Australian children's literature collection were bought when they were needed, so that the titles in that collection would not suffer from wear and tear.

Since children's literature ceased to be taught, the Library has not actively bought any children's fiction or books relating to this subject. If the course is ever reintroduced, it will be necessary to fill this gap with new purchases. All the books that are available on loan to staff and students of the University are also available on inter-library loan to any other library in Australia or overseas. However, there have so far been no overseas requests for works of Australian literature. The Library has the majority of its holdings listed on the Australian Bibliographic Network (ABN), the national network mounted by the National Library of Australia. It is very easy for any library that has access to ABN via a terminal to locate our holdings. Thus any book added to our collection is accessible not only to our own users but also to any other researcher in the country.

Literary periodicals and bibliographies play an important role in support of the literary works. Subscriptions have been taken out to literary periodicals such as *Meanjin, Southerly, Westerly* and *Australian Literary Studies*, which are shelved with all the other periodicals on a separate floor of the Library. As one would expect, bibliographies form a large part of the reference material for Australian literature. The various individual author bibliographies and bibliography series have been purchased and form part of the general reference collection.

The future of the collection will depend largely on funding and the commitments that have to be made to collecting material for subjects that hitherto have not been taught at the University. The collection will continue to grow, but at a slower rate, and some hard decisions will have to be made when purchasing. For example, a bookshop recently offered for sale a collection of around 200 books published by the New South Wales Bookstall Company Pty Ltd. This firm, run by Alfred Rowlandson, produced Australian books between 1900 and 1940. The collection would be a useful asset, but the purchase price is $19,000. One has to be very sure before spending this amount of money that the right decision is being made. It is to be hoped that when collections of this type come on the market they will be bought by a library so that researchers can continue to have access to this material.

The increased use of computerized catalogues in libraries has made it easier for one library to have access to another library's holdings either by remote access terminals or a network. This in turn will signify that collections of Australian literature held in various libraries will be more accessible to library users, who will be able to locate the individual titles and editions they require. This should also assist in collection building so that duplicate sets of material are not acquired in a particular region. The use of CD-ROMs wili enable out-of-print material to be available again. Just as in the 1950s the works listed in the STC were made available in microfilm by University Microfilms, there is no reason, other than cost and demand, why the works of certain Australian authors should not be available on a CD-ROM disk.

However, technology is not likely to replace the printed word as far as creative literature is concerned. People will continue to prefer to read a novel on the train or in bed in book form rather than on a small portable screen. Authors will continue to provide material to satisfy people's reading habits. As the demand for books in Australia grows, either from shops or libraries, so Australian literature will thrive into the twenty-first century.

Notes

1 Barron Field, *First Fruits of Australian Poetry*. Sydney: George Howe Government Printer, 1819.

2 Henry Savery, *Quintus Servinton*. Hobart: H. Melville, 1830-1831.

3 A.D. Hope, 'Australian Literature and the Humanities,' *Meanjin* 13 (1954): 167.

4 Vincent Buckley, 'Towards an Australian Literature,' *Meanjin* 18 (1959): 63.

5 E. Morris Miller, *Australian Literature and Bibliography to 1938*, extended to 1950 by Frederick T. Macartney. Sydney: Angus and Robertson, 1956.

6 Andrew Fabinyi, 'Australian Books Today,' *Meanjin* 13 (1954): 559.
7 Louis Becke, *Pacific Tales*. Salem: Ayer and Co., 1987 (facsimile reprint).
8 Rosa Praed, *Bond of Wedlock*. London: Pandora Press, 1987.
9 Patrick White, Happy Valley. London: Harrap, 1939.
10 *Australian Nineteenth Century Literature in Print*, ed. by V. Crittenden. Canberra: Mulini Press, 1989.
11 Louis Becke, *Rodman the Boatsteerer and Other Stories*. Salem: Ayer and Co., reprint of 1924 ed.
12 Mrs Henry A. Doudy, *Growing towards the Light*. Melbourne: G. Robertson, 1909; 2nd ed. Adelaide: Women's Christian Temperance Union, 1928.
13 Arthur Upfield, *Mr Jelly's Business*. Sydney: Angus and Robertson, 1937; *Murder Down Under*. New York: Doubleday, 1943; *Wings above the Diamantina*. Sydney: Angus and Robertson, 1936; *Winged Mystery*. London: John Hamilton, 1937.

14 Collecting Australian Literature: A British Perspective

Patricia M. Larby

Materials for Australian studies in British libraries are widely available. These immensely rich and varied resources date from the early voyages of exploration in the eighteenth century to the present. Current collection policies are subject to the impact of increasingly stringent financial cuts on acquisition and retention policies. Despite practical difficulties, the future for Australian studies seems buoyant, and Britain's libraries are well equipped to meet demand.

Introduction

The collections of Australian materials in British libraries are amazingly rich and varied. They represent the fruits of an involvement by Britain in Australia affairs from the early European voyages of discovery in the eighteenth century to the present. Interest in Australia has been heightened in recent years by the establishment in 1983 of a Centre for Australian Studies in London and the celebration in 1988 of Australia's Bicentenary which received considerable popular coverage in the British media. Australian films and television series enjoy considerable success with British audiences, while the study of Australia in schools and institutions of higher learning claims a minor, though enthusiastically supported, share of teaching and research.

The Role of the Sir Robert Menzies Centre for Australian Studies

Despite the long-standing historical links between the two countries, it was not until 1949 that the study of Australia in Britain began to feature as a distinct topic of interest. The establishment in that year of the Institute of Commonwealth Studies by the University of London, headed by Sir Keith Hancock, an eminent Australian historian, provided a focus for advanced study and research which has attracted a regular clientele of visiting Australian scholars. When, in the 1970s, there were expressions of interest in a more visible profile for Australian studies, the Institute was seen as the natural home for what became established as an Australian Studies Centre, initially funded by the Australian Government and backing from the Menzies Memorial Fund, but latterly entirely by the Menzies Memorial Fund. The Centre was renamed the Sir Robert Menzies Centre for Australian Studies in 1988, and it has a lively programme of seminars, conferences and publications.

In his paper to the British Library's Colloquium on Australian and New Zealand Studies in 1984, the Centre's first Head, Geoffrey Bolton, reviewed the extent of teaching and research on Australia being conducted at the time in Britain's educational establishments, and outlined what he saw as the Centre's role in promoting Australian studies in Britain.[1] His proposals included an association for Australian studies to promote the interchange of information and experience between individuals with an interest in Australian affairs; the British Australian Studies Association was founded shortly afterwards.

Britain's Library Resources for Australian Studies

When the Centre was founded, the extent of library resources in Britain to support Australian studies was not fully known. The production of a guide to Australiana in British libraries was seen as an essential early priority for the Centre. An experienced bibliographer, Valerie Bloomfield, was engaged and it is her guide, published as *Resources for Australian and New Zealand Studies*, which uncovered the substantial quantities of materials held in British libraries relating to Australian affairs and from which many of the data contained in this paper are drawn.[2] From this and an earlier work describing the riches of Britain's manuscript materials relating to Australia, Phyllis Mander-Jones' *Manuscripts in the British Isles Relating to Australia, New Zealand and the Pacific*,[3] the true extent of Australiana in British libraries was revealed.

Historical Studies

As might be expected, the finest historical collections of Australiana are held in older libraries, especially those of the great museums and learned societies, where they have accumulated, in some cases, from the eighteenth century down to the present. Such collections represent the outcome of exploration, travels, funded expeditions and scientific research which reflect the primary objectives of the institutions concerned. The resources of the British Library are described elsewhere in this volume, but many other libraries have excellent holdings of these early materials. An impressive collection of voyages of discovery is held at the Foreign and Commonwealth Office (FCO). The collections which form the present Library were founded in the nineteenth century, but various earlier travel accounts are held, including a virtually complete set of the records of the voyages of James Cook; some of these have been described by Margaret Cousins.[4] Included among the Library's riches are works on migration and settlement, and an unrivalled collection of official publications dating from the first half of the nineteenth century. Following an instruction in 1837 from the Secretary of State, governors of Australian colonies were required to forward to London copies of legislation, gazettes and other legal and administrative documents. The requirement appears to have been interpreted widely for a considerable volume of other local publications, particularly pamphlets – many of them rare – was also sent. Although the Library now concentrates on international relations, diplomacy, politics, economics and law, the scope of the total collection is very broad. Even within its more narrowly defined current acquisition policy, coverage is still extensive, though state publications, other than legislation which is still collected in its entirety, are more selectively acquired.

The comparable collection at the Royal Commonwealth Society, founded in 1868, is also known for the extent of its rare and unusual holdings which have been built up over the years by many generous gifts from members as well as by purchases and exchanges. Historical works include many of the early classic accounts of exploration and discovery and include E.G. Wakefield's *A Letter from Sydney...together with the Outline of a System of Colonization* (1829); R. Mudie's *The Picture of Australia, Exhibiting New Holland, Van Diemen's Land and All the Settlements...* (1829); and a work of fiction, *Voyage de Robertson aux Terres Australes, Traduit sur le Manuscrit Anglois* (1767), by a pseudonymous author described only as Robertson. Other strengths lie in the collection of nineteenth-century directories, yearbooks, works of reference and contemporary creative writing. The last is well represented in a collection of pamphlets containing literary bibliographies and volumes of verse, which also includes political tracts, town guides and similar output from local presses in Australia. It is difficult to encapsulate in a few short sentences the riches of this great library; they include not only materials for academic research in the fields of history, politics and literature, but also popular works such as cookery books, travel guides, wildlife studies and art books. Its catalogues have been published,[5] as has the catalogue of its superb biographical collection, *Biography Catalogue*, which contains in excess of 800 entries on Australia.[6]

The Royal Geographical Society Library is an outstanding source of information on all aspects of geography and related topics, and contains a substantial quantity of Australian materials, including a collection of nineteenth-century travel; its Polar library also contains items of Australian interest, and a separate biography collection includes many famous Australian names. The National Maritime Museum's collection of early travel and discovery is exceptionally rich; the volumes, some dating from the seventeenth century, are listed in its printed catalogue,[7] but Australian materials are represented throughout the Museum's subject coverage: national and local history, biography, naval history and the two World Wars. The Polar section of the Library includes the achievements of Australian explorers.

Maritime affairs are also covered in some depth by the Library of the Ministry of Defence (Navy). Many of the early voyages to the South Pacific were made under the patronage of the Admiralty, and the Royal Navy was actively involved in the discovery and exploration of Australasia, charting the coasts, mapping the interior and transporting convicts. The works of early British and European explorers are a major resource, and there are additionally extensive holdings of works of the eighteenth and nineteenth centuries on the founding of new colonies, their economies, natural resources, missionary activities and on the goldfields. Australian materials are also held in the sciences: oceanography, meteorology, hydrography and natural history.

Outside London the copyright libraries at Oxford and Cambridge Universities both possess extensive Australian collections, with British publications on Australia being received via legal deposit. In Oxford the Bodleian Library's holdings on Australia are particularly strong in literature, especially poetry, and also in printed ephemera, maps and music, including ethnic music. The Bodleian's subsidiary libraries, the Law Library and Rhodes House, aim to acquire major Australian works in their respective fields. Law reports, legislation, sets of Acts – the last virtually complete at both federal and state levels – are held by the Law Library. Rhodes House, responsible for materials from 1760 in history, politics, economics and social conditions of the Commonwealth of Nations, sub-Saharan Africa and the USA, holds substantial quantities of Australiana maintained by an active buying programme from Australian suppliers. Historical materials are well represented, with many works on early travel, migration and settlement and a series of nineteenth-century directories and handbooks. Rhodes House is one of the few libraries outside the British Library that acquires and files newspapers, some from Australia going back to the 1840s. Cambridge University Library also owns strong holdings of Australian official publications, some going back to the nineteenth century, together with many series of state publications. The Library now houses the

Scriptures Library of the British and Foreign Bible Society, and its collection of the scriptures includes some in Aboriginal languages.

The immense collections of the John Rylands University of Manchester Library contain several thousand works on Australia, early materials being well represented. Particularly worthy of note is the Library's ownership of a complete set of the works of John Gould on the birds and mammals of Australia, published between 1848 and 1888. The Methodist Archives and Research Centre, transferred to the care of the Library in 1977, contains a number of accounts of missionary work in Australia.

The extent of Scottish links with Australia and current Scottish activity in Australian studies was outlined by Ian Donnachie at the British Library's Colloquium.[8] The most significant historical collection is without doubt at the National Library of Scotland in Edinburgh, a depository library for British publications, and where particular emphasis is given to material on Scots overseas. Other Scottish sources include Glasgow University Library's Hunter Collection, which holds contemporary works by James Cook, Sydney Parkinson, J.G.A. Forster and other writers, and the Hunter Museum, which contains specific specimens collected by Sir Joseph Banks. Glasgow's Mitchell Library also contains a range of eighteenth- and nineteenth-century works including ornithological works by John Gould and J.W. Lewin.

Modern Studies

Traditionally, Britain's past involvement with Australia has owed much to political and historical factors, but the growth of area studies as an academic discipline in the post-war period has been responsible for the development of significant library collections in a variety of special fields. A substantial body of creative literature in English, for example, has emerged from overseas writers. Two libraries excel in this field of 'new literatures': the Commonwealth Institute in London and the University of Leeds. The Commonwealth Institute exists to foster knowledge and understanding among the peoples of the Commonwealth of Nations and to that end undertakes a wide range of educational activities for schools and the public. Its Library is strong in audiovisual materials and it maintains a commercial photographic library, COMPIX. Its collection of literature by Commonwealth writers, reckoned to be the finest in London, mostly relates to the post-war period and includes a collection of children's books. Australian authors are well represented. The Institute has recently been badly affected by financial cuts with the result that the literature collection has been 'frozen' until such time as additional funds can be found to revitalize it; even so, it remains a collection of research quality. The University of Leeds collection began in 1967 in support of new courses mounted by its School of English. Total Australian holdings number in excess of 3000 items and, as well as literature, include history, politics, Australian federal and state government publications and a strong collection of literary periodicals.

Australian creative writing and Australian cinema are well represented at the University of Kent, where courses in Australian literature are supported by holdings built up since 1965. A book grant from the Sir Robert Menzies Centre for Australian Studies in 1984 was used to strengthen journal holdings and fill gaps. At the University of London the central University Library is to target the acquisition of Australian literature within its Commonwealth literature collection in direct response to the literature option offered in the MA (Australian Studies) at the Sir Robert Menzies Centre. University College, London, has for many years collected 'little' magazines and publications of small presses; in excess of 3000 such titles are held and some 6000 small press items. Bloomfield's *Resources* lists thirty-nine Australian titles with detailed holdings. A smaller collection of small press publications is held in the Poetry Library of the Arts Council of Great Britain, where its 'Nationality Index' offers a geographical approach to the Library's stock; Australian titles number over 300 and include the works of individual authors, anthologies, standard works and experimental writing from workshops. Bloomfield lists some of the small presses whose output is represented in the stock.

Australian literature is also studied at the University of Exeter within the context of a course on American and Commonwealth Arts and for which a collection on Australian cinema in the Department of Film and Media Studies has been developed. Some funding in support of collecting Australiana has been awarded by the Sir Robert Menzies Centre and the Australian Government.

For modern history, politics and international relations, several libraries in London provide for advanced, scholarly demand. The British Library of Economic and Political Science at the London School of Economics is internationally renowned for the breadth and quality of its research holdings. Extensive coverage is given to official materials from federal and state governments, and within London University the Library has been designated as the University's primary research resource in the political and economic sciences. Also at the University of London the Institute of Commonwealth Studies (which houses the Sir Robert Menzies Centre) specializes in political and economic development, and in particular primary materials such as official publications and those issued by university and research bodies. The Institute's collection of Australian political ephemera is unique in Britain and numbers around 1500 publications from some 150 political parties, pressure groups and trade unions. The collection includes many primary documents such as party constitutions, policy statements and a wealth of minor documentation such as posters and campaign literature mostly acquired through non-trade sources. In common with many other libraries, the Institute has recently revised its book selection policy to reflect more accurately the known demand for Australian materials. This has resulted in a shift of emphasis away from some statistical materials and less used publications, but the Library remains committed to supporting the activities of the Sir Robert Menzies Centre.

For international relations, the major library is that of the Royal Institute of International Affairs at Chatham House. Although its Australian holdings do not match in quantity some of those already described, the Library is pre-eminent in its field and receives on exchange publications of the Australian Institute of International Affairs and other Australian university and research bodies focusing in particular on the period post-1945. The Institute's Press Library, started in 1924, forms a major archive of over 10 million cuttings. Unfortunately, Australian newspapers have not been currently clipped for some years, though Australian news from the presses of Britain, Europe and North America continues to be covered. Pre-Second World War cuttings are now held on microfilm, and those for the period 1940-1971 have been transferred to the British Library's Newspaper Library at Colindale.

Particular specialities in Australian studies include trade union affairs at the Trade Union Congress Library with its collection of trade union documents and current statistics in various government libraries such as the Department of Trade's Export Marketing Information Centre and the Office of Population Censuses and Surveys. The latter aims to achieve comprehensive coverage at national level of Australian censuses, and demographic and vital statistics via an exchange programme with the Australian Bureau of Statistics; state publications are more selectively acquired. At the Royal Air Force Museum and the National Army Museum the armed forces are the subject of interest; of particular note in this field are the collections of the Imperial War Museum with its many historical materials, often received as donations. The Museum's substantial periodical holdings include a special collection of trench magazines; those relating to Australia are listed in *Resources for Australian and New Zealand Studies*.

Aboriginal studies are covered in depth by the Library of the Museum of Mankind which is the Ethnography Department of the British

Museum and to which the Library of the Royal Anthropological Institute was added in 1976. The primary thrust of the subject coverage is social anthropology, archeology, material culture and physical anthropology. The reference collection includes a number of bibliographical works on Aborigines published in Australia, as well as journals, pamphlets and off-prints. Current Aboriginal studies materials are collected by the Institute of Commonwealth Studies and the School of Oriental and African Studies.

The Sciences

Britain is fortunate in the quantity and quality of its specialist scientific organizations where literature within particular subject areas is collected world-wide. The Royal Botanic Gardens at Kew – an excellent example of this type of organization – owns one of the largest collections of botanical literature in the world. Its subject coverage includes plant taxonomy, anatomy, genetics and physiology, and geography, horticulture and economic use on an international scale. Australian materials are represented in all these areas, and the Library receives a number of journals in exchange (some fifteen Australian exchange partners) for the *Kew Bulletin.* Although the Library has no special programme or book selection policy for Australian materials, it uses a good network of contacts and an efficient local supplier to ensure that adequate coverage is maintained. The Kew Herbarium accommodates an Australian Botanical Liaison Officer, funded by the Australian Government, who services requests from Australian botanists. Various publications relating to Australia are issued by the Royal Botanic Gardens, and there is a continuing involvement with the Flora of Australia project.

World-wide coverage of natural history is the aim of Britain's major library in this subject field: the British Museum (Natural History). Australiana are located throughout the several subject libraries which support the research of its botany, entomology, paleontology, mineralogy and zoology collections. Among the historical materials are manuscripts, prints and drawings from Sir Joseph Banks' Library and other works relating to all three of Cook's voyages as well as those of later explorers. Standards of excellence for modern materials are maintained via exchange agreements and professional contacts with Australia. The research literature thus acquired includes journals, conference papers, reports, surveys, off-prints and publications arising from expeditions. Holdings of maps and various indexes to pictorial material all contribute to the Library's bibliographical services.

Pictorial Materials

Britain's library resources for Australian studies are not limited to books and journals. In recent years there has been greatly increased interest in non-book resources: maps, photographs, film and audio materials. The very large photograph collections of the Royal Commonwealth Society, the Foreign and Commonwealth Office and the National Maritime Museum have all been the subject of special cataloguing projects designed to make better known and more easily usable these valuable but difficult to handle records. In recognition of the national value of the Royal Commonwealth Society's collection, the British Library funded a two-year project for its organization and cataloguing. Australian photographers are well represented: the work of several from the nineteenth century, depicting settlers in the Queensland outback, Tasman Aborigines, and views of Melbourne, forms part of the collection. Some of the Society's photographs were exhibited in Brisbane at the time of the Commonwealth Games in 1982; the catalogue of the exhibition was published as *Commonwealth in Focus: 130 Years of Photographic History*.[9] The catalogue of the Society's collection and the photographs themselves have been published on microfiche.[10]

The Foreign and Commonwealth Office also owns a vast collection of photographic and other pictorial material. Photographs of Australian interest include several nineteenth-century views of public buildings in Adelaide, Queensland and Tasmania, panoramic views of Sydney harbour and the arrival of Lord Hopetown, first Governor-General of the Commonwealth of Australia. The Library also owns a watercolour sketch, *North View of Sydney, New South Wales* (1820) by J. Lycett. A handlist to this collection is being prepared. Several thousand photographs relating to Australia are held by the Museum of Mankind; these date from the 1860s, are mostly concerned with Aboriginal culture and include albums of Aboriginal portraits taken between the 1870s and 1890s by J.W. Lindt. Another major holding is that of the Imperial War Museum where, within an archive of over 5 million photographs and negatives relating to warfare in the twentieth century, are over 6000 photographic items concerned with the activities of Australian Forces in the two World Wars. Several hundred photographs and engravings of Australian interest can be found in the BBC Hulton Picture Library, a major pictorial archive founded by the news magazine *Picture Post*, to which was later added the *Evening Standard* picture library. The total collection exceeds 10 million items.

Further pictorial material is to be found in the University of Kent's Centre for the Study of Cartoons and Caricature, where a detailed system of indexing permits easy identification of Australian items; these feature political events, personalities, international affairs and other topical matters. A collection of primarily historical interest is held by the Royal Geographical Society and depicting mostly towns and natural features; its catalogues identify portraits of individuals who have links with Australia, and its framed pictures, paintings and watercolours, including oil paintings by Thomas Baines on the North Australia Expedition of 1855-1856, have been separately catalogued. A portrait index, by which Australian materials held in stock can be located, is also maintained by the British Museum (Natural History).

Photographs, pictures and films are a feature of the Scott Polar Research Institute in Cambridge, where the bias is towards Australian involvement with Antarctic exploration. The Library inherited a collection on early exploration from its first director, but scientific papers from expeditions and research projects form the bulk of stock. The University Library in Cambridge also owns a small collection of topographic views of Australia and a postcard collection containing items on Australian scenery, towns, buildings, natural features and people.

Maps

As might be expected, some of the finest map collections are to be found in the older historical libraries, particularly those noted above for the excellence of their works on early travel and exploration.

The largest collection of maps in Europe is held by the Royal Geographical Society, numbering over 600,000 sheet maps and 4000 atlases. Those for Australia can be identified via the Map Library's card catalogue, which is arranged by geographical area. The Society owns original maps by Matthew Flinders, A.C. Gregory, F.W. Leichhardt and W.J. Wills, together with reproductions of a number of early maps. Current topographical maps are deposited by the Australian Division of National Mapping, and other map producing agencies, such as the Tasmania Lands and Survey Department, donate maps from time to time. Little is purchased, and the library relies on donations, especially for acquisition of older materials.

In Cambridge the University Library's Map Room houses nearly 900,000 maps and over 10,000 atlases. Australian maps are deposited by the Division of Mapping and charts by the Australian Admiralty. Thematic maps cover a wide range of subjects including botany, economic development, geology, population, railways, roads, the whole collection being supplemented by gazetteers, bibliographies, library catalogues and similar works of reference.

The map holdings of the Foreign and Commonwealth Office date only from 1940; earlier items have been transferred to the Public Record Office, where the total for Australia, New Zealand and the Pacific Islands amounts to around 2000 items, many of them manuscripts and often with handwritten annotations. Early maps include a French map of the Southern Hemisphere dated 1714 and a chart of Terra Australis drawn in 1802 by Matthew Flinders. Modern maps still held in the FCO Library number around 300 and cover topography, meteorology, geology and communications.

Other map collections include that of the School of Oriental and African Studies, which has around 2000 sheet maps and 100 town plans for Australia. The National Maritime Museum owns a number of specialized items on Australia and individual states, as well as a quantity of nineteenth-century atlases which are listed in Volume 3 of the Library's printed catalogue titled *Atlases and Cartography*. In Oxford the main centre for maps is the Bodleian Library, where those for Australia are acquired from the Division of National Mapping and various state agencies such as the New South Wales Central Mapping Authority. Maps are also received from specialist government departments such as the armed forces and state geological surveys; thematic maps cover a wide range of topics including climate, communications, land utilization, population, soils and vegetation.

Manuscripts

Uncovering the considerable extent of Britain's manuscript resources relating to Australian affairs has been the aim of the Australian Joint Copying Project. This London-based project was founded in 1945 by the National Library of Australia and the Mitchell Library in Sydney with the intention of copying historical records held in Britain which could then be made available in Australian libraries. A survey of holdings in a large number of institutions resulted in the publication in 1972 of *Manuscripts in the British Isles Relating to Australia, New Zealand and the Pacific* by the then Project Officer, Phyllis Mander-Jones.[11] Within its 700 pages are listed the manuscript holdings of over 200 organizations, more than half in London, and with particular attention given to documents in the Public Record Office. The publication of this volume made a notable impact on historians and led to the Project widening its searches from the Public Record Office and government departments to archives held by local record offices, private organizations and individuals. Although only a fraction of the material listed in Mander-Jones has been filmed, the Project has continued to identify and locate further materials of Australian historical significance and an active filming programme continues. A supplement to, or revised edition of, Mander-Jones would be a service to scholarship but, unfortunately, one that is unlikely to materialize. The quantity of manuscript material available for Australian studies is huge and increases steadily. Much becomes available when individuals die and it then appears in the auction rooms or is donated to libraries with interest in Australian studies. Thus the Institute of Commonwealth Studies has in recent years received the microfilmed papers of the 1st Earl Gowrie (the originals are held by the National Library of Australia) on deposit from the Gowrie family, as well as several smaller collections.

The extent of archival materials held for commercial studies is indicated in Charles Jones' *Britain and the Dominions: A Guide to Business and Related Records in the United Kingdom Concerning Australia, Canada, New Zealand and South Africa.*[12] This volume lists original materials held in a variety of repositories including such obvious sources as county record offices and academic libraries as well as those held by commercial bodies themselves and revealing the extent of their dealings with Australia. International firms such as Unilever, Cable and Wireless, Jaguar and Cadbury Schweppes all own documents relating to Australia, as do many other business organizations: banks, insurance companies and a multitude of smaller firms.

Methods of Acquisition

It would be impossible to quantify the current volume of materials for the study of Australia in British libraries without detailed investigation, but it seems that British publishers have discerned a market in Britain for books of Australian interest. Recent annual indexes to the *British National Bibliography* list some thirty to forty subject headings on such varied Australian topics as philosophy, wine, cinema, airlines, cricket and stained glass, while Aboriginal studies cover languages, music and paintings. Many titles are jointly published with Australian publishers but this is by no means always the case.

There appears, too, to be a healthy intake of publications from Australia by a number of British academic and research libraries. James Bennett Library Services, the premier Australiana bookseller, supplies a number of Britain's major libraries with a wide range of materials, mostly in the social sciences and humanities but also, to a lesser extent, titles of scientific interest. The increasingly high profile of Australian published output may be attributed to the growing reputation of Australian research and scholarship, particularly in the fields of agriculture and climatology, and thus appealing to a wider international readership. Over the past couple of years titles issued by the Australian Government Publishing Service are supplied in Britain via Books Express, based in Saffron Walden, from where current titles can be ordered and paid for in sterling; orders sent to Australia are returned to Books Express. The service is not without its teething troubles, however, and is not as yet an ideal source of supply for official publications. Similarly, Flinders Bookshop in London, while offering a range of Australian titles on its shelves, is not geared to supply the library market; major bookshop chains in Britain stock little that is published in Australia. The serious buyer of Australian materials has little choice but to buy directly from Australia.

While the acquisition of Australiana does not present the intractable problems encountered with, say, African or Caribbean materials, all is not plain sailing. Australia and Britain could hardly be further apart in terms of geographical distance. Supplies despatched via surface mail can take up to three months to arrive and, although communication by air mail takes only a few days, the transaction of urgent business by telephone is unpopular because of the difference in time zones – let alone the cost. The fax machine is increasingly used as the most rapid and efficient means of contact. Distance also means that most book selection is guesswork and is based on information supplied in publishers' catalogues and bibliographies. There are no means in Britain for the examination of titles before purchase, no approvals, and reviews of new works published in Australia do not often appear in British journals. The return of materials wrongly supplied means that accounting queries drag on for months.

It is fortunate that Australia's bibliographical recording is of such a high standard for both historical and current output. The *Australian National Bibliography* appears with commendable regularity; its coverage is more than adequate and cataloguing is informative and accurate.[13] A cataloguing-in-publication facility offers current awareness, and the output of report literature by Australia's many research establishments is well recorded, as is that of many minor and ephemeral organizations. For those who do not require, or do not have access to, the *National Bibliography*, the National Library issues *Australian Books: A Select List of Recent Publications and Standard Works in Print*.[14] This is a most useful compilation listing books published in Australia in the previous twelve to eighteen months to provide a list of current works judged to be authoritative or of outstanding quality. It is a most acceptable alternative selection tool for the general library. To the national bibliography must be added the weekly record of central government output, *Commonwealth Publications Official List,* issued by the Australian Government Publishing Service, the annual *Australian Government Publications* and various sales lists of popular government materials.[15] State government printers produce their own sales lists. Sales catalogues from all types of publisher are readily forthcoming, and the secondhand market appears to be well catered for by a range of dealers.

As well as acquisition by purchase, specialist libraries also actively seek exchange agreements with libraries, research establishments and individuals working in particular fields for the maintenance of current publications. Such exchanges are a normal feature of scientific activity, and a number of journals issued by British organizations, e.g., the *Kew Bulletin*, are the basis for world-wide exchanges of scientific papers. Similarly, many government and academic libraries operate exchanges for certain types of material – journals, seminar papers, library accessions lists – as a means of promoting the exchange of information and maintaining current awareness. The Office of Population Censuses and Surveys acquires all its Australian census materials via exchange with the Australian Bureau of Statistics. Exchanges are, of course, heavily dependent on the value of the materials exchanged being approximately equal and on the benefits justifying the staff time invested in maintaining the necessary records. Exchanges are not cheap: institutions without sufficient of their own publications to offer to an exchange partner must buy materials in order to meet their obligations, and staff must be of sufficient number and calibre to maintain exchanges efficiently; argument over long distances is expensive and time-consuming if things go wrong. As staff costs rise, the investment in such arrangements can be prohibitively costly, and some libraries have reduced their exchanges in favour of purchase via commercial channels rather than engage in this aspect of acquisition.

Future Trends

Libraries do not stand still. Since the compilation of Mrs Bloomfield's directory, various changes have taken place in libraries and their coverage, the most drastic of which is the reduction of official Australian involvement in promoting the study of Australia overseas. This has drawn unfavourable comparison with Canada, which maintains active support for Canadian studies programmes in Britain, including underwriting the cost of operating the British Association for Canadian Studies. A crucial decision was the withdrawal of the funding for the Australian Studies Centre at the Institute of Commonwealth Studies in London. The Centre was opened with great ceremony in 1983 in the presence of the Australian Prime Minister, but five years later pressures on the Australian economy forced the government to withdraw from its commitment. It is only with the generosity of the Sir Robert Menzies Memorial Trust that the Centre's activities have continued. At the same time the Library at the Australian High Commission in London was reduced in scope, premises and staffing levels, despite a high level of demand for its services. The decline in official support has also seen the curtailment of the library services of the Agents-General for Australian states in London. For example, that for Western Australia, which had a detailed entry in the Bloomfield guide, no longer offers any access to the public but confines its information services to commercial bodies seeking trade and investment information.

Lack of funding available to the National and Mitchell Libraries is also responsible for the crisis in the Australian Joint Copying Project. Its collapse has been temporarily averted by a rescue operation involving a wider spread of Australian libraries' support which will allow the Project to continue for another year or two. Beyond 1993 the Project's future is uncertain, despite its acknowledged value to academic research in Australia.

In Britain funding cuts are creating pressures on space and staffing in many academic and research libraries, forcing librarians to examine and revise stock selection and retention policies – to respond more to expressed rather than to anticipated demand. The automation of library systems and availability of online access to other libraries' catalogues are also making a marked impact on library collections. It is now possible to locate individual titles in a large number of major libraries; a decision whether to buy or borrow can be made in the light of known availability elsewhere and enquiries can be targeted accordingly. The use of inter-library loan as a substitute for purchase is likely to increase. Australian materials – a minority interest – are not exempt from the new stringencies.

Pressure on funding is also forcing large-scale changes in two major libraries. The vast collections of the Foreign and Commonwealth Office are undergoing a vigorous programme of weeding and dispersal in preparation for the removal of the library from its present site into more limited accommodation. While it is not intended that Australian materials should be among those to be discarded, all duplicates are being weeded and large quantities of other categories of material are being dispersed on permanent deposit to other libraries.

At the same time the equally extensive library of the Royal Commonwealth Society has been submitted to a slimming programme aimed at reducing stock to a level where it can be accommodated in considerably less space. The slimming programme has already resulted in the transfer of Queensland parliamentary papers, *Journals* and *Votes and Proceedings* to the British Library of Political and Economic Science, and government gazettes to the Royal Philatelic Society. The Library has also experienced transfers of stock of a more unwelcome nature: three real treasures of Australiana were part of a major theft in 1989 – Lycett's *Views in Australia* (1824-1825), H. Neville's *The Isle of Pines* (1668) and Callander's *Terra Australis* (1766-1768). But, worse, with the Society's ability to support the library increasingly in doubt, it may well be that a substantial amount of this valuable historical library will be dispersed via the sale room during 1992.

At the Institute of Commonwealth Studies a revision of book selection policy has resulted in a reduction of intake of Australian titles, particularly of government serials and state publications where supply exceeded demand, and in titles from the Australian Bureau of Statistics where charges have been introduced for items which in the past were supplied free of charge.

In all acquisitions from Australia built-in delays in supply are a factor that needs to be taken into account when placing orders. Almost certainly, the bibliography or sales catalogue from which book selection is made will be several months old before it reaches the librarian's desk. By the time selection and checking procedures have been accomplished a further couple of months may have passed. With such obstacles to supply the chances of a British institution placing an Australian published work on its shelves within twelve months of publication are remote. The speedier alternative use of air mail or surface air lift can be prohibitively expensive when added to other costs such as payment charges.

The costs of making payment to an overseas supplier can come as an unwelcome surprise to libraries which do little such business. A payment in Australian dollars requires the purchase of the necessary currency from the bank. Non-sterling transactions take more time to process– some two to three weeks – and bank charges are not cheap: commission, transaction costs and agents' fees added to the cost of an invoice can result in additional costs of £10-15 per invoice. A cheaper means of payment is the operation of an Australian dollar account, but this is justified only where there is a reasonably high volume of business. It would be expensive tor a small number of transactions.

Conclusion

Despite cuts, rationalizations and the practical difficulties of acquiring source materials, British interest in Australian studies continues; the Sir Robert Menzies Centre remains a focus for scholarly activity; the British Australian Studies Association mounts well supported conferences and its journal, *Australian Studies*,[16] attracts increasing respect. Current research and scholarship are expanding beyond traditional history and politics to new and exciting developments in literature, the arts, archeology and media studies. While there is room for considerable improvement in the availability of Australian-produced publications in Britain's public libraries and book shops, special and academic libraries are serving Australian studies well.

Acknowledgments

A number of librarians and booksellers have provided information for this chapter; the author offers her grateful thanks to them all.

Notes

1 Geoffrey Bolton, 'Australian Studies in the United Kingdom: The Prospect Before Us,' in *Australian and New Zealand Studies: Papers Presented at a Colloquium at the British Library 7-9 February, 1984*, ed. by Patricia McLaren-Turner. London: British Library, 1985, pp. 14-21.

2 Valerie Bloomfield, *Resources for Australian and New Zealand Studies: A Guide to Library Holdings in the United Kingdom.* London: Australian Studies Centre and the British Library, 1986.

3 Phyllis Mander-Jones, *Manuscripts in the British Isles Relating to Australia, New Zealand and the Pacific.* Canberra: Australian National University, 1972.

4 Margaret Cousins, 'Australian and New Zealand Material in the Library of the Foreign and Commonwealth Office,' in *Australian and New Zealand Studies*, ed. McLaren-Turner, *op. cit.*, pp. 79-84; Margaret Cousins, 'FCO Holdings of Early and Rare Australiana,' Paper presented to the British Australian Studies Association Conference, 1985.

5 Royal Empire Society, *Subject Catalogue.* 4 vols. London: The Society, 1930-1937, reprinted by Dawsons in 1967; Royal Commonwealth Society, *Subject Catalogue.* 7 vols. Boston, Mass.: G.K. Hall, 1971; *First Supplement.* 2 vols. Boston, Mass.: G.K. Hall, 1977.

6 Royal Commonwealth Society, *Biography Catalogue.* London: The Society, 1961.

7 National Maritime Museum, *Catalogue of the Library*. 5 vols. London: HMSO, 1968-1976.
8 Ian Donnachie, 'Scottish Resources for Australian and New Zealand Studies,' in *Australian and New Zealand Studies*, ed. McLaren-Turner, *op. cit.*, pp. 179-182.
9 *Commonwealth in Focus: 130 Years of Photographic History*. [Sydney?]: International Corporation of Australia Ltd, 1982.
10 Royal Commonwealth Society, *Photograph Collection: Guide to the Microform Collection*, ed. by John Falconer. Zug: IDC, 1988.
11 Mander-Jones, *op. cit*.
12 Charles Jones, *Britain and the Dominions: A Guide to Business and Related Records in the United Kingdom Concerning Australia, Canada, New Zealand, and South Africa*. Boston, Mass.: G.K. Hall, 1978.
13 National Library of Australia, *Australian National Bibliography*. Canberra: National Library of Australia, 1961- .
14 National Library of Australia, *Australian Books: A Select List of Recent Publications and Standard Works in Print, 1945-* . Canberra: National Library of Australia, 1946- .
15 Australia. Government Printing Office, *Commonwealth Publications, Official List*. Canberra: Australian Government Publishing Service; Australia. Government Printing Office, *Australian Government Publications, 1976-* . Canberra: Australian Government Publishing Service, 1977- .
16 *Australian Studies*, 1- ; 1988- ; available from The Subscription Manager, *Australian Studies*, Department of English Studies, University of Stirling, Stirling FK9 4LA, UK.

Appendix: Libraries and Specialist Holdings of Australian Materials in Britain

Arts Council of Great Britain
 Creative writing; poetry; small press publications
Bodleian Law Library
 Law
Bodleian Library
 British copyright deposit materials; ephemera; literature; little magazines; maps; music; poetry; pre-1760 materials
British Library of Political and Economic Science
 Aborigines; bibliography; history, federal official publications; international relations, politics; state official publications

British Museum (Natural History)
Botany; early travel and explorations; entomology; maps; mineralogy; paleontology; pictorial materials; scientific expeditions; zoology
Cambridge University Library
British copyright deposit materials; federal official publications; maps; pictorial materials; postcards; state official publications
Commonwealth Institute
Audiovisual materials; children's books; literature; photographs
Exeter University
Cinema; literature
Foreign and Commonwealth Office
Diplomacy; early travel and exploration; economics; history; federal government publications; international relations; law and legislation; international relations; maps; migration and settlement; photographs; pictures; politics; state government publications
Glasgow University
Early travel and exploration; geological survey maps; scientific specimens
Imperial War Museum
Armed forces; military history; photographs; pictorial materials; trench magazines
Institute of Commonwealth Studies
Aborigines; bibliography; economics; federal official publications; history; manuscripts; political ephemera; politics
John Rylands University of Manchester
Early travel and exploration; missionary archives; natural history
Kent University
Bibliography; caricature and cartoon history; cinema; creative writing; economics; history; international relations; literature; statistics
Leeds University
History; federal government publications; literature; maps; politics; state government publications
London University Library
Literature; maps; paleography
Ministry of Defence (Navy)
Early travel and exploration; colonization; hydrogeography; map making; maritime studies; meteorology; missionaries; naval history; natural history; oceanography; transportation of convicts
Mitchell Library, Glasgow
Birds; genealogy; nineteenth-century works
Museum of Mankind
Anthropology; archeology

National Library of Scotland
British copyright deposit materials; polar exploration; Scots overseas

National Maritime Museum
Early travel and exploration; history; biography; naval history; maps; photographs; polar studies

Office of Population Censuses and Surveys
Censuses; demography; statistics

Rhodes House
Early travel and exploration; directories; economics; history; migration and settlement; newspapers; politics, social studies

Royal Botanic Gardens, Kew
Botanical sciences, Horticulture; pictorial materials; plant specimens; travel and exploration

Royal Commonwealth Society
Biography; early travel and exploration; federal government publications; history; literature; maps; manuscripts; migration and settlement; photographs; politics; reference works, yearbooks and directories; small press publications

Royal Geographical Society
Biography; early travel and exploration; geography; historical geography; maps; naval history; photographs; polar studies; portrait index; First and Second World Wars

Royal Institute of International Affairs
International relations; press library

School of Oriental and African Studies
Aborigines; languages; maps

Scott Polar Research Institute
Films; photographs; pictorial materials; polar studies

Trade Union Congress
Trade unions

University College, London
Anthropology; bibliography; law; little magazines; small press publications

15 Developing an Australian Literature Collection: An American Perspective

Ross Atkinson

North American libraries can and should improve their holdings in Australian literature. In comparison with European literature collections, Australian literature collections are neither difficult nor expensive to develop. Once the library has determined the level and scope of the collection to be created, the bibliographer can make use of the excellent bibliographic and synoptic sources now available on the subject. As a basis for selection, the bibliographer needs to build up a vocabulary of the key words of which the subject is composed; a frequently updated author list should also be created. Once the collection has been developed to the level desired, a variety of periodic bibliographical sources can be used to maintain the collection at that level. Although North American libraries can develop research collections strong enough to support in-depth research on the subject of Australian literature, it is probably neither desirable nor possible for such libraries to build comprehensive collections in all aspects of the subject.

Literature is verbal art – the use of language for artistic purposes. Literature should be classified and studied, and collections of literary works should be developed, therefore, primarily on the basis of the languages in which those works have been written. English literature, understood in the narrow sense as literary works created by authors living in England, can and should also be more broadly defined and approached as literary works written in English. How English is and has been used for artistic purposes should be a major concern in the study and teaching of English literature, and it is at least partially in support of that goal that English literature collections should be built.

To provide such support, North American libraries need to make available to their users representative samples of primary literature in English created in different geographical locations, as well as the critical (secondary) literature which describes and interprets that primary literature. Probably the most significant contributions to English literature which are consistently underrepresented in United States library collections are those produced in the Commonwealth countries.

While Canada, by virtue of its geographical proximity to the United States, receives some attention, it is much easier for libraries to lose sight of Australian literature – especially if there is no consistent pressure from the user community to build and maintain that collection.

There are, to be sure, excellent collections of Australian materials in North American libraries. Robert L. Ross was recently able to produce a very fine bibliography of Australian literary criticism from 1945 to 1988 by relying entirely on libraries in the United States.[1] Nevertheless, many medium and large academic and public libraries have not traditionally paid adequate attention to their Australian literature holdings. Of the forty research libraries which have completed the literature segment of the Conspectus, only four (Yale, Iowa, the Library of Congress and the British Library) claim to be building their Australian literature collections at a level which will support advanced research. Fifteen other libraries of those forty claim to be collecting at a level which is adequate to support instruction, while the remainder are collecting only at a basic or minimal level. For several reasons some effort should be made to correct this relative underrepresentation of Australian literature in United States libraries. First, Australian literature is a rich and growing subject area, which would do much to enhance and to fill out the English literature holdings of most libraries. Second, the resources needed to build up an Australian literature collection are relatively modest, so that a representative collection can be put in place and maintained without a heavy drain on the resources supporting other parts of the collection. Third, there is a gradually increasing interest in Australian literature throughout North America – perhaps most visible to the library through the appearance of two new journals in the past three years, *Antipodes*, published in New York, and *Australian and New Zealand Studies in Canada*, published at the University of Western Ontario. Libraries need to respond to and participate in this renewed interest by devoting increased attention to the subject.

The purpose of this paper is to describe in very practical terms how to begin developing and to maintain an Australian literature collection, or to enhance one already in place, in a North American library. I need to note at the outset that I am not an expert in this area. I did devote some time to developing the Australian literature collection at the University of Iowa in the mid-1980s, and some of the following discussion is based on that experience. For the most part, however, what follows is simply an effort to apply some of the standard methods of collection development as practised today in North American libraries to the problems of building an Australian literature collection. Since all collection development is based finally upon individual judgments, some of the following discussion necessarily contains subjective assertions or recommendations deriving from personal values and experience.

General Principles

Collection development – especially the initial phases of creating a new collection or expanding one already in place, and especially, also, at a time when only a portion of all that is published can be afforded by any library – is always a reactive, even reactionary, undertaking. What happens, to put it very simply, is that the bibliographer (that is, the library staff member responsible for developing the relevant portion of the collection) studies what users are saying on the subject, what is being said in the literature, what is being said in the materials already available in the collection – and then looks at items newly published or newly available on the same subject. The bibliographer then selects those items which most correspond to – which contain the same words as – those discussions already taking place among users and in the literature. What those words mean is far less important for collection building than the fact that they are currently being used – that they refer to issues people involved in the subject are talking about. In the humanities many of the key words upon which selection is based do not in fact 'mean' anything, because they are proper names – for the most part, the names of major authors. The bibliographer's first step in building a collection, therefore, is to build his or her own vocabulary.

At the same time a decision needs to be made as early as possible about the extent to which the collection segment – in this case the library's holdings on Australian literature – is to be developed. Since the advent of the Conspectus, we normally draw the distinction between collection strength (i.e., the quality or utility of the collection in place) and collecting intensity (i.e., how much effort is being put into collection building). Collection strength and collecting intensity are described by collection levels ranging from 0 to 5, in which basically '0' indicates that no effort is being made to collect anything, while '5' means an effort is being made (seldom with total success) to collect everything.[2] Collection strength and collecting intensity are not necessarily the same: the strength of a collection could be at the 2 level, for example, and the intensity of collecting at the 3 level, or vice versa. Such inconsistency between strength and intensity can persist, however, only for a limited period, because collection strength is necessarily a product of collecting intensity. The level of collecting intensity, if maintained over time, will eventually become the level of the collection's strength. The bibliographer needs to decide, therefore, what the strength of the Australian literature collection ought to be, and should then begin to collect at an intensity which is equal to (or greater than) the strength targeted.

In most instances the bibliographer will want to aim at a 2-, 3- or 4-level collection in Australian literature. A 5-level collection is probably out of the question for the whole literature, at least for a North American library. A 1-level should require little effort beyond acquiring a few standard reference works, and perhaps those titles still in print which are listed in the third edition of *Books for College Libraries*.[3] The purpose of the 2 level, or basic level, is to collect standard bibliographic and reference sources, as well as a small but representative sample of the main primary and secondary literature. The 3 level, or instructional support level, is intended to provide materials needed for an undergraduate curriculum and some graduate work: a collection at that level should include a full and reliable representation of those authors and critical works which form the corpus of the literature. The 4 level, or research level, should include what is needed to do original scholarly research on the subject, which should encompass not only mainstream publishing but also – at least in a strong 4-level collection – some publications of lesser known ('minor') authors and smaller presses.

Which level the library decides to aim for depends upon the needs of current and future users of the collection, and upon available resources. The resources for collection development and management fall normally into three categories. First, there is the budget, i.e., the funds allocated to pay for the materials on the subject. Second, there is staff time, which is the amount of time required for the bibliographer to make selection decisions, and for the processing units in the library to acquire the material, catalogue it, and get it onto the shelf (and, if we want to complete the circle, we would include the time needed by the library's public services units to bring the users into contact with the appropriate information). Third, there is space, which in a paper environment consists mainly of shelving and the buildings which contain it. These three resources are intimately connected, and are constantly played off against each other. The budget as a resource can be stretched by the bibliographer devoting more time to selection. Time can be saved by the bibliographer being less selective and thus spending more of the budget. (In another sense, of course, this practice merely shifts the expenditure of temporal resources from the collection development unit to the processing unit.) Time is also often purchased at the expense of space: weeding is done infrequently in research libraries not simply because it is politically difficult and because a library should serve as a place of record, but also because it absorbs staff time, which in many libraries is a resource in shorter supply than space. During an initial build-up phase, all three resources must normally be increased substantially. Once the desired collection level is achieved, the resources needed to maintain that level should be considerably less than those needed for the initial build-up, at least for well established and gradually evolving subjects like Australian literature.

Subject Matter

The Australian literature collection in most libraries will presumably be built by bibliographers who have been responsible for Western European literatures. Because of the brevity of Australia's history (as a Western European settlement), and because of the relatively good bibliographic control available for Australian literature, experienced bibliographers should find the development of the Australian literature collection well into the 4 level a relatively manageable undertaking.

Australia was claimed for Great Britain by Captain Cook in 1770; the First Fleet (carrying mostly convicts, for one primary function of Australia was to serve as a penal colony) arrived in Botany Bay in 1788, and shortly thereafter the settlement was founded which was to evolve into Sydney. Real economic expansion did not begin in Australia until the second third of the nineteenth century. There was little literature produced during the early years of Australia's colonization by Great Britain, since the settlers were understandably preoccupied with other priorities – like trying to survive. Most of the early writings were travel descriptions, diaries and reports. The first Australian novel was not published until 1830, and there were no significant literary stirrings until the mid-nineteenth century. For all practical purposes, therefore, the literature to be collected spans a period of only a century and a half, making it much easier to survey and manage than the European literatures or even North American literature. The majority of the time devoted by the bibliographer to Australian literature will be focused on the literature produced during the past 100 years.

When we speak of Australian literature, we are referring normally to that literature produced by Western European colonists. The language is predominantly English. Older oral Aboriginal literature will be of interest to anthropologists and ethnologists as well as literary historians.[4] In the bibliographical sources on Australian literature today, Aboriginal authors writing in English, such as Kath Jackson, Jack Davis or Colin Johnson, are always included, and, because the authors' names often do not reveal their Aboriginal origins, the bibliographer may seldom even know which authors selected are Aborigines.[5]

Two of the first questions which the bibliographer charged with developing an Australian literature collection must ask, therefore, are 'what do we mean by Australian?' and 'what do we mean by literature?' Usually Australian literature will be limited to that English-language literature written in Australia since 1788, regardless of the national or ethnic origins of the author. This should include not only Aboriginal authors and those authors who immigrated to Australia from areas other than Great Britain, but also those authors, such as Christina Stead, who were born in Australia but who lived and wrote elsewhere. The decision will also need to be made as to whether literature includes only belles-lettres, or whether it should also encompass the kinds of memoirs and travel literature of which so much of the writing of Australia's early British settlers is comprised. In most cases the Australian literature bibliographer in a larger research library who intends to select only belles-lettres will want to effect some kind of arrangement with the bibliographer responsible for Australian history to ensure that there is adequate coverage of such early travel literature and personal reminiscences.

Anyone used to working in Western European literature will find that the Australian literature collection can be built and maintained relatively quickly, at least at the 2 or 3 level. Development of the collection at the 4 level will obviously take more effort, but the bibliographer familiar with Western European literature collection building will usually notice that the resource shift from budget to time also arrives much more quickly in developing the Australian literature collection: one reaches that point much sooner at which the main library resource being used is the time of the bibliographer (and that of staff in the processing units) to locate and import lesser known, often small press and less expensive items.

Getting Started

At the beginning of any serious collection building project one must invariably ask the same fundamental, three-pronged question: (1) what is the collection strength of the subject collection in place? (2) what is the collection strength desired? (3) what needs to be done and what resources will be required to move from 1 to 3?

If the collection in place includes no Australian literature holdings, or holdings so small as to have a negligible impact on collection planning, then one can proceed immediately with building a core. A visit to PR 9600-9619 or to the 820s in the stacks, or a look through the shelflist in the appropriate classification ranges, will reveal much about the extent of the library's holdings in Australian literature.

Most libraries with any interest in building Australian literature collections will hold some materials in this area already. The first job of the bibliographer is to determine the quality of that collection already in place: where are the strengths, if any, and where are the gaps? The only means to make that determination is to undertake a collection assessment. This is normally best done by comparing current holdings against a list of publications on the subject which together represent an ideal collection. The extent to which the library holds the works on the list will reflect the proximity of the collection to its ideal.

If one is looking only for an assessment of the collection, one can simply compare a representative sample of items on the list with the library's holdings. When undertaking such an assessment as a first step in a building or upgrading project, however, it is always preferable to use the list as a first step in the identification of titles which should be included in the collection – which normally requires a search of the entire list rather than a sample. Which list one uses depends always on the ideal collection toward which one is aiming. In a well defined and relatively manageable subject such as Australian literature the selection of such a list or lists is of critical importance, since a good list can be used to define the core around which the entire collection can be built.

When developing a collection from scratch, one must always build it, so to speak, from the centre outwards. If I had to select one title to place at the centre of any Australian literature collection at this time, I would probably choose *The Oxford History of Australian Literature*.[6] If the library contains nothing on Australian literature, that is the first title the bibliographer should order — and read; and it is from that seed that a 2-, 3- or even 4-level collection can ultimately be created. The book contains synoptic essays on fiction, drama and poetry, followed by a closely packed, sixty-page narrative bibliography by Joy Hooton. The bibliography is by no means comprehensive, but it is a good representation of the corpus of Australian literature; and a collection containing all of the items listed in the bibliography would probably provide adequate support (with a few exceptions discussed below) for most research on the subject. For American libraries striving for a low or medium 4-level collection, the content of the Hooton bibliography, suitably updated and augmented, would constitute much of an ideal collection on the subject. The bibliography begins with a discussion of 'bibliographical and reference aids', followed by an examination of the major 'general studies' on Australian literature. The remainder of the bibliography is devoted to a thorough discussion of the major works by and about seventy-one Australian authors. In the interests of efficiency, I would suggest that the materials listed in this bibliography be defined by any library as the core of Australian literature, at least until 1980. The bibliography does need to be supplemented (it is now over a decade old), and I will discuss methods to do that below. The important point is that time should not be spent searching vainly for the true core of the subject. The Hooton bibliography is close enough for the initial phase of collection building. The time available should rather be devoted to comparing this representative core to the library collection already in place.

If the intention is to build a 2-level collection, then the Hooton bibliography can be searched selectively; this is relatively easy to do, because the bibliography is in narrative form, and includes evaluative comments. While this is perhaps the best way to start building a 2-level collection, it does take some time, and a 2-level collection may not justify ploughing through Hooton. An alternative might be simply to acquire first the most standard, current enumerative and synoptic sources. These should include (but not be limited to Green, Hergenhan, Lock and Lawson, Miller, Ross.[7] Next read one or two shorter summaries of Australian literary history. The article in the *Australian Encyclopaedia* is a good place to start.[8] Based on the authors identified as being most important in those summaries, use Hooton to identify their major works and try to order currently available editions listed in *Australian Books in Print*. Supplement that information by reading the narrative section for the past several years of the annual bibliography published in the *Journal of Commonwealth Literature*. The collection can then be maintained using an abbreviated version of one of the methods described below for 3- or 4-level collections, combined with specific recommendations by users.

If the aim is to build a 3- or 4-level collection, it is worth the investment of staff time to search the entire Hooton bibliography against the library's holdings; only in that way can the quality of the collection in place and the extent of the collection building effort ahead be estimated. Many of the citations in Hooton refer to journal articles, and it is important to determine whether the library holds the issues cited. (The frequently cited periodicals and books listed at the beginning of the bibliography should be searched first, so that the searcher need not check the library's holdings on that list each time an article in a periodical or monographic collection is cited.) For the most part a seasoned searcher is not necessary for this job; a reliable student could do the job as a summer project.[9] The searcher should be trained to record all editions of an item cited, since the library will often not hold the original editions listed in the bibliography.

Once the Hooton bibliography has been searched, the bibliographer's real work begins. The bibliographer gave the searcher a description of the literature, in the form of the Hooton bibliography; when the job is done, the bibliographer receives back from the searcher something very different, namely a collection description. The bibliography itself and the searching in the margins must now be read and interpreted by the bibliographer as a single text which refers to the collection. This new text represents both what the collection includes and what it lacks – what it is, and what it should be. The bibliographer, in reading carefully through this unique text from beginning to end, will usually end up adding notes or rubrics of his or her own, highlighting and distinguishing different kinds of information, and targeting new jobs to be done as the next step in the process. In some cases further searching will be necessary; in other instances holdings will need to be checked to determine whether they are adequate or complete. Much of the bibliographer's effort will be devoted to items which should next be searched in *Australian Books in Print*. The bibliographer will then presumably want to order those items which are presently published, and to list with antiquarian dealers those titles which are no longer in print.

This brings us finally to the subject of editions. A quick glance through the stacks will show that Australian literature, especially when compared with Western European literatures, includes few multi-volume standard editions. There are some collected – or more often selected – works editions, but there is a noticeable lack of historical-critical editions of Australia's most important authors. The standard editions for certain authors which do exist can be found through Hooton and the maintenance sources discussed below. The other method is to find recent articles on the main authors in the standard critical or scholarly journals and to note which editions are being cited. If one is building a 4-level collection, a decision will need to be made at the beginning about the extent to which the library is willing to invest in rare materials. Some of the titles listed in Hooton exist only in early or original editions, which, if available at all, are to be had only through antiquarian dealers, and which can be very expensive. Usually the library will want at most to establish certain authors, genres or periods of Australian literature as suitable for special collections.[10] When building a 3- or 4-level collection in Australian literature, the objective will normally be quite simply to bring in all significant primary literature in whatever editions can be located at the time. If standard or original editions are out of print, the projected level of use will determine whether the collection can make do with a more popular edition, if one is available, or whether the standard edition needs to be sought through antiquarian channels. If no copy of a standard edition is available on the antiquarian market, it is possible to borrow a copy from another North American or Australian library, and to photocopy it and bind it, providing there is no violation of copyright restrictions. Needless to say, photocopy is the best medium for primary literature; it does not lend itself at all to microfilm. This kind of effort should be invested only in the works of the most important authors or those authors of most interest to the library's current users. For many authors in the Australian literature canon it is best and easiest, if funding permits, simply to order everything available by the author currently in print which the library does not hold. If several editions are available, and the bibliographer can find no information on relative editorial quality, the bibliographer can use his or her knowledge of the publishers as a basis for the selection decision.

Vocabulary Building

As noted above, selection depends partly upon learning the key words in the subject field. Every bibliographer makes selections on the basis of some kind of list of key words. It is useful, if possible, to write down this list — with the understanding that it will need to be constantly updated. In the humanities many or most of the key words are personal names. In building an Australian literature collection, one of the first tasks is to create a list of authors which the bibliographer has identified as needing to be well represented in the collection. The bibliographer can then watch for any works by that author which may be newly published (i.e., newly written works, new editions for older authors, new secondary literature) or older materials not held by the library which may appear in antiquarian catalogues.

The author list in its initial form is always a very conservative one, in the sense that it is usually an attempt to define the canon. A 5-level collection in literature aims to include most of what has been *published* in the field. A good 4-level collection is intended rather to include as much as possible of what has been or is being *read and discussed* in the field. The idea initially, in other words, is to buy those authors about whom other people have written. One can start with the seventy-one authors treated in Hooton. If building a 2-level or a low 3-level collection, one might prefer instead the forty-eight authors listed by Lock and Lawson, or the thirty-four listed by Jones.[11] A 3-level collection might concentrate initially on the fifty-four authors listed by Smith, who includes several of the early non-fiction authors.[12] A fast means to build an initial list for a 4-level collection is to combine those lists, and to add – perhaps selectively – the authors treated in the three Gale bibliographies, as well as the more recent authors included in Ross.[13] Although there will be some dispute over individual authors included in or excluded from such a list, the works of these authors are surely the essential primary material in the field, and the list should serve as a reasonable starting point for collection building.

Every 4-level collection is, however, necessarily unique – a product both of the knowledge and the biases of the responsible bibliographer and the users. While most of the authors on the kind of core list described above will presumably be included in every 4-level Australian literature collection, each bibliographer responsible for such a collection will always add other authors to the list. There are basically three types of augmentation for the author list. First, the list will need to be expanded using maintenance sources (i.e., periodic bibliographies) over time. This expansion will represent authors previously of little interest, but who have recently been 'rediscovered' and are now generating scholarly and critical interest. When such names previously unfamiliar to the bibliographer appear in one of the maintenance sources, some judgment must be exercised. I would add such a name to the list if a monograph on such an author were published by one of the standard publishers, or perhaps if two articles of reasonable length were to appear in the standard scholarly or critical journals. If the book were published by a small press previously unknown to me, or if an article were published in one of the smaller magazines, or even if a whole issue of one of the smaller magazines were devoted to a particular author, I would probably not add that author to my list on that basis alone. I would rather need to judge from review information elsewhere that the author may generate enough interest in future for the library to begin to collect his or her works in earnest.

The second way to augment the list is closely related to the first. Many of the 'rediscovered' authors belong to particular categories of writers. In the past decade there has been increasing interest in literature by women, for example, and in literature by Aboriginal authors. If the bibliographer makes the decision to build in those areas, which must be done if the aim is a 4-level collection, then the authors which best represent those areas need to be added to the list, regardless of the amount of critical or scholarly publication they have generated so far. Ross lists recent critical works on women and Aboriginal authors, which can be used to identify representative authors whose works the bibliographer can begin to collect. A new bibliography on Australian women authors has also been published.[14]

The third method of augmenting the list is to begin to include newly published authors, whom the bibliographer expects will generate scholarly or critical interest in future. This is the principal means the bibliographer uses to counterbalance the necessarily reactionary nature of the initial collection building effort. The best source for such information is *Australian Book Review*, as well as any other review sources treating contemporary literature.[15] Here the same rules apply as those which inform the collection of contemporary literature from other countries.[16] It is in this area that the greatest divergences will usually exist between one library collection and anothre. In the case of Australian literature it would probably be very useful for North American libraries which have decided to collect at the 4 level to share the lists of contemporary authors they collect, and then to establish cooperative agreements which would coordinate selection and thus ensure that most of the works of contemporary Australian authors are and will remain available in North American libraries.

As noted earlier, whenever the decision is made to add an author to the list of a 4-level collection, it is normally a good idea to order at once anything listed as available by the author in *Australian Books in Print* which the library does not already hold. To have an author on a 4-level list should mean to accept the responsibility for trying to acquire everything (significant) available written by that author.

Keyword lists, of course, should consist of words other than authors' names. The bibliographer of the 4-level collection will know, for example, that anything with the word 'Jindyworobak' in the title or subject probably needs to be acquired. The best immediate source for vocabulary building of this kind is probably *The Oxford Companion to Australian Literature*, which, like the other Oxford companions, is a one-volume subject encyclopedia.[17] Aside from that, good sources of vocabulary building are the standard histories,[18] and the articles in the usual scholarly journals. The bibliographer should always scan the articles in *Australian Literary Studies*, the *Journal of Commonwealth Literature*, *World Literature Written in English* and the other scholarly or critical journals.[19] The purpose of such scanning should not be to read the articles or to ponder their arguments. The bibliographer should rather concentrate on the titles, the main divisions of the articles and especially the notes to see the materials being cited. Reviews, on the other hand, should be read regularly and routinely whenever possible, even when the decision has already been made to acquire the item reviewed. This is because reviews often provide the best bite-sized synopses of current literary and scholarly trends, and frequently make evaluative comments about titles other than the one being reviewed which the bibliographer will want to ensure have (or have not) been added to the collection.

Maintenance

If we accept the Hooton bibliography as the starting point for collection building, we must be aware of several of its drawbacks. To begin with, it does not cover primary literature which has not been written by one of the eighty-one authors covered by the bibliography. There are some notable absences from Hooton's list, especially those authors (e.g., Elizabeth Jolley, Les A. Murray) who have become quite important since Hooton was published. Expanding the core author list, as described above, will overcome this limitation of Hooton. Ross' bibliography, an excellent source of the more recently published critical works, should be used both to update and to supplement Hooton.[20] Once that work is done, and all of the retrospective material which can be acquired initially has been received, the process of maintenance begins. As always, this consists of retrospective building and current selection.

Retrospective building involves the search for those titles identified in the initial search of Hooton and any sources used to supplement Hooton, as well as the works of any other authors on the author list, which are no longer in print. Searches can be undertaken through the library's favoured American and British antiquarian dealers; there are also excellent antiquarian dealers in Australia. A short list of Australian antiquarian dealers can be found (through the subject index) in the *International Book Trade Directory*.[21] A very useful listing of the types and frequency of catalogues issued by Australian antiquarian dealers for the early 1980s will be found in Howes.[22] It is important to get the library on the mailing lists for these dealers, so that catalogues will be routinely received. This kind of retrospective collection building is an ongoing process, since it is unlikely that all of the historical gaps in a main stacks collection on Australian literature can ever be filled.

The standard retrospective bibliography for Australian literature is Miller, which runs to 1935, and which has been extended to 1950 by Macartney.[23] These provide a wealth of historical and bibliographical information, and serve as the basic record of literary publications by Australians before 1950. Miller is the source which should be used whenever a library is attempting to build a comprehensive (5-level) collection of the works of individual authors.

The national bibliography for works published until 1900 is Ferguson.[24] The first part of this bibliography runs to 1850, and the citations are in chronological order. The second part is in alphabetical order by main entry, and contains few belles-lettres citations, on the assumption that these will be found in Miller. For materials published in the first half of the twentieth century, there is a new four-volume *Australian National Bibliography 1901-1950*.[25] For materials published after 1950, use the *Annual Catalogue of Australian Publications*, which began publication in 1937 (covering the year 1936), and which in 1961 became the monthly *Australian National Bibliography*.[26]

Maintenance through current selection is best achieved by using the standard periodic bibliographies. Such bibliographical sources are quite good for Australian literature, and the amount of time and effort which needs to be expended is relatively slight. For a 2-level collection, it is probably adequate to rely on the two periodic synoptic sources: the introduction to the annual bibliography in the *Journal of Commonwealth Literature*, mentioned above, and the Australian section in *The Year's Work in English Studies*.[27] The latter has had a section summarizing scholarship in Australian literary studies only since 1983; this new section has so far been an excellent, although highly selective, summary, and should be read each year by every bibliographer responsible for collection building in Australian literature. The only problem with *The Year's Work* is that it is slow to appear. In maintaining a 2-level collection, therefore, it is probably most efficient for the bibliographer to defer to the evaluative judgment of the authors of those two periodic summaries, and to select for the collection the items identified as significant in those summaries. Further selections can then be made in direct response to user requests.

The first step in maintaining a 4-level collection – and probably also a 3-level collection – should be regular use of the *Australian National Bibliography (ANB)*. This comprehensive bibliography appears monthly, with annual cumulations. It is obviously preferable to use the monthly version – simply because it ensures that the collection is always as up-to-date as possible, that material ordered has not gone out of print, and that there is an even flow of orders and receipts, which should preclude large blocks of Australian literature material getting stuck in the library's processing stream.

The *ANB* contains everything published in Australia which has been submitted to the Australian National Library for copyright deposit. It is arranged according to the Dewey Decimal Classification. Australian literature can be found very quickly in a special section of the 820s with the letter prefix 'A', following the regular 820s. Subject headings are included, which allows easy identification, for example, of those titles which qualify as children's literature. New serial publications are also listed. Primary literature is best selected through the use of the author list – at least for a 3-level or a low 4-level collection; consideration should normally be given to acquiring all new works by or about authors on the author list, even if the publisher is unfamiliar. For a strong 4-level collection I would recommend, in addition, buying any belles-lettres listed in the *ANB* published by a standard publisher, regardless of whether the author is familiar or on the library's author list. This will ensure that the library's collection is representative of mainstream literary publishing in Australia.

Which are the standard Australian publishers? These the bibliographer learns with experience, after ordering for a time, examining the materials received and reading reviews. Like the author list, it is likely that each bibliographer will have his or her own 'standard' publishers' list, including among others the University of Queensland Press, Angus and Robertson, Hale and Iremonger, Melbourne University Press, and the Australian branches of Oxford University Press, Cambridge University Press, Hodder and Stoughton, Allen and Unwin, and Macmillan. Penguin Books Australia also publishes many significant, well edited works. My list would also now include the Fremantle Arts Centre Press for newer works, and perhaps the Currency Press for drama. This is, as I have said, a very incomplete and subjective list, and is intended only as a starting point for others to build upon. The bibliographer must bear in mind that many works published by smaller publishers will often also be needed for the collection, depending on collection scope and user interests.

For 3- and 4-level collections the safety net is then provided by the annual bibliographies. Titles missed or deferred when selecting from the *ANB* can be caught in this way. There are three main annual bibliographies, one published in *Australian Literary Studies (ALS)*, one in the *Journal of Commonwealth Literature (JCL)* and since 1982 the *MLA International Bibliography*. They are different enough in their approach and coverage that all three need to be used. Probably the major value of the annual bibliography in *JCL* (aside from its excellent synoptic introduction) is its listing of primary literature. Most of the book publications of the standard authors are included; whenever the publication is a reprint, the date of the original publication is noted. If the bibliographer responsible for a 3-level collection is short of time, and if there is no pressure from users for immediate access to the latest literature, then the bibliographer might give consideration to using the *JCL* annually rather than the *ANB* monthly. This method will, however, retard receipt of some items by up to two years, and it does risk missing some publications of smaller presses which may go out of print.

The *ALS* annual bibliography provides excellent coverage of the secondary literature, and it includes material published outside Australia, as well as items which were not included in the bibliography in earlier years. Some primary literature is also included, but this is not nearly as complete as that listed in *JCL*. A major value of the *ALS* bibliography is the listing of book reviews. When a primary or secondary literature title is reviewed, it is listed in the *ALS* bibliography, even if that title has been listed in earlier years. As noted above, reading reviews is an important part of the bibliographer's job, and the *ALS* bibliography can be used to identify reviews both for the bibliographer's routine reading and for use in deciding whether to order a particular title. (The latter will be of more interest to the bibliographer responsible for building the 3-level collection; for a 4-level collection one will normally want to order most of the monographic titles listed in the *ALS* annual bibliography, regardless of reviewers' verdicts.)

The *MLA* bibliography lists no primary literature. Its main value is its listing of sources on Australian literature which are not published in Australia. Most of these are articles, but the bibliographer will want to confirm that such journals are being received by the library. In addition, monographs published in North America and in Western Europe will be readily identified in the *MLA* bibliography, which also includes dissertations on Australian literature summarized in *Dissertation Abstracts International*.

A monthly glance through the *Australian Book Review* will also be an essential job, at least for the bibliographer responsible for the 4-level collection. There is also a new annual bibliography in *Antipodes*, which is intended to list primary and secondary literature either published or reviewed in North America.[28] To date, two instalments (in the spring 1989 and winter 1990 issues) of this new bibliography have appeared, and it is certainly worth consulting as a supplementary maintenance source.

It should be noted, finally, that an online bibliographic database of Australian literature has now been created, AUSTLIT, which contains some 100,000 citations of both primary and secondary literature.[29] AUSTLIT lists both monographs and articles from a wide range of journals and newspapers. It appears that the very detailed topical searching available in AUSTLIT will be especially useful for those building collections on particular authors or subjects. The aim is to create eventually a fully up-to-date, comprehensive database for Australian literature. Access to AUSTLIT is possible from North America, although I am aware of only one institution in the United

States, Pennsylvania State University, at which access is routinely provided to library users.[30]

Periodicals

As is the case with Western European and American literature, many contemporary poems and short fiction, as well as much of the most useful secondary literature in Australian literature, are published in journals. An adequate journal collection is therefore essential, and continuing subscriptions to some of the major journals is preferable in tight budget years to acquiring new critical monographs. Bibliographers should always try to acquire and examine samples of the journals before subscribing, and each bibliographer will have an opinion as to which journals are more essential than others. My personal preference – and it must again be borne in mind that this is a highly subjective judgment – would be as follows. For a 2-level collection I would want as a minimum *Australian Literary Studies*, the *Journal of Commonwealth Literature*, perhaps *Antipodes* because of its North American origin, and one or two of the best literary journals such as *Meanjin* and/or *Southerly.* For a 3-level collection (in addition to the titles just listed for a 2-level collection), I would ensure subscriptions were in place for *Ariel, Australasian Drama Studies, Overland, Quadrant, Scripsi, Westerly, World Literature Written in English.* A 4-level collection would require much more breadth; I would add such titles as *Australian and New Zealand Studies in Canada*, the *Australian Book Review, CRNLE (Centre for Research in New Literatures in English) Review Journal, Hecate, Island Magazine, Kunapipi, Meridian, Notes and Furphies, Outrider, Poetry Australia, Span* and some smaller or newer literary magazines and specialty journals reflecting either strengths already in the collection or interests among the users of the library. For the 4-level collection some retrospective collection building would also be necessary. Bennett and Stuart are good starting points for assessing the library's historical periodical holdings.[31]

Conclusion

A representative collection of materials in Australian literature is useful to any academic or larger public library collection, and can serve well to supplement or round out an already strong English literature collection. As has been shown, such a collection can be built and maintained at a relatively modest cost in terms of staff time and funding. Most libraries will want to limit acquisitions to a carefully selected core, but even a low 4-level collection can be maintained without placing an excessive burden either on the bibliographer or the budget. Few North American libraries will want to aim for a very high 4-level collection, which would doubtless prove very difficult to develop. It is always problematic and risky to try to build an exceptionally strong collection in the absence of an ongoing flow of evaluative information about current trends both in the bibliography of the subject and the subject itself. At most academic institutions and in most libraries in North America there is normally inadequate knowledge of current conditions in Australian literary studies upon which to base decisions for an in-depth collection. If the institution does not contain a coterie of faculty who are experts in the subject area, and if the bibliographer does not have the background or the time to read in depth and to discover such trends, then the development of an exceptionally strong collection in Australian literature is probably not a possibility. Were a North American library nevertheless intent on building up to such a level in Australian literature, the most effective step would be to contract with a research library or a bibliographer in Australia, provide that bibliographer with a reasonable budget, and have him or her build the collection from Australia – in other words, basically ask the bibliographer to duplicate (within carefully defined limits) the selections in Australian literature the bibliographer is making for his or her own research library in Australia. This could perhaps even be done in return for selections in United States or Canadian contemporary literature made by a bibliographer in the North American library.

Most libraries will want to build at most a much more modest collection of Australian literature. Whatever the collection level the library sets as its goal, the excellent bibliographical sources available for Australian literature will ensure that the goal is easily and efficiently attained, and the fine quality of the English literary works thus added to the collection will make such a project well worth the effort.

Notes

1 Robert L. Ross, *Australian Literary Criticism, 1945-1988*. New York: Garland, 1989, p. xvi.

2 See *Guide for Written Collection Policy Statements*, ed. Bonita Bryant, Collection Management and Development Guides, No. 3. Chicago and London: American Library Association, 1989, pp. 7-9.

3 *Books for College Libraries*. 3rd ed. Chicago, Ill.: American Library Association, 1988. Vol. 2, pp. 445-447.

4 See the essays by Stephen Muceke on oral Aboriginal literature, and by Jack Davis and Adam Shoemaker on written Aboriginal literature in Laurie Hergenhan, ed., *The Penguin New Literary History of Australia*, special issue of *Australian Literary Studies*, 13, 4 (October 1988): 27-46.

5 Some Aboriginal writers are changing their names back to original language forms. See the note on Walker and Johnson opposite the contents page in Hergenhan, *op. cit.*

6 Leonie Kramer, ed., *The Oxford History of Australian Literature*. Melbourne: Oxford University Press, 1981. The 'Bibliography' by Joy Hooton is on pp. 427-490.

7 M.M. Green, *A History of Australian Literature: Pure and Applied*. Rev. by Dorothy Green. 2 vols. Sydney: Angus and Robertson, 1984-1985; Hergenhan, *op. cit.* The Appendix in Hergenhan, by John Arnold, is entitled 'Sources for the Study of Australian Literature' (pp. 572-579); Fred Lock and Alan Lawson, *Australian Literature: A Reference Guide*. 2nd ed. Melbourne: Oxford University Press, 1980; Alan Lawson, D. Blair and Marcie Muir, 'English Language and Literature,' in *Australians: A Guide to Sources*. Ed. by D.H. Borchardt. Australians: A Historical Library. Broadway, NSW: Fairfax, Syme and Weldon, pp. 400-411; E. Morris Miller, *Australian Literature from Its Beginnings to 1935: A Descriptive and Bibliographical Survey....* Melbourne: Melbourne University Press, 1940 (facsimile ed. Sydney University Press, 1973); E. Morris Miller, *Australian Literature: A Bibliography to 1938*. Extended to 1950... by Frederick T. Macartney. Sydney: Angus and Robertson, 1956; Ross, *op. cit.*

8 H.P. Heseltine, 'Literature', in *The Australian Encyclopaedia*. 3rd rev. ed. Sydney: Grolier Society, 1979, Vol. 4, pp. 29-38.

9 I recommend photocopying the Hooton bibliography onto legal-sized paper, so that there are broad white margins on which the searcher can record the searching results. This will still make for some very cramped writing by the searcher, with many arrows drawn from the citation in the text to the searching in the margin, but the end result is much more useful for the bibliographer, and much more cost effective in terms of time than trying to copy the citations onto separate sheets of paper.

10 For a current and enjoyable introduction to collecting Australian rare books, see Jonathan Wantrup, *Australian Rare Books 1788-1900*. Sydney: Hordern House, 1987. Information on titles and prices available in the early 1980s will be found in Brian R. Howes, *Guide to Fine and Rare Australasian Books*. Wagga Wagga, NSW: The author, 1986.

11 Lock and Lowson, *op. cit.*; Joseph Jay Jones, *Authors and Areas of Australia*. Austin, Tex.: Steck-Vaughn, 1970.

12 Graeme Kinross Smith, *Australia's Writers*. Melbourne: Nelson, 1980.

13 Barry G. Andrews and William H. Wilde, *Australian Literature to 1900: A Guide to Information Sources*. American Literature,

English Literature, and World Literatures in English Information Guide Series, 22. Detroit, Mich.: Gale, 1980; Grove A. Day, *Modern Australian Prose, 1901-1975*. American Literature, English Literature, and World Literatures in English Information Guide Series, 29. Detroit, Mich.: Gale, 1980; Herbert C. Jaffa, *Modern Australian Poetry, 1920-1970*. American Literature, English Literature, and World Literatures in English Information Guide Series, 24. Detroit, Mich.: Gale, 1979; Ross, *op. cit.*

14 Ross, *ibid.*; Debra Adelaide, *Australian Women Writers: A Bibliographic Guide*. London and Sydney: Pandora, 1988.

15 *Australian Book Review*, 1961-1973; N.S., 1- (June 1978-).

16 A good summary of the general problems will be found in Charles W. Brownson, 'Contemporary Literature,' in *English and American Literature: Sources and Strategies for Collection Development*, ed. by William McPherson. Chicago and London: American Library Association, 1987, pp. 102-126.

17 William H. Wilde, Joy Hooton and Barry Andrews, *The Oxford Companion to Australian Literature*. Melbourne: Oxford University Press, 1985.

18 The standard histories include Green, *op. cit.*, still perhaps the best history, although it concludes at 1950; Ken Goodwin, *A History of Australian Literature*. Houndmills: Macmillan, 1986, a good recent introduction, with the main emphasis on the twentieth century; Geoffrey Dutton, ed., *The Literature of Australia*. Rev. ed. Ringwood, Vic.: Penguin Books, 1976, somewhat dated but still worth looking through, with an excellent narrative bibliography; Hergenhan, *op. cit.*, the latest, which covers a much broader range of genres and literary issues.

19 'Annual Bibliography of Studies in Australian Literature,' *Australian Literary Studies*, 1- (1963-) (usually in the first and third issues of each volume); Horst Priessnitz, 'Australian Literature: A Preliminary Subject Checklist,' *Australian Literary Studies*, 11 (October 1984): 513-540; 'Annual Bibliography of Commonwealth Literature,' *Journal of Commonwealth Literature*, 1- (1965-) (usually in the second issue of each volume).

20 Ross, *op. cit.*

21 *International Book Trade Directory*. 2nd ed. Munich: K.G. Saur, 1989.

22 Brian R. Howes, *A Checklist of Some Recent Australasian Antiquarian Book Dealers' Catalogues*. Wagga Wagga, NSW: The author, 1985.

23 See references to the two Miller titles in Note 7.

24 John Alexander Ferguson, *Bibliography of Australia*. 7 vols. Sydney: Angus and Robertson, 1941-1969 (facsimile ed. National Library of Australia, 1974-1977).

25 *Australian National Bibliography, 1901-1950*. 4 vols. Canberra: National Library of Australia, 1988.

26 *Annual Catalogue of Australian Publications*. Canberra: Commonwealth National Library, 1936-1960; *Australian National Bibliography*, 1961- .

27 *The Year's Work in English Studies*, 64- (1983-).

28 *Australian Book Review, op. cit.*; 'Bibliography of Australian Literature and Criticism Published in North America,' *Antipodes* (Spring 1989-).

29 For a discussion of the origin and objectives of the database, see Jan Blank, 'AUSTLIT: It's No Furphy,' *Australian Academic and Research Libraries* 20 (June 1989): 71-78. AUSTLIT is produced by the Library of the Australian Defence Force Academy, Canberra/

30 I am grateful to Nan Bowman Albinski of the Australian Studies Center, Pennsylvania State University, for this information on AUSTLIT.

31 Bruce Bennett, ed., *Cross Currents: Magazines and Newspapers in Australian Literature*. Melbourne: Longman Cheshire, 1981; Lurline Stuart, *Nineteenth Century Australian Periodicals: An Annotated Bibliography*. Sydney: Hale and Iremonger, 1979.

16 Historical Sources and the Tyranny of Distance: The Achievements of the Australian Joint Copying Project

Graeme Powell and Adrian Cunningham

Since 1945 the National Library of Australia has administered the Australian Joint Copying Project (AJCP). This project aims to identify and microfilm unique, original documents held in the British Isles that relate to the history of Australia, New Zealand and the Pacific. The project has produced over 9000 reels of microfilm which have proved an invaluable resource to Australian historians and researchers. These microfilms, with their attendant lists and finding aids, are widely available throughout Australia and New Zealand.This paper explores the history of Australian copying projects in Britain, outlines the operation and administration of the AJCP, discusses the types of records filmed and the repositories searched, summarizes the finding aids available to researchers, and elaborates on the future of the project which is due to wind up in 1993.

One of the most widely read books on Australian history is Geoffrey Blainey's *The Tyranny of Distance*.[1] Its title, like that of Donald Horne's *The Lucky Country*,[2] quickly became a cliché in Australian parlance. It is not surprising that it was a historian who examined so thoroughly the manifold consequences of Australia's remoteness from Europe, as well as the huge distances within Australia. Generations of Australian historians have had personal experience of the frustrations and difficulties caused by 'the tyranny of distance'. Novelists and other writers can happily live and work in the Kimberleys or the western plains or the Queensland tropics. Historians, however, depend to a greater or lesser extent on written sources, and a substantial proportion of Australian sources are located half a world away in the British Isles.

When Britain first colonized Australia in 1788, the modern British civil service was already in existence. Some departments, such as the Treasury and the Admiralty, were quite ancient, while others, such as the Home Office, Foreign Office and Board of Trade, were recent establishments. Bureaucratic record-keeping was becoming more comprehensive, and sophisticated and voluminous official despatches, registers, ledgers and calendars documented the attention that politicians and officials devoted to the affairs of penal settlements. Away from Whitehall, the generation after 1788 saw the emergence of a plethora of learned societies, museums, missionary and philanthropic societies with a deep interest in the botany, fauna, mineral resources and indigenous peoples of Australia and the Pacific, an interest reflected in their minutes, correspondence, pamphlets and journals. At a somewhat later stage, banks, land and investment companies, and shipping firms started to turn their attention to Australia and New Zealand. Meanwhile, the published accounts of the early settlements and Australian exploration had attracted a wide reading public, and increasingly individuals and families at all levels of British society corresponded with friends and relatives who had been transported or emigrated to the Antipodes. Altogether, it seems reasonable to conclude, as Noel McLachlan has done, that from its very beginning, 'the settlement [was] the best documented ever.'[3]

The extensive published sources, the books, pamphlets, journals, newspapers, broadsides, prints and maps, have generally been available to historians in Australia, although often only in one or two libraries. Much unpublished material, both official and private, is also held in Australian libraries and archives. At the same time a huge body of unique or very rare source material on Australia, New Zealand and the Pacific has survived in Britain and Ireland and, to a much lesser extent, in other European countries. Historians studying many aspects of Australian and Pacific history, in particular the Australian colonial period (roughly 1788-1860), have been hampered by the inaccessibility of these sources. For academic historians, the regular research trip to Britain, facilitated by sabbatical leave and travel grants, became a rite of passage that was sometimes the envy of researchers in other parts of the post-colonial world. For non-academic historians, the distance between Australia and Britain has often been insurmountable.

Since the mid-1970s university-based researchers have been faced with shorter sabbatical leave and less generous travel grants. Consequently, many of them have joined the freelance historians, the genealogists and undergraduate and postgraduate students in making much heavier use of the 9000 reels of Australian Joint Copying Project microfilms held in Australian and New Zealand libraries. The microfilm may strain their eyes and place certain constraints on their research, but it has to a considerable extent overcome the tyranny of distance that overshadowed Australian and New Zealand historical studies.

History

Some of the earliest Australian historians and librarians recognized the need to make British sources on Australian history more accessible by copying and publishing. In the mid-1980s James Bonwick began the formidable task of transcribing by hand both official and private records relating to New South Wales held in a variety of repositories in London and other British cities. He laboured at the task for fifteen years. Many of the transcripts were reproduced in the series, *Historical Records of New South Wales*, eight volumes of which were published between 1892 and 1901.[4] Following Federation in 1901, the Commonwealth Government reluctantly accepted responsibility for publishing early Australian documents. The series, *Historical Records of Australia,* appeared in thirty-three volumes between 1914 and 1925 under the editorship of Frederick Watson.[5] While of great value to historians, the publication was far from complete, with not even Series 1 (Governors' despatches) reaching the period of responsible government.

In the early decades of the century further transcribing projects, on a much smaller scale than Bonwick's, had been carried out in London. With the emergence of photocopying and microfilming technology in the 1920s and 1930s, Australian libraries decided that they would no longer sponsor the time-consuming and imprecise practice of transcribing original documents. In 1939 the Mitchell Library in Sydney and the National Library in Canberra both announced that they intended to microfilm all the records in the Public Record Office in London relating to Australia. Their plans were thwarted by the outbreak of war and the dispersal of many of the records to the safety of the English countryside. Negotiations were resumed towards the end of the Second World War, and it was recognized that the establishment of two distinct Australian copying projects in London was neither practicable nor sensible. The two libraries therefore agreed in October 1945 that they would share equally the cost of microfilming records in Britain of Australian and Pacific interest. The project would be administered by the National Library Liaison Officer at Australia House. Other Australian libraries would be encouraged to acquire copies of the film, thereby eliminating the need for publication.

The first reel of Australian microfilm was produced at the Public Record Office in August 1948. It had been suggested that filming could continue for as long as five years, a prediction based on a widespread misapprehension about the sheer quantity of records in existence. In fact, filming has continued without a break for over forty years, with an average of 200 reels produced each year. There are now some 5 million pages of documents available to researchers in Australia and New Zealand. The Australian Joint Copying Project (AJCP) has claims to being the oldest manuscript microfilming project in the world.

The Project has had a fairly peaceful history. It was administered by the National Library Liaison Officer until 1960, when the first full-time AJCP Officer was appointed. Later the staff was increased to two. Both officers have always been based in Australia House, although much of their time has been spent in repositories throughout Britain and Ireland, searching for material of Australian and Pacific interest. Neither the method nor the scale of copying has changed significantly since 1948. The Project has on occasion resorted to xerox copies, photographs, transparencies and 16mm microfilm, but the overwhelming majority of records have been copied on 35mm microfilm. Most of the film has been produced by photographers employed by the repositories that hold the original records, although from time to time commercial photographers have been engaged to copy large private collections. In 1977 the AJCP acquired a portable camera which has been useful for small collections, especially those in private homes. The output of film has inevitably varied from year to year, but it has never exceeded 400 reels, nor has it ever dwindled to nothing.

The Records

Throughout its history the AJCP has concentrated on locating and copying unique records that can only be found in Britain. While some attention has been given to unpublished maps, plans, drawings and photographs, the principal concern of the Project has always been with handwritten and typescript records.

Of the 9300 reels produced so far by the AJCP, almost 7000 have been filmed at the Public Record Office (PRO) in London. Indeed, for the first ten years filming was confined entirely to the PRO. The pattern changed suddenly with the appointment in 1960 of Phyllis Mander-Jones, a former Mitchell Librarian, as the first AJCP Officer. While not neglecting the PRO, she immediately set off in pursuit of private records of Australasian interest throughout the British Isles. In 1972 appeared her great work, *Manuscripts in the British Isles Relating to Australia, New Zealand and the Pacific.*[6] It has received heavy use by Australian and New Zealand historians, and it has been an invaluable guide to AJCP staff in planning the surveying and filming of collections, especially in the smaller and lesser known repositories. In the last twenty years a greater proportion of the Project's resources has been devoted to filming outside the PRO.

For purposes of arrangement and description the AJCP microfilm is divided into two series: the Public Record Office (PRO) Series and the Miscellaneous (M) Series. Within the PRO Series the records of the Colonial Office, joined more recently by those of the Dominions Office, are predominant. Nearly 30 per cent of all the AJCP film is taken up by the despatches, correspondence, letterbooks and registers, dating from 1788 to about 1954, of these two departments. In addition to the huge classes dealing specifically with the Australian, New Zealand and Pacific colonies, film has been acquired of many general classes referring to such subjects as colonial appointments, honours, emigration, overseas settlement schemes, the involvement of the Dominions in the First World War, and imperial policies and relations generally. The filming of this material represents the greatest achievement of the Project, for no other Australasian records in Britain are so extensive, cover such a long period, or contain information on such a wide range of subjects.

Apart from the Colonial Office records, the most heavily used group of films produced by the AJCP are almost certainly the records of the Home Office. The Home Office was responsible for administering the system of convict transportation which dominated the first sixty years of British settlement of Australia. The film of criminal registers, transportation registers, convict musters and the famous 1828 census (Australia's Domesday Book) has been used extensively by both academic historians and genealogists.

The vast geographical area which the Project has sought to cover, much of it comprising ocean, has meant that Admiralty records are a major source, entailing many years of searching. The despatches, letters, logs, musters, court-martial records, surgeons' journals and other records of British warships and exploring vessels that visited the Pacific have been located and filmed. Other Admiralty records copied include hydrographic surveys and papers on naval defence and the formation and operation of the Royal Australian Navy. Prior to 1870 there was a continuous British military presence in Australia and New Zealand. War Office records of the 1788-1870 period relating to British regiments stationed in the Australasian colonies have been comprehensively filmed. They include musters, pay lists, service returns, correspondence and court-martial records.

Other relevant material has been identified and filmed in several Public Record Office record groups: Foreign Office, Treasury, Board of Trade, Audit Office, Board of Customs, Meteorological Office, Air Ministry, Cabinet Office. The AJCP has also filmed, usually on a selective basis, nine collections of personal papers at the PRO. Among them are the papers of two Prime Ministers (William Pitt and Lord John Russell) and four Secretaries of State for the Colonies (Russell, Edward Cardwell, Lord Granville and Lord Carnarvon).

The Miscellaneous Series now totals about 2400 reels. The first collection of private records, the archives of the London Missionary Society, was filmed in 1958, and since then collections in over 200 repositories have been listed and copied. They range from large general institutions such as the British Library, the National Libraries of Scotland, Wales and Ireland, the Public Record Office of Northern Ireland and the Bodleian Library to specialized collections such as those of the House of Lords Record Office, Lambeth Palace Library, the Post Office Archives, the Royal Society, the Royal Botanic Gardens, and the Fawcett Library and the Hydrographic Department. In addition, records have been filmed in almost all the county record offices and in many city record offices as well. At a few of the large repositories searching and filming have extended over several years. However, compared to the Public Record Office classes, most of the selections of private records are relatively small and only a few exceed ten reels. The largest collections filmed have been some of the missionary society archives, especially the United Society for the Propagation of the Gospel and the London Missionary Society, and business archives, such as the records of the New Zealand and Australian Land Company at Edinburgh and the Port Line at Liverpool.

In addition to material in public and private repositories, the AJCP has copied papers held by over 100 families and individuals. They mostly consist of diaries or small groups of letters written in the nineteenth century by emigrants to Australia and New Zealand. Papers have also been lent for copying by the descendants of some notable figures in Australian history: the governors Sir Richard Bourke, Sir William Denison, Sir William Jervois, Lord Carrington and Lord Hopetoun, the officials Sir Saul Samuel, Sir Timothy Coghlan and E.T. Crutchley, and the Reverend Samuel Marsden. In locating such papers the Project has relied heavily on information and clues passed on by researchers. The papers located in private homes have been a valuable supplement to the personal papers filmed in institutions, such as the politician Lord Derby (Liverpool City Record Office), the governor Sir Thomas Brisbane (Royal Astronomical Society), the feminist Vida Goldstein (Fawcett Library), the anthropologist Baldwin Spencer (Pitt Rivers Museum) and the scientists Sir William Bragg and Sir Lawrence Bragg (Royal Institution).

A discrete group within the Miscellaneous Series are the 105 reels of Irish convict records presented to the Australian people by the Irish

Government as a Bicentennial gift in 1988. The original records are in the State Paper Office in Dublin Castle and comprise transportation registers, convict reference files and prisoners' petitions. There is also an online index to the records. Both the index and the microfilms have been purchased by a large number of Australian libraries and genealogical societies. They fill a major gap in the convict records filmed in the early years of the AJCP.

Limitations on Searching and Filming

The librarians who set up the AJCP in the 1940s boldly declared that it would locate and copy all the unpublished records in Britain that related to Australia and the Pacific. In practice, the ideal of comprehensiveness has proved impossible to attain, even after more than forty years of toil. This is partly due to the nature of the records. At the Public Record Office references to Australia can be found in thousands of classes, comprising hundreds of thousands of volumes, boxes and files. The AJCP staff often undertake page-by-page searches, but there needs to be a reasonable return for days or weeks of searching. Consequently, some classes will never be examined, even though it is likely that they contain isolated references to Australia and New Zealand. Moreover, the AJCP has no cut-off date, and every year the PRO releases a further quantity of files containing papers on Australia. In smaller repositories it is sometimes possible to undertake exhaustive searches, but again the problem of bulk often arises. For instance, ledgers and other financial records of companies tend to be very bulky, they may be difficult to use or interpret, and their contents may be of limited research interest. The AJCP staff have often sought expert advice before deciding whether the high cost of searching and filming various categories of business records would be justified by their likely research value.

The problem of bulk affects filming far more than searching. It has sometimes been argued that filming has been too selective, and certainly many Public Record Office classes and most collections of private records have been filmed selectively. Selective filming can lead to relevant items being accidentally missed and it can also distort the true significance of papers that have been copied. The geographical limitations can be arbitrary and are frustrating for biographers, imperial historians, historians of science, and other researchers seeking to study an Australian subject within a wider context. Nevertheless, filming is a very costly process, and the AJCP has never had the resources to film in their entirety huge classes or collections that consist predominantly of non-Australian material. Moreover, it is unlikely that proposals to film on a more comprehensive basis would be acceptable to many of the repositories which own the records and which usually carry out the selective filming. All filming must be, to some degree, selective, and historians in Australia who are forced to rely on the microfilm alone work within constraints not shared by their colleagues in Britain.

Other limitations on searching or filming have been imposed by the repositories that own or have custody of the original records. The AJCP has been fortunate in obtaining the cooperation of the great majority of British libraries, record offices and other archival institutions. A very small number, including the Imperial War Museum, Royal Geographical Society, Trinity College Library, Dublin, and the Greater London Record Office, have so far declined to allow any documents to be filmed. At other repositories archivists have shown in recent years a greater awareness of the rights of depositors and of the financial interests of their institutions as owners of unique and valuable documents. Occasionally, records are too fragile or faded to permit filming. The Copyright Act can be a major barrier to filming. Observance or interpretation of the Act varies considerably, but at a number of major libraries, such as the Bodleian Library and the British Library, filming has had to be confined to records over 100 years old.

Finding Aids

With such a quantity and such a variety of records copied, it is not surprising that inexperienced researchers often retreat in dismay from the AJCP microfilms. A knowledge of archival practices and of both British and Australian history is a definite advantage for the researcher seeking to steer a course through the multitude of classes and record groups. Even so, many researchers are left with the uneasy feeling that they have probably missed valuable material lurking in unfamiliar classes with vague or confusing titles. The fact that researchers using the original records in Britain experience the same difficulties is little consolation. (In some cases the film is actually listed in much more detail than the original records.)

Most of the records that have been filmed are described in varying detail in the *Australian Joint Copying Project Handbook*, nine parts of which have been published by the National Library.[7] The early parts listed material filmed in particular PRO record groups, such as the Colonial Office, Home Office and Admiralty. Part 8 provides general descriptions of the collections in the Miscellaneous Series; Part 9 describes in some detail the contents of the nine personal collections filmed at the PRO; Part 10 will list the pieces and files in the Dominions Office classes and will be by far the largest of the parts so far published.

In addition to the *Handbook*, the AJCP staff have compiled typescript lists of most of the collections that have been searched. They vary in format and length, but usually provide far more information than can be found in any published guides. Most PRO classes filmed comprehensively are not listed, but if they have not yet been described in the *Handbook*, basic information about them can be found in the *Kew Lists*, published on microfiche.[8] Similarly, the Mander-Jones guide remains extremely useful; its descriptions are often more detailed than those in Part 8 of the *Handbook*, and it covers many collections not yet filmed by the AJCP.[9]

While a comprehensive, cumulated subject index to the contents of the AJCP microfilm does not exist, the patient researcher, using the *Handbook* and other finding aids, should be able to locate any records on particular topics. A separate problem is the need to make a greater number of researchers aware of the very existence of the microfilm. There is a general impression that the film is still underutilized, a fact that is not wholly explained by the complexity of the arrangement and user resistance to the microfilm format. In an attempt to increase awareness of the film among both researchers and librarians, the National Library has begun to enter brief descriptions of PRO classes and M Series collections onto the Australian Bibliographic Network (ABN). Over 1000 libraries throughout Australia currently participate in this network. Apart from publicizing far more widely the existence of the film, it will be possible for participating libraries to add their holdings of AJCP film to the ABN database, which may in turn lead to greater usage.

Availability of Film

From 1945 to 1988 the AJCP was jointly administered by the National Library of Australia and the Mitchell Library, State Library of New South Wales. Both libraries hold full sets of the film, as does the State Library of Victoria. The Alexander Turnbull Library in Wellington and the National Archives of New Zealand have, since the beginning of the Project, acquired copies of all films of New Zealand interest. Several other state and university libraries have quite good holdings, while a number of other libraries in Australia, New Zealand and the Pacific Islands have purchased small quantities of reels. A list of institutions holding AJCP film appears in Part 1 of the *Handbook*.

Future of the AJCP

The locating and copying of Australian records in Britain could never be brought to a neat conclusion. Important collections of Australian interest will continue to find their way into libraries and archives, and researchers will continue to identify useful material held in private possession. It is unlikely that major Australian research libraries will ever stop acquiring, by various means, copies of such collections. At the same time the maintenance of a fully staffed office in London has been a costly operation, and it was always assumed that a time would come when the office would be closed and the continuous searching and filming of more than forty years would be brought to an end.

In 1988 the State Library of New South Wales, one of the two original partners, withdrew from the Project. This placed a severe financial strain on the remaining partners. The National Library was opposed to a sudden cessation of searching and filming, especially as work was proceeding on some major collections. It appealed for support and was relieved to find that eleven state and university libraries were prepared to make financial contributions to the Project for a period of five years. The AJCP will, therefore, continue until June 1993.

The reprieve granted to the Project has already enabled it to complete some important filming tasks: the papers of W.E. Gladstone at the British Library, the collections at the Post Office Archives and the Fawcett Library, the Aborigines Protection Society archives at Rhodes House Library, and early surveying records at the Hydrographic Department. At the Public Record Office some large Colonial Office, Admiralty and Air Ministry classes have been filmed and a huge Foreign Office class searched and listed. In the remaining time left to the Project special attention will be devoted to the collections of the British Museum (Natural History), National Maritime Museum, London University and Cambridge University. The AJCP Officer will also try to achieve a better coverage of repositories in northern England, Scotland and Wales. The filming schedule will be tight, but suggestions from researchers or librarians about collections of possible interest to the Project will still be welcomed.

Of the various national copying projects in Britain, only the Canadian can compare with the AJCP in longevity, productivity and the extraordinary diversity of records located, listed and copied. The Project was perhaps fortunate in that Australian and New Zealand records in Britain are extensive but manageable, whereas material of American or Indian interest is overwhelming. On the other hand, records of some of the other former British colonies are very thinly scattered among the hundreds of repositories.

Australian and New Zealand researchers are fortunate in that a small group of libraries was prepared to fund the AJCP for over forty years, far longer than had originally been envisaged. If the Project had been dissolved in 1970 or even 1980, there would have been glaring gaps: to take one example, searching at the British Library only commenced in 1980. By 1993 the gaps will be far less apparent. There will be weaknesses: in particular, the coverage of twentieth-century records will be, for various reasons, far less comprehensive than the coverage of nineteenth-century records. At the PRO some large classes in the War Office and some of the economic ministries remain neglected and, inevitably, filming of post-1945 records has been very patchy. Elsewhere, the most obvious weakness is probably the archives of businesses and financial institutions.[10]

Despite these reservations, it is safe to assume that Phyllis Mander-Jones and her successors, working continuously in England for over three decades, were able to identify a great deal of valuable Australian and New Zealand sources which would otherwise have been overlooked and, in some instances, lost forever. In general, it has been possible to reproduce both the obscure sources and also the large or famous collections which were well known but inaccessible to most Australasian researchers. Some researchers may still be reluctant to use microfilm for any length of time, and microfilm of handwriting in various inks, often faded on deteriorating paper, must vary greatly in legibility. Almost all researchers, if they have the chance, will still prefer to visit Britain and work on the original documents. Nevertheless, the Australian Joint Copying Project has increasingly given historians relatively easy access to a much greater range of sources than had previously existed in Australia and New Zealand. In doing so, it has alleviated to a considerable degree the historiographical problems that had long been an effect of the 'tyranny of distance'.

Notes

1 Geoffrey Blainey, *The Tyranny of Distance: How Distance Shaped Australia's History*. Melbourne: Macmillan, 1968.

2 Donald Horne, *The Lucky Country: Australia in the Sixties*. Harmondsworth: Penguin, 1964.

3 Noel McLachlan, *Waiting for the Revolution: A History of Australian Nationalism*. Ringwood, Vic.: Penguin, 1989, p. 13.

4 F.M. Bladen and A. Britton, eds, *Historical Records of New South Wales*. 7 vols in 8. Sydney: Government Printer, 1892-1901.

5 F. Watson, ed., *Historical Records of Australia*. 33 vols. Sydney: Government Printer, 1914-1925.

6 Phyllis Mander-Jones, ed., *Manuscripts in the British Isles Relating to Australia, New Zealand and the Pacific.* Canberra: Australian National University Press, 1972.

7 National Library of Australia, *Australian Joint Copying Project Handbook.* 9 parts. Canberra: National Library of Australia, 1974-1990. (Part 1: Shelf List; Part 2: Colonial Office; Part 3: Home Office; Part 4: War Office; Part 5: Foreign Office; Part 6: Board of Trade, Treasury, Exchequer and Audit Department, Privy Council, Board of Longitude; Part 7: Admiralty; Part 8: Miscellaneous [M Series]; Part 9: PRO (Personal collections); Part 10: Dominions Office [forthcoming].)

8 Great Britain. Public Record Office, *Kew Lists* [microfiche]. Norwich: Her Majesty's Stationery Office, 1988.

9 Mander-Jones, *op. cit.*

10 Charles A. Jones, *Britain and the Dominions: A Guide to Business and Related Records in the United Kingdom Concerning Australia, Canada, New Zealand and South Africa.* Boston, Mass.: G.K. Hall, 1978.

17 Documenting Multicultural Australia

Derek Whitehead

This paper outlines the issues, problems and current directions in collecting documentary materials of Australia's ethnic minorities – particularly materials in languages other than English. The sense in which the term 'multicultural' is used is explained, and recent significant developments in government policy in the area of documenting multicultural Australia are outlined. Different levels and types of collecting are examined, and the experience of the author's library, the State Library of Victoria, is used to highlight some issues and problems. Included is a survey of what is published and its bibliographical control. Problems of acquisition are summarized, and in conclusion it is suggested that documenting multicultural Australia is a complex matter, but that problems are not insoluble if collecting institutions cooperate to carry out the task.

Introduction

Documenting multicultural Australia is inevitably more difficult than documenting the Australian mainstream. The written record of a society's minorities is more fugitive, less evident, less well documented than that of its dominant groups, and poses different problems and issues.

Australia is a multicultural society in two ways. First, the term is a description of the nature of Australian society, in that 30 per cent of the Australian population does not originate in the dominant English-origin Australian culture. Second, the term also describes a set of attitudes and policies whereby diversity is embraced and facilitated, and where the cultures of majority and minorities are seen as equally valid and acceptable, combining to make up a single, diverse Australian culture. In both senses the term 'multicultural' relates to all cultural groups in society, majority and minority, and does not simply refer to ethnic and cultural minority groups.

This paper, however, deals narrowly with the written documentary output of Australia's ethnic and linguistic minority groups. It does not deal with written material relating to them, nor does it deal with the documentation of the Australian Aboriginal people, whose case is distinct and unique. There is an inevitable focus on language, because what is in English is thereby more in the mainstream, more accessible to the person seeking it, and less marginalized. Therefore, this contribution eschews the approach of Buttlar and Wynar, whose guide to building 'ethnic collections' is the major such work, but is almost exclusively a guide to materials in English: dubiously multicultural, and even more dubiously 'ethnic'.[1]

The title of the paper is therefore a misnomer. It does not deal with multicultural Australia, because the term is synonymous with Australia itself. It deals with the most elusive elements of multicultural Australia's documentary heritage, and deals with this from the point of view of the collecting institution – the library in particular. This introduction briefly surveys the diversity of Australian society, and examines the evolution of official policy on documenting Australia's diverse multicultural heritage.

The Diverse Nature of Australian Society

The 1986 Review of Migrant and Multicultural Programs and Services (ROMAMPAS) described the variety of the Australian population in this way:[2]

	(percentages)
Indigenous Australians (Aborigines and Torres Strait Islanders)	1
From the British Isles three or more generations ago	60
From non-English-speaking backgrounds (NESB) three or more generations ago	5
First and second generation of English-speaking background	14
Second generation of NESB	8
First generation of NESB	12
And in linguistic terms:	
Monolingual in English	83
Proficient in English and other language(s) to varying degrees	14
Proficient only in languages other than English	3

Expressed another way: 'At least one hundred distinct ethnic groups have an organised presence within the non-indigenous population, while over 80 immigrant languages and 150 indigenous languages are spoken, used or understood in Australia.'[3] The Australian Special Broadcasting Service broadcasts in forty-five different languages,[4] and the Australian press is one of the most linguistically diverse in the world. The linguistic diversity of Australia has been well documented by Clyne, who lists thirty-two languages with over 1000 speakers in Australia.[5]

These statistics are quoted simply to give an idea of the range and scope of Australia's cultural diversity. Over 3 million of Australia's 16 million people use a language other than English in one or more contexts; over 4 million people are of ethnic backgrounds other than from the British Isles (and the term 'British Isles' itself disguises considerable ethnic diversity). The themes of range and diversity inevitably recur throughout this paper. The fact that over 15 per cent of Australians have a first language other than English makes collecting multicultural Australia both a formidable and essential task.

New Responsibilities: Government Policy

'New Responsibilities: Documenting Multicultural Australia' was the title of a conference held in November 1988 and sponsored by the Commonwealth Government.[6] It brought together people representing museums, libraries, archives and other historical collections. It represented the first foray by an Australian government into the policy issues involved in collecting multicultural Australia.

Previous reports, such as those which preceded the adoption of a national policy on languages,[7] dealt with education or with services (such as public library services), but dealt only sketchily or not at all with the development of collections of cultural material relating to Australia. The Australian Institute of Multicultural Affairs (AIMA), created in 1979, might have taken on a collecting role, but surrendered it; as it turned out, AIMA did not itself survive. The major report of the 1980s on migration and multiculturalism, that of the *Review of Migrant and Multicultural Programs and Services* (1986), did deal with documentation in a section on 'ethnic archives'. It concluded: 'There is no national responsibility for the safeguarding of this archival heritage or its cataloguing in such manner as to make it accessible...they make up a basic resource for anyone attempting to understand the history of Australia.'[8] The idea that the collection and preservation of such material was the responsibility of government collecting institutions was implied, but not proposed. Neither the role of the National Library of Australia nor that of the six state libraries was mentioned.

Two years later even the discussion document, *Towards a National Agenda for a Multicultural Australia*,[9] issued at about the same time as the New Responsibilities conference, did not refer to the collection of cultural materials in its statement of the principle of the right to cultural maintenance and development; in dealing with issues such as basic rights, social justice, participation and cross-cultural understanding, the paper made no reference at all to the collection and preservation of the documentary heritage of Australians of all cultures. Only at the end, in a section on 'Arts Policy for a Multicultural Society', was it stated:

> The reality, however, is that Australian cultural institutions and the public generally are not very familiar with the cultural expressions and heritages of NESB [non-English-speaking background] Australians. This is evidenced in access to popular outlets..., in funding levels, in educational environments, in arts policy and in the collection policies of galleries, museums and historical repositories.

The report concluded that there was a tendency for 'ethnic' and 'migrant' artistic expression to be seen as 'peripheral to Australian artistic expression'.[10] That the collection, preservation and use of documentary heritage were seen in the same way was not stated.

The New Responsibilities conference dealt with the role of Australian institutions in documenting our multicultural heritage. It included papers on the National Library of Australia, the State Library of Victoria and the State Library of South Australia. The conference was the first on the subject, and was significant because it articulated an agenda for government and government institutions, set out in 'Recommendations to the Office of Multicultural Affairs'.

The major outcome was the following decision within the Commonwealth Government's *National Agenda for a Multicultural Australia*:

> The Commonwealth considers the coordination of policy and resources between collecting institutions funded by the different levels of government to be an immediate priority if institutions' collections are to be enhanced appropriately in the medium to longer-term. A plan will be developed to coordinate efforts by cultural heritage institutions, including libraries, to reflect the cultural diversity of the Australian heritage in their collections and practices. Representatives from the three levels of government, community organisations and collecting institutions will be

involved in the process which is to be completed within six months.[11]

This process took place in 1990. The Commonwealth Government appointed a Consultative Committee on Cultural Heritage in a Multicultural Australia, and the Committee engaged consultants (Insearch Ltd) to collect data through a questionnaire and interviews. The main areas of interest were:[12]

1. the degree to which collecting institutions in Australia 'include information and items' relevant to the different cultural groups and how this is used;
2. the role of cultural collecting institutions 'in reflecting and preserving Australia's cultural pluralism';
3. the amount of contact between ethnic communities and cultural institutions, the degree to which communities are consulted by institutions, and the barriers between institutions and the community;
4. the existence of written or other policies and statements on cultural diversity;
5. policies on research, education, exhibitions, access and community relations.

The conclusions of the consultancy will provide a great deal of information about patterns of collecting in Australia. The Committee's report, it is hoped, will provide a national approach to the means by which this may be improved and coordinated.

Government is now recognizing the importance of documenting not only the lives of the majority, but of all Australians. Institutions which acquire printed and other written and published materials are also beginning to recognize this, and this paper is intended as an introduction to the subject.

Varieties of Collecting

Collecting at Different Levels

Collecting occurs for a variety of purposes and at a range of levels. At the most comprehensive level, the National Library, state libraries and other state collections may wish to collect the full range of research materials, including original materials such as photographs and letters. That none approaches adequacy in collecting at a comprehensive (Conspectus level 5) level is a reflection of both limited aspirations and significant difficulties.

At another level are substantial research collections which aim to collect most of the published material available in their areas of multicultural specialization. Collections within academic libraries are likely to focus on multiculturalism and ethnicity as subjects – not dealt with here – or on literature, history and other subjects where the collection of Australian heritage material is relevant. Recently established special collections at Deakin University and Footscray Institute of Technology (the Vaccari Collection), both in Victoria, aim more widely in their aspirations.

Major collections have also been developed by some community organizations or interests. For example, the Greek archive at Phillip Institute of Technology includes not only printed books, newspapers and periodicals, but original photographs and manuscript materials, newspaper clippings and other material. Large community libraries, especially those which have been established for some time, have developed significant collections of printed materials; an example is the Latvian Library in Melbourne, with over 15,000 items, and which now plans to collect manuscript material as well as printed books and periodicals and sound recordings.

Finally, some libraries seek a representative range of monographs and serials relating to ethnic minority Australia, or to particular groups, or in languages other than English. Public libraries may wish to include the main periodicals or newspapers, together with what monographs are available, for the main ethnic or linguistic groups they serve. Individual institutions may wish to emphasize the contribution of a particular group within Australian society.

The State Library of Victoria

The experience of the State Library of Victoria is used here to illustrate one type of collecting. The Library is the principal publicly accessible library for the state of Victoria, which has an ethnically diverse population of over 4 million. The Library is a legal deposit library, entitled to receive on deposit one copy of every item published in the state.

Its general policies also emphasize the collection of materials relating to the heritage of all Victorians, regardless of cultural background or language. Its *Selection Policy* (1986) refers to a goal of developing 'a comprehensive collection of material published in Victoria regardless of format'. For other materials, the policy emphasizes the four languages other than English most widely known in the state (Italian, Greek, French, German) and states: 'Some emphasis is also given to languages which are widely spoken as first languages by Victoria's ethnolinguistic minorities, or which are widely learned or known in Victoria.'[13] The State Library of Victoria in fact aims to collect Australian material in any language, and actively seeks both Victorian imprints and significant non-English-language publications, including newspapers and periodicals, from other parts of Australia. The State Library of Victoria is probably less successful in collecting Victorian publications in other languages because of lack of language expertise, the often fugitive and marginal nature of publishing and distribution, and the greater time required to seek and identify an area of publishing which is, apart from the press, mainly non-commercial.

The Library also collects original materials: principally pictures and manuscripts. Its experience in a project to collect Italian materials has been documented by Tom Griffiths.[14] The Library, through the Building a Country project, has mounted a series of exhibitions based on the collections, which document the presence and contribution to Victoria of five groups of immigrants and their descendants since 1848: Chinese, Greek, Italian, Lebanese and Vietnamese. The material has mainly been acquired recently, by donation, copying from photographs lent, or occasionally by commissioning of photography. The archive thus developed has been extended to Maltese people, and will be extended further to take in German and Japanese Australians. Through the Library's Field Historian, there are plans to contact these and other communities in order to seek manuscript and other material.

Griffiths highlighted two major problems in the Italian programme, which involved a cooperative venture with the Italian Historical Society; other lessons can be drawn from the experience of the State Library of Victoria in documenting multicultural Australia. First, Griffiths suggests that libraries are not oriented to exhibition and display but tend to be 'passive and reactive'; they are less able to work dynamically with the community. In collecting the heritage of Italian people, libraries need to be different. The current programmes of the State Library derive their success from their dynamic nature and their involvement with ethnic minority communities. Second, documenting multicultural heritage is time-consuming and expensive, and Griffiths doubts that the commitment of state institutions is adequate to meet the challenge of entrepreneurial collecting. The major activities of the State Library of Victoria to date in collecting in this area have been financially supported by outside bodies, and the Library has had great difficulty in matching outside support, whether this is financial (the grants from the Schutt Foundation for Building a Country) or community-based (the Italian Historical Society). This difficulty stems from a resource base which is declining in real terms, and from an unwillingness to reorient resources to make its collections more representative of Victorians. A third problem arises from the second: Italians are Victoria's largest ethnic minority group, but there are many others. Documenting the heritage of all Victorians becomes a complex and substantial task. Finally, the issue of language is very significant. Collecting materials which the staff cannot understand poses problems, requires working with outside groups, and requires double interpretation and additional costs.

The efforts of the National Library of Australia have been documented by Thompson. He discusses the library's manuscript, oral history, musicological and pictorial holdings. Discussing holdings of printed material, he says that the National Library 'has developed a strong collection of newsletters and newspapers of the older European communities.' He notes some recurring problems for all collecting institutions: 'ignorance of legal deposit arrangements, suspicion of bureaucracy, and the need for a better community contact in order to establish a link and to maintain thereby a productive relationship, so that a regular supply of material can be achieved.... The problem of many divisions within a single ethnic community – each division producing publications – also presents challenges.'[15]

The experience of the State Library of Victoria, and of similar institutions, is that there is no major barrier to providing as thorough a documentation of Victoria's ethnically diverse population as is provided for the mainstream. The main barriers in practice are a lack of resources for what may be a time-consuming and therefore expensive area of collection, and the attitudes of librarians.

Collecting Literature – and Other Subjects

Collecting of multicultural heritage inevitably focuses most commonly on literature: 'multicultural writing'. While defining multicultural writing is no simple task, academic libraries in particular tend to focus on it as an element in their general coverage of Australian writing. Although there is some collecting of literature in other languages, they primarily collect literature in English.

Lumb and Hazell in their collection of reviews seek 'to make a contribution to education for a multicultural society.'[16] Its scope is fiction, poetry and biography by ethnic minority authors, and the work describes and evaluates works by about fifty authors: thirty-three monographs and 188 short stories in all. Its criterion for authorship is that authors are 'born outside Australia in a country where English is not the first language' – a subset of the broader category, documenting the ethnic minority experience. As the editors point out, most literature which does this has been written by members of the ethnic majority. The writing represented 'tends to be covered in small-circulation journals and self-publishing efforts with their attendant distribution problems'.[17] Although the book lists only works in English, it is particularly useful as an overview of leading bilingual authors at the time.

Houbein produced various editions of her bibliography from 1976 to 1984. She wrote, in the introduction to the fourth edition (1984): 'Sitting in the cold blast of critical comparison with Eng. Lit.-trained writers or native grassroots talent is not conducive to a state of literary well-being.' The scope includes all literary works and biography, and authors are included 'if they were born outside Australia with a language other than English and have published in English.' However, a particular value of the book is that it provides biographical notes listing works in other languages as well. Houbein acknowledges that overseas birth is an increasingly dubious criterion.[18]

The 1988 cumulation of the *Australian National Bibliography* listed only thirty-one monographic works classified as literature, and either bilingual or in languages other than English. They included fifteen in Greek, five in Ukrainian, four in Vietnamese, two each in Latvian and Hungarian, and one each in Spanish, Russian and Croatian.

Literature has been the focus of people working on documenting multicultural Australia, and collections edited by Deszery, Jurgensen, Gunew and others have focused on this area.[19] *Writing in Multicultural Australia 1984* is a particularly useful collection of thirty-two papers on multicultural writing, including writing in English and in other languages, and translation.[20] In its fairly broad scope, including writing in other languages, translation and publishing, it is a key collection in this area. Other subjects are less well collected: there are few significant collections outside the state and national libraries of the major source of minority writing (widely defined): newspapers, or of genres or subjects other than literature.

Bibliography

A general starting point is the impressive encyclopedia, *The Australian People*.[21] This monumental work, comparable to the *Harvard Encyclopedia of the American People*, includes articles on Aboriginal Australians and on all but the smallest of the many ethnic, racial and linguistic groups which make up the Australian population. The bibliography, of almost 4000 titles, is grouped at the end of the work and follows the arrangement of the main text. The bibliography is very selective: it includes 100 items on Greeks and ninety on Germans, for example; it does not generally cite primary sources unless these are the only sources, and the great majority of works listed are in English. Generally, the periodical and daily press are excluded. A further deficiency of the encyclopedia is that although it includes a valuable select bibliography, the work does not itself include a guide to the bibliography of the subject. However, the encyclopedia is a good starting point, particularly for individual groups.

Much bibliographical work is being undertaken. Examples include the unpublished bibliography of Greek-Australian materials compiled by Mimis Sophocleous (Phillip Institute of Technology, Victoria) and the massive bibliography of Germans in Australia compiled by Leslie Bodi and Stephen Jeffries, to be published by Otto Harrassowitz (Germany).

The gap in overall bibliographical work has been partly filled by Nash's *Migrant and Ethnic Studies: A Guide to Doing Research.*[22] This is, unfortunately, closely oriented to the holdings of Monash University, but nevertheless constitutes an invaluable bibliographic introduction, and a guide to starting research or, indeed, collecting in this area. The coverage of databases was surveyed by Middleton and Norris;[23] the establishment of *MAIS: Multicultural Australia Information Service* in 1989 created a new database for this specific purpose; *MAIS* is available online from the National Library of Australia.[24]

Nash's bibliographical chapter lists predominantly general bibliographical works, and they primarily relate to secondary literature. However, Loulo Houbein's valuable bibliography of 'ethnic writings in English' and Lumb and Hazell's work have already been mentioned. Liberman, on Australian Judaica, is an example of ethnospecific bibliography which also includes, for example, works by Jay and Robe.[25] A particularly useful source of ethnospecific bibliography is found in monographs on particular groups. Titles in the Australian Ethnic Heritage Series include bibliographies, while there have also been a number of monographs on the history of particular ethnic groups: thirty are listed by Nash. Another significant bibliographical source is *Chomi-Das*, a bibliographical quarterly published by the Ecumenical Migration Centre in Richmond, Victoria.[26]

Publishing

Publishing in Australia has always been multilingual, and has always reflected ethnic and linguistic diversity: both the publishing output of the majority and of those with a self-conscious minority approach. It is the latter with which this paper is mainly concerned. What kind of material is available? The main categories include commercially published monographs (including educational publishing), self-publishing and other non-commercial, periodicals and the ethnic press, and material published overseas. The volume, varieties, bibliographical control, availability and distribution of this literature are described below.

Monographic Publishing

It was originally intended to describe two categories: commercial and non-commercial. However, if it is true, as Ron Harper suggested, that 'publishing of this kind cannot be regarded as a commercial enterprise in Australia',[27] then such a division is irrelevant; and, substantially, it is. Harper says: 'I believe that people who are writing in languages other than English will have an impossibly small commercial market here for any period that I can foresee.' Only where an overseas market can be added to that in Australia could any publication be commercially viable. Exceptions may exist with the publication of curriculum materials, but even there the market is small. The Melbourne firm, CIS Educational, based on the Centro Italiani Studi, is an example of a publisher which has achieved commercial success, but only by diversifying beyond non-English-language publishing. The reason is, of course, that the non-English-language market is not one, but scores of markets.The largest market is the 400,000-strong population of Italian-speakers, most of whom are bilingual; their reading needs are met by English-language materials, the Italian-language press, and books imported from Italy and borrowed from libraries or purchased.

Commercial publishing may be accessed through the *Australian National Bibliography (ANB)*. The main problem is that very little multicultural writing is published commercially. The landmark award of the National Book Prize to Dimitris Tsaloumas for his bilingual work of poetry, *The Observatory*, in 1983 has not been followed by a rush of mainstream publishing of this kind.[28] Collections of translated Australian poetry by Tsaloumas and Wright are not really exceptions, since the poems are from the Australian mainstream.[29]

The representation of minority-language works in *ANB* is remarkably heterogeneous, although some generalizations can be made: the main one is that most works published have probably escaped the net of *ANB*. Virtually nothing listed is published by the mainstream commercial publishing sector. For example, the thirty-one literary works referred to above were mainly published by small societies, privately, or, in the case of Greek-language books, by several semi-commercial publishers: Leros Press, Elikia, Spring, and in two cases by university presses.

A survey of non-English-language publishing listed in *ANB* shows some trends among the several hundred titles listed for a year. First, governments are major publishers of material in other languages: predominantly works in English providing basic information, and translated into a wide range of languages; government publications dealing with migration or multiculturalism also tend to be translated into other languages. Second, different communities have very different types and levels of publishing. For example, those longer-established communities where publishing in the country of origin is not free have given rise to world-wide networks of exile publishing and distribution, of which Australia forms a part. In Australia, Ukrainians, Yugoslav communities, Latvians and other Baltic groups, Hungarians, Russians, Vietnamese and others produce small numbers of books in their own languages. The main subjects are literature, biography and autobiography, and history, but also sometimes religion, philosophy and other areas of the arts.

The example of the Latvians is illustrative. The community was established in the 1940s, and has a high proportion of well-educated people. It now supports a large library in Melbourne, book shops in three states, and community centres with libraries in other states. It boasts a fund, the Jansons Fund, which supports publishing, and a national cultural journal, *Archivs*. There are Latvian writers' groups, mainly interested in writing in Latvian, and consciously (sometimes formally) part of an international movement of Latvians outside Latvia which holds regular congresses and meetings. Latvian writing and publishing are therefore not oriented towards Australia, but towards Latvia in exile. Of the subjects of publications, literature, including underground literature from Latvia, predominates; the writers are mainly Latvian-born. The effect of greater freedom in Latvia and in the other countries of Eastern Europe remains to be seen.[30]

A contrasting example is that of the Greek community in Australia, which perhaps possesses the strongest publishing among ethnic communities. Greek publishing is enhanced by opportunities for Australian writers to be published in Greece, and also by the size of the Greek community in Melbourne and Sydney. This supports a number of newspapers, the teaching of modern Greek at many universities and the consequent health of writing in Greek in Australia, a vigorous literary movement, and the fact that the Greek community is now well established and able to support the publishing and purchase of books and journals. Like the groups described above, Greek writing has a strong international dimension: based only in Australia, it would be much less strong.

Another significant category of publishing consists of bilingual and other teaching materials produced for the growing school, TAFE and informal education (Saturday school) markets for curriculum materials.

Monographic publishing is not evenly distributed over all subjects, but focuses heavily on literature, history and politics, autobiography and other personal narrative, some educational material and, in some communities, religion. It is diverse, heterogeneous, varies greatly from one group to another, and is largely unrecorded in the major bibliographies of Australian publishing.

Periodicals and the Ethnic Press

Australia maintains a numerous and vigorous ethnic minority press, documented in standard bibliographies of serials and newspapers, as well as in some secondary works. Gilson is the only attempt at a thorough bibliography, but is current only to 1964.[31] For current titles, *Ethnic Press* is useful, while Nash has a select listing of the main titles.[32]

The non-English-language or 'ethnic' press is a neglected area of collecting. Much of it is endangered too, represented sometimes only be single known backsets, or none. In Victoria little has been microfilmed and few efforts have been made to preserve it. Examples of exceptions (in Victoria) have included the donation of funds to microfilm early German-language newspapers, and the microfilming by the State Library of the national Greek newspaper, *Neos Kosmos*. However, although newspapers are the major published source of information about most groups, little is available on microfilm; the likely market for it has not been assessed.

Ethnic Media in New South Wales indicates the range and diversity of the ethnic press in Australia.[33] The listing includes newspapers circulating in New South Wales but published elsewhere (mainly in Victoria). Titles in over thirty languages are listed; this information is summarized in Table 1. The forty-four titles published weekly or more frequently include many published more frequently than weekly, usually two or three times per week, in Arabic (one title), Chinese (two dailies), Greek (two), Italian (two), Spanish (one), Vietnamese (two, including one daily) and Yugoslav (one). The total circulation of all titles is over 700,000, although this figure covers titles of varying frequency. The number of newspapers in languages other than English bought each week in Australia is certainly very substantial – probably between 1 and 2 million – and dwarfs the publication and circulation of monographs. The larger newspapers are also publishers of other material: the occasional monograph or commemorative publication.

Table 1. Newspapers Circulating in New South Wales by Language

Language	Frequency W	F	M	Circulation
Arabic	7	1	1	131,000
Chinese	3		1	30,000
Dutch		1	1	5,000
Estonian	1			1,500
Filipino			1	3,000
Finnish		2		3,800
French			1	7,000
German	1			9,000
Greek	6	1	2	150,000
Hungarian	1			6,500
Indian/Pakistani	1		1	7,000
Italian	2		2	90,000
Japanese			2	20,000
Jewish	2	1		10,000
Khmer			1	
Korean			2	8,500
Latvian	1			
Lithuanian	1			1,200
Maltese	2			12,000
Persian		1		600
Polish	1			6,000
Portuguese	2			12,000
Russian	1			4,500
Scandinavian			1	1,500
Spanish	3		2	54,000
Turkish	2	3	1	28,000
Ukrainian	1			
Vietnamese	3		1	88,000
Yugoslav	3		1	26,000

Key: W = weekly or more frequently; F = fortnightly; M = monthly or less frequently. Circulation is total circulation of all titles.

In addition to newspapers, there is a substantial number of journals. *Australian Periodicals in Print* lists eighty newspapers and journals.[34] Some journals, particularly from groups where publishing is restricted in the home country, such as Poles and Vietnamese, produce journals (such as the Polish *Tu I Tam*) which are professionally produced and substantial. Many communities also support literary and cultural groups which publish journals; such titles may have short and erratic lives, but some have continued for many years. The majority of journals have escaped listing in the major reference sources.

Overseas Publishing

Many Australian authors are primarily published overseas, or find their principal market overseas, Tsaloumas included. It is interesting to note that most of the non-English-language or bilingual authors represented in *Writing in Multicultural Australia* are also binational in their publications.

Problems of Acquisition

Problems of acquisition have been discussed above, and this section summarizes that discussion and adds a little more. The main problems are:

1 Lack of bibliographical control, because of the inability of legal deposit libraries to track down and record the published output. In part this problem is also one of language: neither the national bibliography nor the Australian Bibliographic Network supports non-roman scripts, and this means that works in non-roman scripts are not adequately recorded in them – if they are recorded at all.

2 Community relations is a broad heading, and includes the difficulties referred to by Griffiths and Thompson in establishing relations with ethnic communities. Libraries are not oriented towards establishing close relations with the general community, and this has inhibited their abilities to collect. The problems are accentuated, as Thompson suggests, by suspicion of bureaucracy or just by a sense among ethnic communities that state institutions are not relevant to them or interested in them: a perception which is often justified.

3 The labour-intensive nature of searching for, identifying, acquiring and describing material is also a factor. The degree to which it is more labour-intensive than acquiring fugitive material in English is questionable, and it has often been a

mere excuse. Two other problems are intrinsically more significant.

4 Language variety may make for additional time and expense in locating and acquiring materials. This is partly because institutions are not language-conscious, and find other languages baffling and best left alone. These problems are much wider than library problems, and run through all aspects of Australian society.

5 Complexity is another factor: there are so many different groups, many of them deeply segmented by religion, politics, language or other factors. Complexity has also been used as an excuse; it is sometimes felt that if we cannot represent all groups in our collections, we represent none.

Publishing by ethnic communities, and especially publishing in languages other than English, is fugitive, ill-documented, often ephemeral, and this has been documented above. The frequent failure of libraries, such as academic and public libraries, to collect the major source of information – newspapers – is one which is hard to explain. Ultimately, many of these difficulties go back to timidity and a lack of commitment: timidity in trying new approaches and in grasping the unfamiliar, and lack of commitment to ensuring that Australia's libraries represent the whole community, the 15 per cent as well as the majority.

Conclusions

The library which wishes to document multicultural Australia in more than a nominal way will need to seek it diligently. While a few publications may be obtained through normal commercial or library supply channels, or located through standard bibliographical and book trade tools, many more cannot. For original materials, the key to developing successful collections clearly lies with the quality of the relations between the collecting institution and the community itself.

Documenting multicultural Australia is not a simple task, and no one institution is really able to carry it out comprehensively. The problems described will only be overcome, at a national or regional level, by cooperation and acceptance of diversity. The difficulty of collecting material from linguistically, culturally and socially diverse peoples will best be overcome by institutions specializing, and by a wide mix of cooperating institutions at that. The National Library, state libraries, academic libraries, public libraries, and ethnic community institutions all form part of an embryonic network of collecting institutions. No network exists, no agreements or even discussions on these issues exist. They will need to be developed if documenting multicultural Australia is to be taken seriously by Australian institutions and by the people themselves.

For the future, the Commonwealth Government's recent foray into these issues is to be welcomed, as is the growing interest among other state institutions in collecting the documentary testimony to multicultural Australia. The hope that the current exploration of policy and coordination may lead to a more effective documentation of multicultural Australia and a greater commitment to the task is a suitable place to finish.

Notes

1 Lois Buttlar and Lubomyr R. Wynar, *Building Ethnic Collections: An Annotated Guide for School Media Centers and Public Libraries*. Littleton, Colo.: Libraries Unlimited, 1977.

2 Review of Migrant and Multicultural Programs and Services. *Don't Settle for Less: Report....* Canberra: Australian Government Publishing Service, 1986, pp. 41-42.

3 *Ibid.*, p. 42.

4 Joseph Lo Bianco, *National Policy on Languages*. Canberra: Australian Government Publishing Service, 1987, pp. 40-41.

5 Michael G. Clyne, *Multilingual Australia*. Melbourne: River Seine, 1982. The languages were, in order of size, Italian, Greek, German, Croatian and Serbian, Dutch, French, Polish, Arabic, Spanish, Maltese, Hungarian, Chinese, Turkish, Ukrainian, Russian, Macedonian, Slovenian, Portugueses, Czech and Slovak, Latvian, Lithuanian, Finnish, Estonian, Japanese, Swedish, Romanian, Danish, Indonesian/Malay, Welsh and Irish. Clyne, if he had had the data, might well have added a number of other languages with well over 1000 speakers (Albanian, Armenian and Yiddish, for example), while since the 1976 Census, upon which his book is based, other languages have arrived too (Cambodian, Tagalog and Vietnamese, for example).

6 *New Responsibilities: Documenting Multicultural Australia; A Record of the Conference for Museums, Libraries, Archives and Historical Collections...11-13 November 1988*, ed. by Margaret Birtley and Patricia McQueen. Melbourne: Museums Association of Australia Inc., Victorian Branch and Library Council of Victoria, 1989.

7 Lo Bianco, *op. cit.*; Senate Standing Committee on Education and the Arts, *Report on a National Language Policy*. Canberra: Australian Government Publishing Service, 1984.

8 ROMAMPAS, p. 290.

9 Advisory Council on Multicultural Affairs, *Towards a National Agenda for a Multicultural Australia: A Discussion Paper*. Canberra: Australian Government Publishing Service, 1988, p. 140.

10 *Ibid*., p. 141.

11 *National Agenda for a Multicultural Australia: ...Sharing Our Future*. Canberra: Australian Government Publishing Service, 1989, p. 49.

12 Correspondence from Insearch Ltd and the Department of Arts, Sport, the Environment, Tourism and Territories to the State Library of Victoria.

13 State Library of Victoria, *Selection Policy*. Melbourne: Library Council of Victoria, 1986, pp. 16-17.

14 Tom Griffiths, 'Investing in the State: Victoria's Italians,' in *New Responsibilities, op. cit*., pp. 63-66.

15 John Thompson, 'Serving Multicultural Australia: What Role for the National Library?' in *New Responsibilities, op. cit*., 128-134.

16 Peter Lumb and Anne Hazell, eds, *Diversity and Diversion: An Annotated Bibliography of Australian Ethnic Minority Literature*. Richmond, Vic.: Hodja, 1983.

17 *Ibid*., pp. xi, xiii.

18 Lolo Houbein, *Ethnic Writings in English from Australia: A Bibliography*. 3rd rev. ed. Adelaide: Adelaide University, Department of English, 1984.

19 Andrew Deszery, ed., *English and Other Than English*. Adelaide: Deszery Ethnic Publications, 1979; Manfred Jurgensen, ed., *Ethnic Australia*. Brisbane: Phoenix Publications, 1981; Sneja Gunew, comp., *Displacements: Migrant Storytellers*. Geelong: Deakin University Press, 1982.

20 *Writing in Multicultural Australia 1984: An Overview*. Papers presented at the Multicultural Writers' Weekends...1984. Sydney: Australia Council, 1985.

21 James Jupp, ed., *The Australian People: An Encyclopedia of the Nation, Its People and Their Origins*. General editor, James Jupp. Sydney: Angus and Robertson, 1988.

22 Vivien Nash, comp., *Migrant and Ethnic Studies: A Guide to Doing Research Based on the Collections at Monash University*. Occasional Publication, 5. Clayton, Vic.: Monash University Library, 1988.

23 M. Middleton and S. Norris, 'Multicultural Affairs Documentation: Coverage by Databases and Indexing Services,' *Multicultural Libraries* 1 (1985): 18-31.

24 Thompson, *op. cit*., p. 131.

25 Serge Liberman, *A Bibliography of Australian Judaica*. Sydney: Mandelbaum Trust, 1987; W.E. Jay, *Italians and Australia*. Armidale, NSW: University of New England, Department of Romance Languages, 1977; Stanley Robe, *Poles and Australia: A Bibliographic Record 1775-1980*. Melbourne: Australian Institute of Multicultural Affairs, 1986.

26 *Chomi-Das*. Richmond, Vic.: Ecumenical Migration Centre, 1975- ; quarterly.

27 Ron Harper, 'Multicultural Publishing,' *Writing in Multicultural Australia 1984, op. cit.*, pp. 158-160.

28 Dimitris Tsaloumas, *The Observatory*. St Lucia, Qld: University of Queensland Press, 1983.

29 Dimitris Tsaloumas, *Synkhrone Australiane Poiese/ Contemporary Australian Poetry*. St Lucia, Qld: University of Queensland Press, 1985; Judith Wright, *Many Roads Meet Here = Qui s'incontrano molte strade*. Adelaide: Deszery Publications, 1985.

30 Information from Isolde Forstmanis and Valda Liepins.

31 M. Gilson, *Foreign Language Press in Australia*. Canberra: ANU Press, 1967.

32 *Ethnic Press*. Melbourne: Ministry of Immigration and Ethnic Affairs, 1981. Continued by *Guide to Ethnic Media in Victoria*. Melbourne: Victorian Ethnic Affairs Commission, 1983- ; Nash, *op. cit.*

33 *Ethnic Media in New South Wales*. 5th ed. Sydney: Ministerial Press Office, Premier's Department, 1987.

34 *Australian Periodicals in Print 1989*. Melbourne: D.W. Thorpe, 1989.

18 Conspectus and Australiana Collections, with Some Comments on the Distributed National Collection

John Horacek

In the late 1980s Conspectus became a topic of interest among Australian librarians, and the Libraries Summit in 1988 urged libraries to produce collection development policies using Conspectus. So far the National Library of Australia and certain state libraries have done so, but the description of the Australiana collections is generally treated as a special case, outside Conspectus. Among other developments, the appointment of a Conspectus Officer and the Australianization of the documentation are noteworthy. Applications of Conspectus in the academic library sector are increasing. Conspectus is also seen as a means towards achieving a Distributed National Collection, another Summit objective.

In the short time which has elapsed since the promulgation of the idea of Conspectus in two key articles in US library journals in 1983, considerable interest and activity in the application of the methodology can be observed around the world, Australia not excepted.[1]

Basically, Conspectus was developed in the United States by the Research Libraries Group (RLG) as both a standardized methodology for evaluating library collections and the resulting database containing the collated information gathered via this process. The first formal manifestation of Conspectus in Australia can be traced to 1986, when the Committee of Australian University Librarians recommended that, for collection evaluation, libraries should use the RLG levels and definitions as a national standard, instead of the scale which had been developed by the National Library of Australia (NLA). Some experimentation with Conspectus soon followed, and the writer is aware of at least three projects – one involving highway engineering collections in a group of three university libraries, one relating to theology collections in Victoria, and a project at Australian National University (ANU) to develop a collection development policy using the RLG structures and levels.

The next step forward occurred in 1988, when the Acquisitions Section of the Library Association of Australia (as it was then) organized a Seminar in conjunction with the Biennial Conference in Sydney, on 'The RLG Conspectus and Collection Evaluation', at which the keynote speaker was Dr Paul Mosher. This attracted a considerable amount of interest, and the papers were published in *Australian Academic and Research Libraries*.[2] Soon after that, in October 1988, the Australian Libraries Summit endorsed the Conspectus methodology, and recommended that a Task Force working under the sponsorship of ACLIS (Australian Council of Libraries and Information Services) be set up to produce an Australian version.[3] This Task Force produced its report, *The Australian Conspectus*, in December 1989.[4] This contained thirty-six recommendations, both general and specific. Most significant were those which urge ACLIS to support the establishment of an Australian Conspectus; that the Dewey Decimal Classification based scheme used by the Pacific North West (PNW) group be used; that there be an Australianization of the worksheets and supplemental guidelines; that a Conspectus Officer be appointed, and that the PNW software be used as a basis for the Australian Conspectus database, to run on a PC with diskettes for input and output. The Task Force also spent a considerable amount of time and thought on the rephrasing of the definitions of the levels, which were rejected by some librarians as too oriented towards academic libraries with their stress on teaching and research functions.

While the Task Force was deliberating, training sessions had been held in both Melbourne and Sydney, organized by the Australian Information Management Association, and led by Jeffrey Gardner (of the Association of Research Libraries Office of Management Studies). All this activity, which was supported by a range of meetings organized by various professional bodies, resulted in a good deal of awareness of Conspectus among Australian librarians. But awareness is not necessarily achievement, and it must be admitted that completed Conspectus-based projects are not numerous.

One important factor is that despite the generally favourable reception accorded to Conspectus in Australia, support has not been unanimous; witness the critical article by Geoff Allen, 'A Case against Conspectus', published in 1989, and Margaret Shaw's dismissal of Conspectus as having any value for Australian art libraries.[5] These public statements of opposition are supported by a less vocal group who are also opposed to Conspectus, or at least sceptical of the benefits which its proponents claim.

Conspectus and Australiana

Given the paucity of Conspectus surveys, it is only logical that applications of Conspectus to Australiana would also be very few. Nevertheless, there are some achievements worthy of record.

First, one should cite the work of the National Library of Australia (NLA), as published in its *Collection Development Policy*, distributed in September 1990.[6] The NLA Council had, in December 1987, endorsed the RLG methodology as the basic means for describing the Library's collections, and the Library 'expects to adopt any agreed ACLIS standard for collection descriptions for the description of its collections.'[7] The *Policy* does use the Conspectus levels almost throughout to describe the Library's collecting intentions and Overall Collection Levels, but there is an important exception to this, which is the extensive section dealing with its Australiana collections. Because these are in the majority of cases aimed at the comprehensive level, the Conspectus approach was seen as of limited value. Instead, the section on Australiana is organized by form, and any variations and limitations in the NLA collecting activity are expressed with some detail in the text.

Almost simultaneously with the NLA document, there appeared policies from two of the state libraries, one for the State Library of New South Wales (SLNSW), the other from the Library and Information Service of Western Australia (LISWA).[8] The NSW policy is almost entirely organized by subject, in Dewey sequence, and Conspectus levels are used, both for the Estimated Collection Strength (SLNSW variant on the usual Existing Collection Strength) and the Current Collecting Intensity. Although the preliminary work which the SLNSW did on the collection policy was based on the use of a four-level scale (following the earlier policies of the NLA and the State Library of Victoria), 'following the acceptance by the Australian Libraries Summit...of the need for an Australian version of the Conspectus, the State Library chose to accept the Conspectus levels in the interest of national conformity.'[9] As Janine Schmidt reveals in her paper, 'Conspectus: The State Library Perspective', there was considerable discussion in the State Libraries Council on the merits and defects of the Conspectus methodology, and not all state libraries are committed to using it.[10]

The SLNSW document includes Australiana in its overall structure, but much relevant information is included in the final section, which covers 'Specialist Collections and Services'. This section does not use Conspectus levels or a DDC structure, which is only to be expected as there is more stress on various forms and categories of material (e.g., manuscripts, rare books, ephemera) which cut across all classification numbers, and which need to be described in detail, verbally, rather than in Conspectus shorthand. This parallels the experience of the NLA.

The policy issued by LISWA (which so far covers only the Alexander Library Building; the second volume dealing with public libraries is due shortly) also has many resemblances to those of the SLNSW and NLA. This is not surprising as the 'Acknowledgements' indicate that: 'In the preparation of this document we have unashamedly borrowed ideas for layout and presentation.' This shows itself in the overall organization of the policy, which is basically in DDC order, followed by sections on 'Special Collections' and on 'West Australian Collections'. However, LISWA did not follow the example of the other two institutions in the matter of assigning Conspectus levels to the various subject areas of the collection. The reason cited is that this is premature given the present state of development of the Australian Conspectus: 'The Library and Information Service of Western Australia is committed to a thorough investigation of the Conspectus methodology and to its implementation if appropriate. As work on the Australian version of Conspectus is only in its early stages it does not seem appropriate to assign collection levels at this time.' However, *Past Imperfect, Future Imperative* describes the various collections in the Alexander Library Building in some depth, and also indicates the desired collecting intensity, so it should not prove very difficult in the future to assign Conspectus levels to the text.

The Library Board of Queensland policy similarly uses a DDC-based arrangement and Conspectus level indicators to describe the State Reference Library Collections, but the section dealing specifically with the Australiana (Queenslandiana) material in the John Oxley Library is expressed in verbal terms.[11]

As far as the other state libraries are concerned there is little to report in the way of real achievements. The policy of the State Library of Victoria is a BC (Before Conspectus) document, and there are no specific plans to reissue it in a modified version, though much of the information gathered during its compilation would lend itself to analysis using the Conspectus methodology. The staff are, however, committed to using Conspectus for any amendments or additions to their selection policy. The remaining state libraries have no immediate plans to implement Conspectus in any systematic way.

It is noteworthy that the evidence of the documents discussed above strongly suggests that Conspectus is of limited benefit in the area of Australiana as far as major collecting institutions with specific local responsibilities are concerned. It almost goes without saying that the various state libraries should collect material published in their respective states ('stateiana', to use the new coinage) at a comprehensive level, and therefore what is of interest is the peripheral material and the inclusion and exclusion of unpublished materials (such as manuscripts or realia), as well as those instances where published materials are *not* being collected. At this level of detail Conspectus is less useful, and while one would applaud attempts to gather such data on the Conspectus database, if only for comparative purposes, it would be of limited value only.

At present, academic libraries are considerably behind the state libraries in their achievements. On the basis of information gathered by correspondence and discussions with colleagues, the author can state unequivocally that no academic library has published a Conspectus-based collection development policy. There are many reasons for this, the main ones being uncertainty as to the benefits which could be expected to follow, lack of commitment to Conspectus, the lack of the final Australian manual and worksheets, but, most notably, the amount of work involved and the cost of the staff needed to do it.

In connection with one of the above points, it is worth recording here that progress on the Australianization of Conspectus, and indeed on other matters to do with the implementation of Conspectus in Australia, should receive a fillip as a result of the appointment of a Conspectus Officer. This position, which (as earlier mentioned) was recommended in the ACLIS Conspectus Task Force Report, is jointly funded by ACLIS and NLA, and in September 1990 Margaret Henty was appointed to it. Ms Henty presented a verbal report at the First ALIA Conference in Perth, indicating that a considerable amount of work has already been done in the modification of the schedules from their existing American orientation to reflect Australia, and that the revised schedules are already available – there is now a preliminary edition in looseleaf format of the *Australian Conspectus Manual*, and accompanying Australianized worksheets. The implications of this are that now Australian libraries wishing to proceed with applying Conspectus to their collections can do so, secure in the knowledge that they are working to a national standard. Among the important aspects of the duties of the incumbent will be proselytizing and training, to foster greater awareness of the advantages of the Conspectus for both collection evaluation and the framing of collection policies. The Conspectus Office is also expected to perform a valuable function in acting as a clearinghouse for information and experience arising from projects undertaken by various institutions.

This last task is likely to be of great benefit to the library community, since the present approach to Conspectus projects is a 'let's-all-learn-together' one, and there is likely to be much interest in completed projects. Evidence of this can be found in the numerous enquiries received regarding a Victorian ACLIS Pilot Project on Chemistry.[12] This makes a good deal of sense, since one of the most difficult steps in Conspectus surveying is to come up with the right set of tools for checking, given the fact that material available from the US is often not relevant to local conditions, and even for a subject such as chemistry, which would normally be considered to be unaffected by geographical considerations, the tools recommended in the PNW manuals are considered inadequate for local needs – the lack of currency is also an obvious problem.

The information supplied to the author in response to his enquiry regarding the use libraries had made of Conspectus suggests that similar cooperative, regional ventures may be a useful way to proceed. For instance, the group of university libraries based in Brisbane have organized group training sessions. They have also had a series of meetings to discuss possible joint ventures in Conspectus evaluation of specific subject collections, though apparently progress has been slow due to lack of time of staff committed to other functions.

Individual libraries reported various degrees of progress, ranging from a complete collection development policy based on Conspectus being prepared, through partial surveys of specific collections in branch libraries, to a commitment in principle without (as yet) any specific implementation. There is also a group of academic librarians who are entirely opposed to Conspectus, but this appears to be a clear minority: of the twenty-three responses received by the author, fewer than 20 per cent fall into this category.

This is a promising situation, as it indicates that the climate surrounding Conspectus is generally favourable, and that the habitual scepticism of Australian librarians is gradually being converted into an acceptance of the fact that, while Conspectus is not perfect, it is the best methodology available, and that there are many advantages to libraries using a common tool for the collection evaluation which, in the present environment of needing to demonstrate accountability, is fast becoming a requirement for libraries. Derek Whitehead, referring to Conspectus as a management tool, forcefully comments: 'Libraries which do not map out existing collections and chart collection policies, but instead manage in some kind of intuitive way, are not managing at all. And on the other hand, libraries which rely on introspective means of setting out policy and practice are wasting their efforts, since those efforts are not usable by anyone else.'[13]

The benefits of using Conspectus have been set down in the Task Force Report, and reiterated in a paper by Eric Wainwright given in Perth in October 1990.[14] It is not necessary to list them here, merely to draw attention to the fact that librarians are gradually being convinced, and the NLA and some of the state libraries are performing a very useful function of teaching by example. The account by David Toll of the NLA experience identifies some of the processes and consequences of the development of the collection policy in Conspectus terms.[15] A paper by Suzanne Clarke, also prepared for the Perth ALIA Conference, highlights the work undertaken in the Royal Melbourne Institute of Technology Library in creating a course-related policy using the Conspectus methodology, and the use that was made of the collection analysis for justifying submissions for additional funding.[16]

These case studies must not be dismissed because they are few in number; rather, they should be seen as evidence of the potential, even at this early stage, of the methodology.

In the academic experiments with Conspectus, there appear to be no specific instances of Australiana oriented surveys to date. What the future holds is obviously difficult to foretell. Certainly, when the Australianized schedules developed in the Conspectus Office are readily available, there may be libraries which will wish to implement them immediately. On the other hand, the sorts of strategies Wainwright suggests as most beneficial for the Australian application of Conspectus would probably be best served by concentration on bibliographically large areas. Australian publishing is not voluminous, and hence its contribution to most subject areas is limited, with the obvious and notable exception of Australian history. This area is probably less likely to need Conspectus-style surveys, given what is already known of collections in state and national libraries, though a Conspectus database could draw attention to holdings in other types of libraries, e.g. the older universities, parliamentary libraries and special historical collections.

Another reason for suggesting that implementation of Conspectus would be most valuable if applied to non-Australiana is that the current interest in the Distributed National Collection would be advanced considerably by the identification of areas of special, distinctive collecting strengths – and, because Australiana is both a relatively small area and a crucial one for most institutions, it does not fit the bill.

The concept of the Distributed National Collection (DNC) is becoming a major matter for discussion following Resolution AA1 of the Australian Libraries Summit, that the following principles of a national collection be accepted:

a. aggregation of all library collections in Australia whether in the public or private sector;
b. comprehensive in relation to Australia;
c. selective in relation to the rest of the world as present and future needs require;
d. adequately recorded and readily accessible.

Since this resolution was passed in October 1988, exegesis of its meaning has been widespread, as has discussion of the consequences of its adoption (in some interpretation or other).

ACLIS has adopted DNC as one of the major planks of its platform, and Eric Wainwright has been involved in a series of public meetings on it. At the Perth ALIA Conference, the Acquisitions Section organized a pre-conference seminar on the DNC, and a few days later (in the first week of October) ACLIS distributed the second draft of its 'Statement' on the topic (reproduced here as an Appendix).

There is little point in elaborating on this statement beyond stressing that the issue is extremely complex, even contentious, and any progress from sanctimonious endorsement of the concept to actual implementation, in howsoever limited a way, will test the will of Australian librarians to determine the future growth of library collections, rather than accepting the present Topsy-like situation.

The link to Conspectus is spelled out in the 'Statement', and certainly the more information we have, the better the base for making decisions. However, there is a risk that this link might also serve to delay adoption of DNC in any practical way, since progress on the development of the Conspectus database will almost certainly be quite slow, depending as it does first on individual libraries doing their collection evaluation, and second on the collation of these statements.

Conclusion

Both Conspectus and DNC represent exciting opportunities and challenges for Australian librarians, and there is ample evidence that many are ready to seize them. That all librarians are not converts should neither surprise nor alarm, since unanimity is a utopian ideal, and developments toward more controlled collecting which these concepts represent can occur with the support of the enthusiastic few. A critical mass of implemented projects can soon develop, and this will attract others to participate.

However, as far as Australiana is concerned, there would be fewer benefits and fewer possibilities of implementation in both Conspectus and DNC. It is in the broader areas of collecting that our priorities should lie, and our success can be felt.

Postscript

By way of update to this paper, little needs to be added save to record some achievements of the Conspectus Officer, notably the production of a preliminary edition in looseleaf format of the *Australian Conspectus Manual*, and the publishing of Australianized worksheets. The implications of this are that now Australian libraries wishing to proceed with applying Conspectus to their collections can do so, secure in the knowledge that they are working to a national standard.

One other development is marginal to the comments made regarding Australian collections, and that is the announcement that the National Library is finalizing plans for a conference on access to Australian published material. The conference, to take place in March 1992, has been given the title 'Towards Federation 2001: Linking Australians and Their Heritage'. The few details so far available suggest it will make little use of Conspectus.

Notes

1 Nancy E. Gwinn and Paul H. Mosher, 'Coordinating Collection Development: The RLG Conspectus,' *College and Research Libraries* 44, 2 (1983): 128-140; Paul H. Mosher and Marcia Pankake, 'A Guide to Coordinated and Cooperative Collection Development,' *Library Resources and Technical Services* 27, 6 ((October/December 1983): 417-431.

2 *Australian Academic and Research Libraries* 20 9 (March 1989), available as a separate issue entitled *The RLG Conspectus and Collection Evaluation: An Australian Perspective*, from DA Books, 648 Whitehorse Road, Mitcham, Vic. 3132.

3 Australian Libraries Summit, *Final Report*. Canberra: National Library of Australia, 1988.

4 Australian Council of Library and Information Services. National Task Force on Conspectus, *Final Report*. Canberra: ACLIS, December 1989.

5 Geoffrey G. Allen, 'A Case against Conspectus,' *Australian Library Journal* 38, 3 (August 1989): 211-216 (with a rejoinder by Eric Wainwright, pp. 216-218); J. Margaret Shaw, 'Conspectus as a Tool for Art Libraries in Australia,' *Australian Academic and Research Libraries* 21, 1 (1990): 33-38.

6 National Library of Australia, *Collection Development Policy*. Canberra: National Library of Australia, 1990.

7 *Ibid.*, p. 18.

8 State Library of New South Wales, *Collection Development Policy*. Sydney: SLNSW, 1990; Library and Information Service of Western Australia, *Past Imperfect, Future Imperative: Collection Development at The Library and Information Service of Western Australia. Vol. 1: The Alexander Library Building Collections*. Perth: LISWA, 199.

9 State Library of New South Wales, *op. cit.*, p. 31.

10 Janine Schmidt, 'Conspectus: The State Library Perspective,' in Australian Library and Information Association, *1st Biennial Conference (Perth, 1990): Conference Proceedings. Vol. 2*, pp. 260-264.

11 Library Board of Queensland, *Collection Development Policies*. Brisbane: Library Board of Queensland, 1989.

12 John Horacek, 'The Victorian Chemistry Conspectus Pilot Project,' *Australian Academic and Research Libraries* 21, 4 (1990).

13 Derek Whitehead, 'The Development of Conspectus in Victoria,' in *Australian Library and Information Association, 1st Biennial Conference (Perth, 1990): Conference Proceedings. Vol. 2*, pp. 265-269.

14 Eric Wainwright, 'Long Time Coming? Conspectus in Australia,' in *Australian Library and Information Association, 1st Biennial Conference (Perth, 1990): Conference Proceedings. Vol. 2*, pp. 271-284.

15 David Toll, 'Collection Development and Management: The Experience of the National Library of Australia,' in *Australian Library and Information Association, 1st Biennial Conference (Perth, 1990): Conference Proceedings, Vol. 1*, pp. 591-599.

16 Suzanne Clarke, 'Creating a Conspectus Based Collection Development Policy,' in *Australian Library and Information Association, 1st Biennial Conference (Perth, 1990): Conference Proceedings, Vol. 1*, pp. 611-626.

Appendix: Second Draft for Discussion; The Distributed National Collection – A Statement by the Australian Council of Libraries and Information Services

Introduction

Libraries recognize their interdependence and have developed a strong tradition of cooperation by making their holdings known to other libraries and through the interlibrary loan of material needed by the clients of other libraries.

Library managers, in seeking ways to further improve performance in relation to:

* meeting users' current information requirements;
* making best use of financial resources for the benefit of all Australians;
* preserving recorded information to meet future needs;

have considered the possibility of further strengthening arrangements for voluntary cooperation through the development of coordinating mechanisms (strategies) which attract broad support amongst libraries of all types.

This approach was reflected in much of the discussion and in many of the resolutions of the Australian Libraries Summit in October 1988. Relevant topics included:

the national database
preservation strategies
document delivery systems
access to electronic information
serving users with special needs
and the national collection

Notably, in relation to the national collection, resolution AA1 stated:

That the following principles of a national collection be accepted:

a. Aggregation of all library collections in Australia whether in the public or private sector.
b. Comprehensive in relation to Australia.
c. Selective in relation to the rest of the world as present and future needs require.
d. Adequately recorded and readily accessible.

The idea of an Australian 'national collection' which is in fact distributed, i.e. there are parts of it held in different libraries throughout Australia, is neither a conceptual break-through, nor is the idea new. There is, however, a genuine desire in the Australian library industry to identify and implement strategies to further the achievement of the above principles, through what has come to be called the 'Distributed National Collection' (DNC).

Role of the Australian Council of Libraries and Information Services

The Australian Council of Libraries and Information Services (ACLIS) exists because Australian libraries and other information service providers choose to join the organization which has as its primary objectives (in brief):

* To promote and encourage cooperation.
* To foster and develop effective utilization of libraries and information services.
* To provide effective public advocacy.

Through its broadly based membership, elected National Council and strong State and Territory level involvement, ACLIS is well placed to provide the necessary coordination required to develop the strategies to achieve the 'Distributed National Collection'.

In doing so, ACLIS recognizes the basis for success will be the voluntary cooperation of libraries and that it has no mandate to impose solutions. It is also to be expected that strategies which are recommended and followed by many libraries will not be taken up by all libraries. ACLIS will, however, have a significant role in informing and explaining, with the object of persuading as many libraries as possible to adopt strategies which are in the long term national interest, whilst not impinging on the right of every library to regard the needs of its immediate clientele as paramount.

Definition

It is clear that whether one considers the total number of *volumes* in Australia, or simply the range of *different titles* held, we have in fact a network of collections in which material is dispersed among different libraries.

For the 'Distributed National Collection' to have a meaning, however, it must exist as something more than an ad hoc aggregate of collections built up by different institutions. The 'Distributed National Collection' *has* in fact existed in Australia as a semi-coordinated system for many years. Libraries have, by and large, listed their holdings in various union catalogues, mainly through ABN in recent years. They have also, in varying degrees, permitted access to all or most of their collections by persons from outside their institutions, either directly, or more usually through interlibrary document supply.

These activities represent the minimum for the 'Distributed National Collection' to function as a system, i.e.:

* collections are acquired by a number of institutions;
* holdings in those institutions are made known to other institutions;
* access to those collections is provided to other persons from other institutions, directly or indirectly.

This leads to a recommended definition of the 'Distributed National Collection' as being:

> The aggregation of all collections in Australia which are recorded in generally accessible databases and are accessible, either in person or via interlibrary document supply, to users with bona fide reasons for access. The Distributed National Collection is comprehensive in relation to Australiana and selective in relation to the rest of the world as present and future needs of Australia require.

Vision

The vision behind the Distributed National Collection (DNC) is to maximize the ability of libraries to meet the information needs of all Australians as effectively as possible. The DNC as defined is a target towards which libraries could collectively aspire. In doing so attention must be given to collecting, bibliographical control, preservation, access and national coordination.

Objectives

1. Collecting
   To put in place mechanisms such that libraries of all types can base their collecting decisions on knowledge of the collection strength and collecting intentions of other libraries.
2. Bibliographical Control

To develop the computerized record of items in the DNC. This national bibliographical database (NBD) will enable libraries of all types to record their holding such that any library can determine which other libraries have particular titles in their collections. Materials of national or regional significance will be recorded in the NBD as soon as possible after acquisition.

3. Preservation

   To put in place a preservation plan which will result in the Australian documentary record and as much as possible of the relevant non-Australian resources being preserved for future availability.

4. Access

   To make known the access policies of libraries which will be as liberal as local circumstances permit. Libraries will supply, on request from other libraries, the majority of items (or copies of them) in their collections.

5. National Coordination

   To develop parts of the collections of some libraries in the national interest and as part of a national plan, where to do so would build on existing strengths and would complement rather than conflict with the needs of their primary clientele.

Strategies

Strategies adopted to implement the DNC will need to be kept continually under review by the library community subject to the needs of users, evolving technology and refinement following the experience gained when strategies are applied.

The detail of DNC strategies, including the priorities to be assigned to them, will require considerably more debate and development than has currently occurred. In outline the strategies are expected to include:

1. Collecting
   - A. The Australian Conspectus will provide the framework for libraries to describe their collection strengths and collecting intentions with some consistency and for that information to be gathered together and made available to other libraries.
   - B. Collecting and preservation decisions of libraries can be rationalized in the knowledge of the intentions of other libraries in order to make the best use of resources to meet the needs of their primary clientele.

C. Key collections can be identified which together provide the combined strength to meet the needs of the nation or a region in designated subject areas.

D. Subjects can be identified for which there are no collections with significant strength and the needs of the nation to develop collections or rely on overseas supply can be assessed.

E. Negotiations can occur with identified libraries to determine on what basis they can take on a designated national or regional role in collection, retention and preservation of collections in particular subject areas. Such arrangements need not necessarily involve additional funding.

F. If arrangements for designated national or regional roles involve additional funding (or other support) then libraries could be expected to accept contractual obligations as negotiated with the funding body.

2. Bibliographical Control

A. The national bibliographic database (NBD) is the computerized record of the items in the DNC. The best mix of databases and networks which will contain the records of the DNC will need to be investigated.

B. Libraries, large and small, with collections which in part or whole are of national or regional significance but are not currently recording their holdings in the NBD could be identified.

C. Negotiations could occur with those libraries to determine on what basis or by what mechanisms their holdings could be added to the NBD.

D. Given that the NBD is likely to involve the aggregation of a number of different databases, the development of gateways providing access points to link the proliferating range of library systems should be investigated.

3. Preservation

A. National and regional plans to preserve significant collections in all formats, including electronic, should be implemented to ensure the availability of information resources for future use.

4. Access

A. Directories of the access policies of libraries for both personal access and/or borrowing and also for interlibrary lending should be compiled and made available in appropriate ways, including online.

B. A uniform national system for interlibrary loans should be further developed, promoted and supported, with component parts including the interlibrary loans code and recommended scales of charging to apply when reciprocal arrangements are not in place.

C. Arrangements should be encouraged whereby libraries with interests in common develop reciprocal access arrangements that would mutually benefit their clientele.

5. National Coordination

A. The DNC will involve libraries of all types, large and small, contributing to whatever level they are able through collecting, bibliographical control, preservation and access policies.

B. Within that overall context certain subject collections within particular libraries should, by voluntary arrangement, be designated as national or regional collections of significance within the DNC.

C. Such libraries would accept a responsibility for collecting, recording, preserving and making available their collections in the designated subjects. This may occur without additional funding but when funding is provided, a formal contractual arrangement is likely to be required.

Summary

In a country the size of Australia, with its limited population and resources, and dependence on acquisitions from overseas for an increasing proportion of the information needed for its successful development, there is an argument for establishing mechanisms which provide for better exploitation of the 'Distributed National Collection' than currently exist. If this is to occur, then the necessary building blocks have to be put in place. The technology which could underpin more coordinated collection development certainly now exists – whether the will is there is a matter for ACLIS and the library community as a whole to determine and then pursue with governments in cooperation with Australian libraries.

Notes on Contributors

John Arnold is Senior Research Fellow at the National Centre for Australian Studies at Monash University in Melbourne. He was formerly La Trobe Research Librarian at the State Library of Victoria and has also worked as an antiquarian bookseller. His publications include *The Imagined City: Melbourne in the Mind of Its Writers* and *Biographical Register of the Queensland Parliament, 1930-1980*. Address: National Centre for Australian Studies, Monash University, Clayton, Victoria 3168

Ross Atkinson is Assistant University Librarian for Collection Development and Preservation at Cornell University in Ithaca, New York. Before coming to Cornell, he was Humanities Bibliographer at Northwestern University Library and later Assistant University Librarian for Collection Management at the University of Iowa Libraries. He is the author of numerous articles on collection development, preservation and bibliographical theory. Address: Olin Library, Cornell University, Ithaca, New York 14853-5301

Jerelynn Brown is Manager of Sales and Customer Service at James Bennett Library Services, the major supplier of Australian publications to libraries throughout the world. This is her third stint with James Bennett, where she has also managed the School Libraries Division and served as a director of the company. Mrs Brown has also been Bibliographic Services Manager for New South Wales TAFE Library Services and has taught in the School of Library and Information Studies at the University of Technology, Sydney. Address: James Bennett Library Services, 4 Collaroy Street, Collaroy, New South Wales 2097

Toby Burrows is Divisional Librarian (Technical Services) at the University of Western Australia. He is also editor of the *Australian and New Zealand Journal of Serials Librarianship*, author of a book on British university libraries and of several articles in librarianship and medieval history. Address: University Library, University of Western Australia, Nedlands, Western Australia 6009

Graham P. Cornish works at the British Library in Boston Spa as Programme Officer, IFLA Universal Availability of Publications Programme and Copyright Officer. In relation to the latter position he has written a major guide to British copyright law. In addition he has a strong interest in inter-library lending and related international issues of document procurement and supply. Address: British Library, Boston Spa, Wetherby LS23 7BQ, West Yorkshire

Adrian Cunningham is currently a librarian in the Manuscripts Section at the National Library of Australia. He previously worked as a librarian at the State Library of New South Wales, including four years in the Mitchell Library. Address: National Library of Australia, Canberra 2600

James D. Egles is Curator of the Overseas English Language Section of the British Library, which he joined in 1973 after training as a teacher and working in a number of different occupations. He has also served in the Slavonic and East European Section of the British Library and in his present position is responsible for the Australian, New Zealand and Canadian collections. Address: British Library, Boston Spa, Wetherby LS23 7BQ, West Yorkshire

G.E. Gorman is Senior Lecturer in the School of Information Studies at Charles Sturt University - Riverina, where he specializes in collection development and acquisitions. As an editor of the *Australian Library Review* and *Library Acquisitions: Practice and Theory* he actively supports scholarly and professional publishing in Australia. His most recent books include, with John Mills, *Indexing and Abstracting Services in the Third World* and a second edition of *Collection Development for Australian Libraries*; a companion volume, *Acquisitions in Australian Libraries*, is currently in preparation with Derek Whitehead as co-author. Address: School of Information Studies, Charles Sturt University - Riverina, PO Box 588, Wagga Wagga, New South Wales 2650

Lyn Gorman is part-time Lecturer in the School of Humanities and Social Sciences at Charles Sturt University - Riverina and a part-time freelance editor. Her editorial work includes Centre for Information Studies publications and series such as *Australian Library Review*. She is also responsible for the indexes to the present volume. Address: School of Humanities and Social Sciences, Charles Sturt University - Riverina, PO Box 588, Wagga Wagga, New South Wales 2650.

Michael Harrington is Product Development Manager at the Australian Government Publishing Service. He has also worked at the

National Library of Australia and at the State Library of Victoria. His most recent book, *The Guide to Government Publications in Australia*, was published by AGPS Press in 1990. Address: Australian Government Publishing Service, GPO Box 84, Canberra 2601

John Horacek is currently Divisional Librarian (Acquisitions) at La Trobe University in Melbourne. He has been at La Trobe since 1966 and in the Acquisitions Division since 1971. Within the Australian Library and Information Association he has long been active in matters related to acquisitions and for many years was editor of *Australian Academic and Research Libraries*. Address: Borchardt Library, La Trobe University, Bundoora, Victoria 3083

Wallace Kirsop is Associate Professor of French at Monash University in Melbourne, where he has taught since 1962; he is also Chairman of the University's Centre for Bibliographical and Textual Studies and has edited the *Australian Journal of French Studies* since 1968. His Sanders Lectures at Cambridge University have recently been published as *Books for Colonial Readers: The Nineteenth Century Australian Experience*. Address: Department of Romance Languages, Monash University, Clayton, Victoria 3168

Patricia M. Larby is Librarian of the Institute of Commonwealth Studies in the University of London and has worked in libraries in Uganda, Kenya, Malawi and the USA. For many years she was Secretary of the Standing Conference on Library Materials on Africa and has contributed bibliographical papers to a number of journals, including *African Research and Documentation* and *African Affairs*. Her current projects include a bibliographical volume, *The Commonwealth*, for Clio Press. Address: Institute of Commonwealth Studies, 28 Russell Square, London WC1B 5DS

Wendy Lowenstein gave up being a librarian to pioneer oral history in Australia with her *Weevils in the Flour*, an oral record of the Depression, and *The Immigrants* with Morag Loh. She considers *Under the Hook*, a self-published history of Melbourne waterside workers, her most important work. She was a founding member of the Folk Lore Society of Victoria and edited its journal, *Australian Tradition*, for many years. She is currently publishing a handbook on self-publishing. Address: Bookworkers' Press, PO Box 33, Hawksburn, Victoria 3142

Carol Mills, recently appointed acting University Librarian at the University of the South Pacific, has been the William Merrylees Librarian at Charles Sturt University - Riverina since 1984. Prior to that she was a librarian at the University of Canberra, working in acquisitions and collection development. She has written widely on topics related to Australian bibliography, publishing and bookselling. Her most recent monograph is a history of the Australian publisher, the New South Wales Bookstall Company. She also has participated in several Federal government inquiries into Australian publishing. Address: William Merrylees Library, Charles Sturt University - Riverina, PO Box 588, Wagga Wagga, New South Wales 2650

John Mills has been Lecturer in the School of Information Studies at Charles Sturt University - Riverina for eleven years, specializing in reference work and Australian bibliography. He has served as a consultant on reference collection development for public libraries in Australia. Among his more notable publications is *Information Resources and Services in Australia*, now in its second edition. Address: School of Information Studies, Charles Sturt University - Riverina, PO Box 588, Wagga Wagga, New South Wales 2650

Graeme Powell joined the staff of the National Library of Australia in 1967. He was Manuscript Librarian from 1969 to 1975 and returned to that position in 1987. From 1979 to 1987 he was the Australian Joint Copying Project Officer in London. Address: National Library of Australia, Canberra 2600

Robert L. Ross, Director of the Edward A. Clark Center for Australian Studies at the University of Texas at Austin, is the author of *Australian Literary Criticism, 1945-1988* and editor of *International Literature in English: Essays on the Major Writers*. He has published widely on Australian writers, including Patrick White, Thea Astley, Peter Carey and Christina Stead. He is also editor of *Antipodes: A North American Journal of Australian Literature*. Address: Edward A. Clark Center for Australian Studies, University of Texas at Austin, Austin, Texas 78713-7219

G.A. Stafford is Associate Librarian (Reader Services) at Flinders University of South Australia. Prior to taking up this position he worked in Western Australia and in the United Kingdom. Having been at Flinders University almost from its inception, Mr Stafford has developed a detailed knowledge of Australiana collection development and of the growth of Australian publishing. Address: University Library, Flinders University, GPO Box 2100, Adelaide 5001

Richard Stone has worked at the National Library of Australia for more than twenty years, primarily in the areas of selection and acquisitions for both Australian and overseas materials. He was the

Library's North American Liaison Officer between 1972 and 1975 and has been Chief Librarian of the Australian Selection Unit since its inception. At present he is closely involved in the refinement of the Library's Australiana collection development policy. Address: National Library of Australia, Canberra 2600

Derek Whitehead is Director of Collection Management at the State Library of Victoria in Melbourne, where he has also been Orders Librarian and Acquisitions Librarian. He is the author of several books on multicultural librarianship, including *Buying Books in Other Languages*, a handbook for acquisitions, and *Not Enough to Read*. He has been President of the Acquisitions Section of the Australian Library and Information Association and is currently collaborating with G E Gorman on a forthcoming textbook, *Acquisitions in Australian Libraries*. Address: State Library of Victoria, 328 Swanston Street, Melbourne 3000

Author Index

Subject Index

Title Index